AMERICA'S GREATEST GAME BIRD

AMERICA'S GREATEST GAME BIRD
Archibald Rutledge's Turkey-Hunting Tales

Edited by JIM CASADA

THE UNIVERSITY OF SOUTH CAROLINA PRESS

Copyright © 1994 Jim Casada

Hardcover edition published 1994
Paperback edition published 2025 by the
University of South Carolina Press
Columbia, South Carolina 29208

uscpress.com

Printed in the United States of America

Library of Congress Cataloging-in-Publication Data can be found at
http://catalog.loc.gov/

ISBN: 978-1-64336-593-0 (paperback)

For Parker Whedon, who has generously shared with me turkey-hunting wisdom accumulated over the course of more than five decades dedicated to pursuit of His Majesty. He has opened up before me the most wondrous of sporting worlds even as he rightly warned me that it would lay claim to a corner of my soul. Thanks to him, I have been privileged to experience some of the same joys of the wild that so entranced Rutledge.

Contents

Acknowledgments ix

A Note on Selection x

Introduction—Archibald Rutledge: Lifelong Turkey Hunter 1

Part I The Way of the Wild Turkey 7

Wild Turkeys 11
Beautiful Wings 22
Wild Watchers 24
Reconnoitring 25
The Ways of the Wild Gobbler 27
Wingéd Mountaineers 33
Catching a Wild Turkey 37
The Great Bird Comes Back 39

Part II The Way of the Turkey Hunter 47

Any One's Turkey 51
Calling a Wild Gobbler 55
Talking Turkey 58
Daybreak in the Ocean 65
Ain't a God's Turkey 70
Oh, These Hunters! 74

Part III Memorable Hunts 77

The Bishop Earns a Gobbler 81
Gil-Obble-Obble-Obble 88
A Stalk on the Dunes 94
Big Toms in Big Timber 100
Fireworks in the Peafield Corner 107
My 339th Gobbler 112

Part IV Great Gobblers — 119

Four Bearded Men — 122
Big Tom — 128
Tall Man of the Twilight — 134
The Rajah of Bellefield — 139
The Old Bronzed Men of the Hills — 146
That Twenty-five-Pound Gobbler — 150
The Rogue of Orquic Valley — 157

Part V Magic Moments — 163

Wild Turkeys of the Delta — 167
Steve Knows How — 173
Joel's Christmas Turkey — 178
Magic on Mound Ridge — 185
The Wrong Gobbler — 191
The Lady Was Kind — 197
Miss Seduction Struts Her Stuff — 203

Bibliography — 208

ACKNOWLEDGMENTS

This is the third of three story collections that I have edited for the University of South Carolina Press. As was the case with the two earlier volumes, *Hunting & Home in the Southern Heartland* and *Tales of Whitetails*, I owe a singular debt of gratitude to Judge Irvine Rutledge, Rutledge's only surviving son and a man who figures prominently in some of the stories in this book. Irv's interest in this project, along with his constant support and encouragement, is a tribute to his father's memory. Dale Arenz, a voracious reader of outdoor literature of the past, has provided articles from his extensive collection of sporting periodicals. Fred Hendrickson has been helpful in a similar fashion. Various members of the reference department at Winthrop University's Dacus Library have assisted me by procuring materials on interlibrary loan. Warren Slesinger, Peggy Hill, and their colleagues at the University of South Carolina Press have stoically endured my prodigality in meeting deadlines even as they provided needed prodding and support. What Parker Whedon has meant to me as my turkey-hunting mentor only I can truly know. Suffice it to say that the dedication of this book to him is at best an inadequate tribute to a master turkey hunter. Mom and Dad have, over the course of parts of five decades, consistently encouraged my love of nature and sport. Finally, as ever, the two people I hold nearest and dearest—Ann and Natasha—mean more to this work and to me than I can ever hope to express.

A Note on Selection

Archibald Rutledge was America's most prolific writer on wild turkeys and wild-turkey hunting during the first half of the twentieth century. Part of his productivity can be ascribed to his admirable work ethic. He was also fortunate enough to grow up in South Carolina's Santee Delta, one of our country's last strongholds of the bronze barons of hardwood sloughs and pine ridges. Rutledge's productivity on the subject is little short of amazing. Prior to 1950 only four books had been published which were devoted exclusively to the sport, and only a handful of outdoor scribes even knew enough about turkey hunting to give it the attention and understanding it deserved.

We are fortunate that Rutledge was among their ranks, for he possessed both the literary skills and the sporting savvy to make the glories of the most alluring of all shooting sports come alive. The nature of the turkey-hunting experience has changed since Rutledge's heyday from a late-fall and winter sport to one practiced in the spring mating season. The shift in seasons aside, Rutledge's pieces consistently remain timely, possessing an appeal that will endure so long as hunters take to the field.

The selections included in this book have been chosen primarily on the basis of two criteria—as the most readable and, in my view, most meaningful and representative of Rutledge's writings on wild turkeys. Several of these pieces will be familiar to Rutledge devotees. Others are obscure, and a number have never appeared in book form before. For those interested in other turkey-related writings by Rutledge, the bibliography will provide a guide. What follows is one devoted turkey hunter's choice of thirty-four personal favorites among Old Flintlock's writings on this wily, wary, and wonderful bird.

AMERICA'S GREATEST GAME BIRD

—Introduction—

ARCHIBALD RUTLEDGE
Lifelong Turkey Hunter

"Some men are mere hunters; others are turkey hunters." Thus did Archibald Rutledge succinctly describe the entrancing, almost addictive appeal turkey hunting held for him. During the span of a long, active life that came to an end just short of his ninetieth birthday, Rutledge spent countless days afield in the quest for wild gobblers. More important for posterity, he wrote prolifically about this aspect of his experiences as a sportsman and naturalist.

His first love was deer hunting, in part because he so enjoyed the camaraderie of the large gatherings typical of dog drives for deer. Yet for all that he cherished the deeply rooted traditions of deer hunting, Rutledge—Old Flintlock as he was known to family and friends—reserved a special place in his heart for the wild turkey.

In some senses, the difference between the two types of hunting was striking. One involved noisy companions, both canine and human, and a frenzied air of hustle, bustle, and hullabaloo; the other was a sport of silence and stealth, best pursued alone or in the company of a single comrade. Turkey hunting has always been a contemplative man's sport, filled with prolonged periods of watchful waiting and uncertain anticipation. It lends itself to quiet reflection, to immersion in the remote woodlands, secluded sloughs, and distant field edges which the beautiful bird calls home. Indeed, the consummate hunter enters turkey woods not as an intruder but as an individual capable of coming as close to oneness with nature as a human can.

Rutledge hunted turkeys from the time he was a lad until he was well into his eighties, with most of his activity focused on the familiar world around his ancestral plantation home, Hampton. As it remains in large measure today, the area was a wild world, home to alligators and rattlesnakes, wild boars, and an abundance of deer. It was also, as Rutledge recognized and deeply appreciated, one of the few places in America where wild turkeys untainted by any hint of contact with their domestic brethren were found in significant numbers.

The two types of hunting which Rutledge loved best are now going the way of punt guns and unposted land. Deer hunting with dogs is a thing of the past in all but a handful of Southern states, and the standard approach to turkey hunting focuses on "gobblers only" during the spring mating season. Although old-timers have accepted these changes begrudgingly, they represent two of the great wildlife management success stories of the twentieth century. Once seemingly destined to go the way of the bison, both the turkey and deer populations are today at all-time highs. Rutledge was an early and eloquent proponent of restoration efforts and ethical hunting. He was not a game hog. He did not take more birds than the law allowed, and a sound sense of conservation guided his sport.

In pursuit of turkeys Rutledge enjoyed the sort of experiences that no law-abiding hunter will ever know again. Annual limits of wild turkeys in South Carolina during his heyday allowed a hunter twenty birds, and one of the stories included in the present work recalls the outing which ended with him killing his 339th gobbler. The piece was written in the mid-1950s and describes an event which took place earlier. A number of active years of hunting still lay ahead of him, and in all likelihood Rutledge's lifetime bag of toms was close to 400. That number is phenomenal. For purposes of comparison, it might be noted that South Carolina's current limit is five birds annually, and that allowance is higher than the number permitted in virtually every other state in the country.

Interestingly, Rutledge scorned the practice, which is today standard, of hunting gobblers during the spring, when they are most vulnerable. "In the mating season," he wrote, "it is nothing to call a gobbler to you. Before it was against the law, nearly all the old birds were killed this way." Even though things have come full circle, were he still among the ranks of turkey hunters, Rutledge would be among the first to acknowledge that spring hunting has proved beneficial to the wild turkey.

As is frequently revealed in his accounts of turkey hunts, Old Flintlock had a deep appreciation for his quarry. Like all ethical hunters, Rutledge emphasized the importance of making proper table use of the game he harvested. He was constantly concerned about how wild turkeys around Hampton were faring, and he sought regular reports from those he called his "black henchmen" about sightings of flocks.

Rutledge's astounding feats as a turkey hunter were thus largely the product of his skill and personal circumstances. His views of what constituted proper hunter behavior and acceptable hunting techniques are somewhat at variance with today's perspective, but he was unquestionably correct in his assertion that it was much more difficult to call a mature bird within range during the winter than during the breeding season. A propos of Rutledge's personal wealth of turkey-hunting wisdom, it is important to remember that precious few individuals of his day were deeply immersed in the lore of the sport. Far too many modern hunters fail to appreciate this fact. There were only isolated pockets of sizable turkey populations in existence nationwide during the first half of the twentieth century. Most were found in the South and in Pennsylvania and, with a few exceptions, turkey hunters of the time tended to be a reclusive, uncommunicative lot. Calling abilities, knowledge of the whereabouts of birds, insight into their behavior, and other bits of turkey-hunting wisdom were carefully guarded secrets passed on from father to son and seldom shared with outsiders. Only Rutledge, Edward A. McIlhenny, Tom Turpin, Henry Edwards Davis, Simon Everitt, and one or two others of their ilk offered induction into the sport's mysteries through their writing.

Among the men just mentioned, only Rutledge did not produce a book on turkey hunting. Yet in terms of total literary productivity, in the years between publication of the first book devoted exclusively to turkey hunting (McIlhenny's *The Wild Turkey and Its Hunting*, 1912) and the beginning of modern restoration efforts around mid-century, Rutledge wrote more about the sport than anyone. Rutledge's writings do not belong to the "how to" and "where to" genre so popular today. Instead, he was a teller of tales, a scribe who excelled at capturing mood and setting. In that regard, no other has been more adept at depicting the excitement of turkey hunting. His stories, tales of breathless anticipation, frequent failure, and constant uncertainty, reflect well the circumstances and moods of the sport. They hold the reader enthralled in precisely the same fashion as the hunter falls victim to the great bird's allure.

Rutledge's stories of grand turkey-hunting experiences convey the delicious unpredictability and unexpected delights of this demanding sport. Flintlock was an "old master," although by his own standards of judgment, no man even approached mastery in the sport. When Rutledge was well into his sixties he wrote: "Turkey hunting has been with me a kind of religion ever since a hatchet was a hammer; and perhaps I have learned a little of the art. Yet even after almost a half-century of hunting of the noblest game bird that graces America's wild, I am going to confess that I am still in the kindergarten; and I doubt if any human being ever acquires a complete education in this high art."

There is an element of truth here, but Rutledge was being overly modest. Take, for example, his lifelong study of the art of calling turkeys. For years he experimented with dozens of calling devices, studying the notes they produced and attempting to ascertain which best replicated the bird's natural sounds. The end product of his researches was a rather crudely fashioned box call he dubbed, with his customary feel for words, Miss Seduction. Rutledge produced copies of Miss Seduction and for a time advertised the calls, complete with printed instructions on their proper use, in the pages of major sporting periodicals such as *Outdoor Life*.

Apparently the calls never sold particularly well; today they are treasured collector's items. Yet the box call's lack of commercial success had nothing to do with its effectiveness. I have had the opportunity to "run a box" made by Rutledge. It produced all of the basic sounds which can readily be elicited from a box call—yelps, clucks, and purrs—with convincing accuracy. In all likelihood the reason Rutledge's box calls were not a roaring economic success is that there was a small market for them. Veteran turkey hunters of his era for the most part crafted their own calls—wingbones, Jordan-type yelpers made from cane; boxes; and slates—or else called with their natural voices or by using leaves of the greenbrier or other plants.

When it comes to matters of calling, the reader of Rutledge's stories will be both entertained and educated. For example, in the last couple of years the use of two or more calls simultaneously to simulate turkeys fighting has become very popular in the turkey-hunting world. These so-called aggressive purrs have been touted as a new, noteworthy breakthrough in the sport, and in the sense that this is the first time such a tactic has come into widespread use, this is true. Yet a half century ago Rutledge hinted at the manner in which curious turkeys flock to witness a supposed fight, and in the story "Oh, These Hunters!" he even suggests one way, albeit not by means of calls, of "staging" such a struggle.

On calling techniques, Rutledge was of the old school. He subscribed to the belief that the most effective type of calling was, as I once heard Parker Whedon describe it, "Get the gobbler's attention, then lay a heavy dose of silence on him." Rutledge proffered instruction along these lines in an eloquent fashion. "To call too much is fatal. You have to vamp him [the gobbler you are trying to lure within gun range]. Like a man, he does not care for the ripe fruit which falls into his hand. What he gets stirred up over is a siren, an enchantress, a wildwood princess, shy and wonderful, hard to obtain, full of shadowy avoidance, and therefore greatly to be desired."

Rutledge also recognized that meaningful instruction on how to imitate the actual sounds of the turkey lay beyond the capabilities of the printed word. "Calling," he wrote, "is a thing to be learned rather than told of." Rutledge passed decade after decade afield, constantly endeavoring to improve his own performance as a caller. In that regard he lived according to words of wisdom offered by Horace Kephart, the dean of American campers: "There is no graduation day in the school of the outdoors."

For all the considerable attention he devoted to learning the voice and vocabulary of the wild turkey, Rutledge did not overlook other elements of the sport. Many astute hunters would argue that sound woodsmanship and solid understanding of turkey behavior are more important ingredients in turkey-hunting success than calling, and certainly Old Flintlock paid close heed to these qualities. He emphasized just how important it was to avoid spooking the quarry, driving home his point in the easygoing yet firm tone so often found in his works. "A man," he reckoned, "is as likely to be able to call a scared wild gobbler as he is to make a hole-in-one straight for nine holes." Or, as he addressed the turkey's inherent wariness from another perspective: "You may hear of men who have stalked wild turkey; and perhaps the thing can be done—if the turkey is blind."

Humorously tendered tidbits of this sort give spice to his tales of turkey hunting, yet often they are such an integral part of the story's flow that the reader, caught up in a rousing adventure, overlooks the practical advice they afford. Indeed, I would argue that Rutledge's writings on turkeys should be read twice—initally for the sheer pleasure of armchair adventure; subsequently for information and instruction. Incidentally, it was precisely this twofold approach that Rutledge used for his own forays afield after wild turkeys. Each outing, every new day, was for him an exciting adventure, but it was also yet another educational session in nature's incomparable classroom.

Rutledge once said of adherents of the sport: "A real turkey hunter follows his sport as if it were a religious rite; he is a man of infinite caution, woodcraft and patience. . . . He is a consecrated, a dedicated man; admirable, too, in the sense that his virtues are those the pioneers had." Consciously or not, Rutledge was describing himself. He was a hard hunter, a man of single-minded purpose motivated by a zest in no way diminished by the taking of scores of fine gobblers or the difficulties of old age.

Even in his final years, when increasing frailty left him first unable to go afield and finally bedridden, Rutledge continued his lifelong love affair with wild turkeys. As dawn wrapped the eastern horizon in a shawl of scarlet on still spring mornings, he could hear lordly gobblers proclaim dominion to all within earshot. The incomparable sound sustained his soul just as the raspy yelp of a gobbler approaching had once brought him a rush of adrenalin.

Today Rutledge's remains rest in the family cemetery at Hampton Plantation. Massive live oaks, mingled with towering cypresses in the low spots and lofty pines on the sandy rises, shade his grave and stretch away toward the Santee River. Those trees still provide roosts for the bronze, regal birds that were so important in the hunter's heart. As spring's annual reawakening brings new life and love to the earth, gobblers serenade hens from the treetops at daybreak and greet the raucous caws of crows or the eerie eight-note call of the barred owl with thunderous declarations of the wild gobblers' preeminence.

Rutledge's gravesite offers an ideal spot to pause and listen to the symphony of spring to which the hunter so readily harkens. The meditative visitor to the family plot, straining to hear each gobble resounding through the budding trees of April, is moved by the realization that he is listening to direct descendants of the turkeys that gave Old Flintlock so much pleasure. These sounds belong to the ages; so too do Rutledge's wonderful stories of tribute to the great game bird of which he wrote so often and so well.

The Way of The Wild Turkey
~ Part I ~

The vast majority of Rutledge's turkey-hunting stories focus on one aspect or another of the sport, and one of the key ingredients to his success as a scribe, no less than as a hunter, was his keen observational powers. His comments on the characteristics of the wild turkey, many of them tendered in humorous fashion, attest to his profound knowledge and understanding of the bird. When he wrote that "the oil shares of the stock market are absolutely regular in their behavior compared to the shiftiness of the wild turkey," you can be assured that these words were a direct product of the turkey-hunting school of hard knocks in which days of empty game bags far outnumbered days earmarked by success. His description of the turkey's incredible vision painted a memorable and apt word picture: "The turkey's eyes are such that he can see a bumblebee turn a somersault on the verge of the horizon." It was Rutledge's studied opinion that "if a plain wild turkey is not the most intelligent bird afoot or awing, then the dodo isn't dead." Likewise, when he asked "Is there anything more trimly alert in nature than a wild gobbler?" the foregone conclusion was that his answer to the question would be a resounding "No!"

Great admirer of the turkey that Rutledge was, it is not surprising that once he had moved from Pennsylvania back to his boyhood home at South Carolina's Hampton Plantation, he missed no opportunity to watch the flocks living in the hardwood sloughs of the Santee swamps and the nearby pine ridges. He studied the seasonal variations in turkey behavior—the mating rituals of spring, the precarious days of summer as poults grew toward adulthood, the banding together of hens and their now nearly grown broods in the fall, and the establishment of a pecking order among birds of both sexes as the hard times of winter passed and the days began to lengthen. This knowledge served him well as a hunter and as a man attuned to natural history.

One of the hallmarks of the most accomplished turkey hunters is a deep appreciation, approaching reverence, for their quarry. When Rutledge writes of the antics of baby turkeys or the extraordinary alertness of mature birds, it is not sport but admiration that is his motivation. "I have," he once commented, "the same reverence for a turkey that I have for a julep, a dollar, and some of those other delightful, elusive things." He might have added, as he surely believed, that the quintessential wildness of the bird stirred him to the depths of his soul.

His writings give insights on turkey behavior that are drawn straight from the wellsprings of experience. With old Flintlock, we discover that as we "learn more about the way wild things live," we are rewarded by "knowing better how to live ourselves." Rutledge also always maintained that closeness to nature was the perfect balm for those who were troubled: "most people who are sick are heartsick and homesick. They ought to go back to the woods and the fields; there they'll find man's ancient home." There is more than a touch of pantheism in this outlook, but it comes from genuine conviction and for that reason it is convincing. As we learn more about the ways of wild turkeys in the pages that follow, let us do so with gratitude that the comeback of "the great bird" Rutledge predicted well over seven decades ago is now an accomplished fact.

WILD TURKEYS

Wild turkeys have always had for me a peculiar fascination. Within sight, indeed within call, of my house, wild turkeys nested every year. During more than one season I have watched a brooding turkey hen come from her nest into the bowed and brown cottonfield for her noontime foraging. I have found nests close to the rail fences that border the home fields. Anyone who has watched a tame turkey's craft in nesting time—her patient, tedious secretiveness, her gentle self-effacement—will have a correct idea of the behavior of the wild turkey at such a season.

But, touching and strange to relate, this most wild and astute bird, once on her nest, can sometimes be approached. For a man to catch a wild turkey on her nest is no difficult task. "Perfect love casteth out fear." Even so, I have seen it with my own eyes.

In due time her brood comes forth, and she knows the mystic and infinite pride of motherhood. She watches with delight the behavior of every one of her helpless little children. She radiates maternal affection and that constant sacrifice that is the chief charm of deep devotion.

I remember watching one day in late spring such a brood in a wild tangle of greenery just beyond a field of young corn. The turkeys had been hatched in an adjacent thicket, a dim, sweet place, where jessamines tossed their showers like golden fountains playing, where smilax rioted over hollies, scrub oaks and myrtles. Shimmering little sunny glades beneath huge pines were here, lonely fair paths beside which the tall wood violets grew.

I was sitting on a stump in a small clump of myrtles when I heard the turkeys approaching. But for the noise they make walking through the leaves and brush, a flock of grown wild turkeys can be singularly silent. But it was not so with these children. I heard a faint elfin piping—flute noises of a quality most delicate, yet almost piercing in their soft sweetness. And for every plaintive or excited call that the little ones gave, the old mother had an instant reassuring answer.

From *The Woods and Wild Things I Remember* (1970).

The infants seemed to stray a great deal, running into blind alleys among the deep greenery, getting into dense heaps of leaves and, not being able to extricate themselves handily, lagging behind the flock to gaze about at the great new world into which they had come. Whenever he was in doubt, one of the little wanderers would pause and gaze about for a moment with glistening eyes, finally complaining of his plight in a dulcet treble. The old mother never failed to supply an answering note of comfort. For his dismay, even though childish and imaginary, she was always the solace.

One tiny turkey got his foot caught in a jagged strip of bark. He tugged manfully, his gleaming feathers fluffily disheveled, but the grip hurt his ankle. He complained. Instantly the old mother went to him, looked carefully at the situation, drove her black beak in the offending bark, and so freed the tiny captive. I shall never forget with what delicate abandon and grace that little wild thing fled joyously down the sun-flecked pathway toward its companions, its tiny wings held up, its feet twinkling, its faint pipings sounding on the still forest air with pathetic, winsome charm—as if a child of Titania were taking music lessons on a fairy flute.

They love their home woods—these wild birds, the noblest, I think, in all the world, and certainly one of the most splendid in our own country. They follow a certain routine every year which, when understood, proves their attachment for the place where they were born.

Near the old hearthstone they lived until the first gun of the hunting season was fired. Then, with admirable sagacity, they betook themselves across the river into the mysterious fastness of a mouldering swamp. There they stayed as long as the sportsman was abroad in the land.

But during all those months they did not forget home. When the first bull alligator began to moan his profound and ludicrous love lyric; when the first yellow jessamine began to hang out its golden bells; when the first warm, cloudy weather set the frog chorals going, then the turkeys would come back, their ranks thinned, perhaps, but all of them wiser and warier birds. But no fear would ever keep them from the old home woods. The flock would break up; mating would begin, and the great cycle of life would once more commence.

Few indeed are the places left in North America today where the pure-blooded wild turkey is found. I hunted more than forty years for this wonderful bird in many states. As far as I know, the blood of birds of the Santee River swamps is absolutely uncontaminated by the admixture of any of the barnyard variety. These beautiful bronzed kings of the wilderness do not attain great weight (twenty-two pounds was the weight of the heaviest gobbler I ever saw); but when you consider that the breast is as plump as that of a ruffled grouse, if you get one you have something that you may well be proud to bring home. Such a turkey will have all the features characteristic of the pure wild strain; the rich bronze plumage, with much purple iridescence in certain lights; the long keen neck and blue head; the pink legs.

The wild turkey is commonly considered a bird of the deep forests; but these birds I have in mind are lovers of swamps and marshes. They are at home in mud and water; indeed, I have rarely killed one in his native habitat without finding his legs and feet stained with yellow river mud. Much of his foraging is done in the gross marshes of the Delta, and one big gobbler I killed had his crop entirely filled with the tender shoots of aquatic plants. One of their favorite foods is the acorn. In the autumn, when my plantation crops were ripe, they frequently flew across the river to forage in my fields. They are great gleaners of peas, corn, and rice. When fattened on these foods, and on the sweet acorns of the live-oaks, there is no finer bird in the whole world for the table.

But you want action. All right. Late one afternoon one of my sons, then but a child, and I were walking down an old bank near the river. The bank was so straight, and the great trees made so perfect an arch over it that we could see, as if through a clear tunnel, for a distance of two hundred yards. Suddenly, near the far end of the bank and upon it three graceful shapes appeared. By their trim alertness and their high-held heads I knew that they had already made me out. Controlling a brainstorm, I squatted down and pulled my boy close to me.

"Son," I whispered, pointing down the bank, "those are wild turkeys yonder. You stand right here until you hear me shoot. Don't move."

If one hunter tells another in cold blood that he has stalked a wild turkey, the man addressed has a perfect right to try to get somewhere so that he can have his laugh out. A wild turkey may often come to you, but it is almost a miracle if you can go to him. However, in this case, there were circumstances that made the feat seem to me possible. And here let me suggest (what nearly every hunter knows) that, in stalking, the hunter should be keen to take advantage of anything other than himself that may be distracting the game's attention. I knew the turkeys would be watching my boy; and if he did not move, their curiosity but not their alarm would be increased.

Edging over the side of the wooded bank, I began the crawl of my life. Fortunately, for the first hundred yards there was a screen of bushes. Then came brier patches. Then there were canes and young willows. During my stalk I did not again attempt to look at the turkeys; for this bird's eyes are such that he can see a bumblebee turn a somersault on the verge of the horizon. I knew at what place on the old bank they were, and I trusted to luck and to my boy.

Pulling myself up at last gingerly to the edge of the bank, I espied the three turkeys, within gunshot, and standing almost as they had stood when first seen. At this moment, however, one began to move toward another. Both heads were held high. When the shapely necks crossed, I let drive.

A great time my little sportsman and I had gathering in those two big wild turkeys and carrying them home. And when I told him that he, by distracting their attention from my approach, had made the thing possible, I told the truth.

I want to say a word about the proper load for one of these great birds. It is by no means a tragic thing to miss one; but it is a genuine tragedy to wound one and let him get away, to die in the wilds, or to be devoured there by some predator. The wild turkey is a big bird, and it takes a heavy load to break him down. Of course, if he should happen to walk right up to you, you can kill him with tens. But I am thinking of the average chance. I always traveled in turkey country with fours in my right barrel, twos in my left. In hunting where there are both deer and turkeys, it is sometimes hard to change shells in time; and while a turkey can be killed with buckshot, he is more likely to be missed. I have shot point blank at sixty yards at a gobbler standing, my load being buckshot, and I never cut a feather.

One day the mother of a hopeful young turkey hunter interviewed me as to how to go about the business. I told her about the shells I used, and added, "Of course, if the gobbler comes close enough, your boy can kill him with a stick."

"Dear me!" she exclaimed. "I never thought of that. And a stick is so much safer for my boy than a gun, isn't it?"

On one occasion, while flanking a deer drive with one of my sons, the drive being close to the river, and therefore a good place for turkeys, a huge gobbler walked out of the gallberry bushes ahead of my son, and took wing with ponderous yet speedy grace. He fired one barrel at him with buckshot. I saw the turkey's left leg drop, but he continued to fly far out of sight. As it was then twilight, we made no pursuit, but I told my boy that we could get him next morning. He did not believe me; but it is a fact that, while a wild turkey with a broken wing is likely to escape a hunter, one with a broken leg can hardly ever get away. He has to make a little run (as an airplane taxies before rising) in order to take wing; and if he has but one leg, he just can't take off.

At daybreak next morning, taking my bird dog, I repaired with my son to the place where I thought the turkey must have come to ground. Almost immediately we came to him; the dog pointed; and the gobbler couldn't rise. It was a wonder, though, that a fox or a wildcat had not picked him up during the night.

In a country as full of predators as mine was, you might suppose that this splendid bird would have a difficult time breeding. But two things protect the nesting mother: Like all other game birds, she appears to give out little scent in the spring and summer (or are there so many other lush and dewy scents in the woods then that hers is not readily distinguishable?); and then she makes it a practice to fly both from and to her nest so that she will not be trailed. To me, one of the most interesting and touching sights in all nature is to see a nesting wild turkey flying far through the woods and swamps when undisturbed. I have found her nest by watching her flight.

They take good care of themselves on the ground, and they use their heads in the trees as well. It has been my observation that these birds rarely roost in trees perfectly bare when there are others to be had. I have known them to settle for the night in the dense tops of young pines, sometimes not more than twenty feet from the ground. They are partial to live-oaks, which are evergreens, and to cypresses, gums, and tupelos. But these latter have no leaves in the winter.

Wild turkeys have a regular range. Sometimes this is of great extent, but they usually make a daily round of it. If the hunter knows the country and can plot this range, he is almost certain to see the great birds. My strategy was to intercept them at a certain place at a given time of day. If undisturbed, they often arrive on the minute.

Having roosted a great many flocks of turkeys, both while I was hunting and while I was not, I have watched very carefully their behavior at night. When disturbed from roost, they seldom fly far; indeed, sometimes not farther than sixty yards. They will invariably alight in a bare tree, the limbs of which, I suppose, they can distinctly see. They will never fly to the ground at night. But if you flush one from his roost in the morning, he will almost invariably come to earth.

It is sometimes very easy to call up a wild turkey. For this purpose I designed a box-call, the box being of yellow willow and the top of locust (black walnut is also good for the top). These woods I finally selected after trying about twenty other varieties. Its tone was mellow and alluring. It had IT. I found it almost indecent to use, so seductive were its persuasions. But it is one thing to have a good call, and it is another to call up a wild bird. Much depends on the season, on the mood of the turkey, and the question of whether a flock has been scattered. A turkey will often simply refuse to come; sometimes he will answer and will not come. A single bird is most likely to be responsive. I have had a flock answer me; but I have never been able to call a flock up to me, their attitude seeming to be: "Here we are; why don't you come over to us?"

At dusk one December evening I was calling on the riverbank near home. It was so late I was doubtful whether any turkeys were still on the ground. At last I heard a sound; but it was in the marsh across the river; and it seemed too big a noise for a turkey to make. I thought it was a deer or a wild hog. But across the wide expanse of the Santee here came a gobbler flying. He alighted on the bank within thirty yards of me, and was promptly collected. Five minutes later two other gobblers walked up to me. One of these I shot. I did not want to have to carry three wild turkeys all the way to the house.

There is a psychology about turkey-calling that the hunter should do well to heed. The old gobbler is an aristocrat, a patrician. When he hears a call, what stirs him is exactly what stirs a man. He visions some wildwood princess, some enchantress, demure and elusive. If ever I get an answer, however faint and far away, I stop calling. That silence intrigues the gobbler's soul. He just has to see what kind of wonderful creature shows indifference toward him. If I call too much, he will not come; not because he is afraid, but because he is disgusted. He says to himself, "That girl must be a common sort after all; she's too eager."

Another reason for not continuing to call after you have your turkey coming is that, however admirable your call may be, as he gets nearer to you, he is likely to detect its artificial nature. In calling, if you make a false note, don't dare to stop on that. If you do, your gobbler will think that the false note was the other turkey's clearing his throat.

It occasionally happens that a hunter will enter into competition with calling turkeys. Late one afternoon I roosted a flock on an old bank running through the mouldering heart of the great swamp. I left home long before daylight the next morning, but I ran into a head-tide. By the time I got near the turkeys, they were coming to ground. They come down, of course, not as a flock, but separately; and often alight at considerable distances from one another. Then they immediately begin to call together. Some of this calling had commenced as I stole down the old muddy bank toward them. Here was a case that called for some maneuvering.

Listening intently, I decided that most of the birds were already together, and were moving off into the deeper swamp. But one gobbler was all by himself, and he was asking the gathered flock to come to him. The flock meanwhile was telling him not to be silly and stubborn. I knew that he would eventually come to them. I therefore refrained from calling. My game was to get between this lone bird and the retreating flock. I noticed that these birds did not call in the ordinary way. They just kept repeating "Put! Put!" in very high and resonant tones. Satisfied of the direction that the flock was taking, I got between that point and the place where the one bird was still calling. Then I sat down and got ready to shoot. It is an unusual experience to have one wild turkey call up another wild turkey for a hunter. But it happened here, and he weighed twenty-one pounds.

In waiting for wild turkeys, a man has to be a good deal more cautious than if he is in waiting for a deer. If a hunter does not move, and the wind is in his favor, he may reasonably expect a deer to come within easy range, even if he is just standing against a tree or a rock. But the wild turkey's eyes are among the keenest and most discriminating in all nature; and when I expect one to approach me, I hide myself as completely as possible. So ready is the wild turkey to detect in the woods what does not belong there that in the old days, when turkeys used to be shot from blinds, these blinds had to be built with extreme caution. They had to be constructed a little at a time. If a blind were built in a day, a wild turkey would never come near it. It had to be made with such a degree of deliberation that it had the semblance of growing.

Of all the watches set by wild game, that of the wild turkey is one of the very best. As sensitive to sound as he is to sight, his wariness is of the hair-trigger variety. Having often observed them feeding, I never saw a flock without a sentinel—trim, alert, his serpentine head and neck almost rigid. This same guard or outpost is usually to be seen with a flock of turkeys traveling through the woods, sometimes two or three taking it upon themselves to act as warders. I once watched an old gobbler taking a dust-bath; beside him stood another, doubtless his partner in many adventures and escapes. Finally the first gobbler arose, shaking clouds of dust and little feathers from him. Thereupon he took up the sentry business while his pal relaxed himself in the sand for his bath.

The hunter of these bronzed monarchs of the swamps need have, I think, no misgiving about killing one. According to the present law, gobblers only may be shot. They have for some years been on the increase. At the close of every season, at least in my part of the country, there are plenty of gobblers left for breeding. But the main reason why the hunter can justify his pastime is that this bird is just about the most difficult in the whole world to hunt. Of course, even an amateur may stumble on one; but as a rule, this sport exacts from the woodsman the maximum of patience, endurance, intelligence, and woodcraft. And I believe that any sport that lays down these exactions is a mighty good type of recreation to have in these days when too many men expect to get their game with no more effort on their part than to pull a trigger with a lazy and effete finger.

Make no mistake about this: Some men are mere hunters; others are turkey hunters. These two strains of sportsmen are radically different. In every community there will be many ordinary hunters; they are just medium fellows. "But Jim—he's a turkey hunter," you will hear. That means that Jim is in a class by himself. All my life I have been hearing this kind of thing. What does it mean? Why is a real turkey hunter a *rara avis?* Well, as the poet says: "Listen my children and you shall hear." There's a real answer, and we may be able to give it.

Several hunting clubs I know specialize on ducks and quail. As a rule the members take small interest in deer hunting; they are wild about ducks and quail; and they appear indifferent to turkeys.

The concensus of their replies was: The work involved is too hard and too uncertain.

That it is difficult and uncertain is a fact; but, as is the case with all arts, it can be mastered, and the dividends paid are worth all the time and effort spent, all the failure and disappointment. As is the case with most other things in life, the pleasure and sport derived are in proportion to the energy expended, but more especially to the degree of mental craft employed.

I guess the best way to go about this business is simply to tell of some of the turkey hunters I have known—the real ones; the men who, coming on a gobbler's track or any other sign of wildwood majesty, would forsake all else to follow him.

Tyler Somerset was a turkey hunter. As I remembered him, even in his prime, he had a lot of boyish characteristics: Slight, keen, active and tireless, he had in the woods what I call a melting quality. Now I'm not referring to the oomph of Hollywood. I mean that now you would see him, and now you wouldn't. Even in comparatively open woods he could fade out. Every step he took was a wary one. He could keep long silences. I have been with him for more than two hours at a time without having him speak a word. He was oblivious to such trivialities as the weather and the passage of time. Miles from home, in the most desolate and Godforsaken swamp, the coming of eerie and obliterating darkness meant nothing to him. He was perhaps the best listener I ever knew; and he could wait. Now, other hunters can wait; but Tyler waited differently. I can see him now, as alert as a just awakened sentry who has been tipped off that an officer is approaching; his head a little on one side, his blue eyes glinting—looking, listening, actively waiting for his True Love. He had that rare sportsman's trait: The ability to outwit a wild turkey.

I myself at times have been a hunter of turkeys, and I know what it takes; among other things it requires boundless persistence, endless patience, and the ability to absorb more than a normal degree of disappointment. I might add that an incurable turkey hunter must either discipline his wife to his vagaries, or else suffer a good many domestic shocks. When a man does not come home until several hours after dark, with nothing to show for all his time and effort, his lad's attitude may faintly suggest that he is something that might be sold to a circus. Despite their reputation for sentiment, women (especially wives) are very practical. They love game on the table, and they love a man who can put it there.

Successful hunting of this great bird calls for an almost perfect knowledge of its habits, and requires also a high degree of individual initiative. As a rule, the deeper you go into the wilderness, the better your chance of success will be. Nor is the hunting standardized as is the case with practically all other game. It takes a lot of personal scheming and hard work. For it is to be remembered that this bird has legs that enable it to outdistance a good horse; he has wings that can carry him a mile or more out of danger; his eyes and ears are among the most perfect in all nature; his behavior is as unpredictable as his mentality is high. As a general rule, if you move, he will see you and hear you long before you are aware of his presence. "Not many hunters can kill a turkey," as an old friend, Phineas McConnor, says. And that remark makes you realize the difference between the ordinary variety of hunter and the turkey-loving tribe.

Not far from me, but in the gross wilderness, lived Phineas, a matchless Negro woodsman. He was small in stature and physically he was frail. But he was one of the best turkey hunters I know. When I asked him why he had such luck, he said, "I outquiets them." And then I knew it was not luck at all, but rather a kind of wildwood genius: A capacity to wait for hours without motion and without sound. When I walked the woods with this lithe and wary Negro, I felt clumsy. He went through brush like a cat crossing a carpet.

I can see Phineas now, almost creeping ahead of me down the old pineland road, his eyes scanning the apparently undisturbed pine straw. Suddenly he stops, "Ah, ha!" he whispers, pointing out to me a piece of bark that has just been turned over. "I think a turkey did that," he says.

I am unconvinced until we come to a damp place in the road. Then, in a perfect ecstasy, Phineas spreads wide the fingers of either hand in imitation of the huge turkey tracks we see in the sand. The delight of Phineas is such that one might imagine that the old bearded men were already his. In a way, they are. Woe to the wild turkey upon whose track a real turkey hunter comes!

Of course, of all wild game the turkey is perhaps the most difficult to stay with. If he ever discovers that you are after him, he will literally quit the country—almost quit the world. And, unlike most other game, he does not persist in having regular haunts. For that reason, while I could always promise a man a shot at a buck, I made no such promises about a gobbler. He is here today; tomorrow he may be ten miles away. Often, for no other apparent reason than a love of travel, he will fly across rivers and lakes, pass from one mountain to another, and traverse huge tracts of country. Nor do I believe there is another bird in the world that uses both his legs and his wings to carry him over so great distances. Compared to the travels of a wild turkey, the grouse, quail, pheasant, and wild duck hardly go anywhere on their feet. When he is doing nothing but merely ranging for food, a wild turkey may travel several miles a day; and when he is getting out of the country he has become suspicious of, he may even go farther.

Turkeys are subject to vagaries; they get *notions;* and with apparent purpose, but for no discoverable reason, will suddenly quit good quiet territory and wander for miles. You cannot count on turkeys. They sometimes act as if they had something on their minds that not even a turkey hunter can fathom, and perhaps they themselves don't quite know why they act as they do. And no man can be sure, even by means of what he calls perfect planning, of coming up with these big birds which, either from secret wisdom or from aberration, occasionally act as if they were plain goofy.

A hunter's success with game is usually in proportion to the game's wariness, and to his knowledge of what moves to make in this life-and-death chess game of the wilds. He may bring in twenty rabbits for every single ruffled grouse; ten grouse for every wild turkey.

When I lived in the beautiful Cumberland Valley of Pennsylvania, I found there, as I found elsewhere, that a real turkey hunter is one who really stands quite apart from the ordinary lovers of hunting. In the village in which I lived, there were perhaps thirty men who hunted quail, rabbits, grouse, squirrels; perhaps half that number hunted deer. "But Seth," I was told—"he's a turkey hunter."

I cultivated the acquaintance of Seth, and I hunted turkeys with him in the wilds of Path Valley, clear up to the Huniata; in Bear Valley, on Sideling Hill, in the Big Cove, and on Two-Top Mountain. We even got into West Virginia on a hint from a friendly mountaineer that there were turkeys at a place called Seldom Seen.

As I had regular work, I always had to get home by night. But Seth's regular work was to kill a gobbler. I have known him to spend the night alone in those wild mountains just because he had come upon some turkey scratchings that looked not over a day old.

"To kill a gobbler," he used to tell me, "you got to see him first; and after you see him first, you mustn't let him see you at all. A wild turkey that sees a man is a turkey that gets away."

Seth had a good wife. She understood him. "I like him the way he is," she once said to me with shy pride.

She had a right to be proud; for during all the years I knew him, he got his gobbler every season.

Seth knew much more than I did about hunting wild turkeys in the Pennsylvania mountains. Following his advice, I enjoyed some grand sport in that matchless country. His advice was simple: "Stay high on a ridge, where you can look down both sides; let them come up to you; and outwait them."

Yet for all his smartness, for all his equipment for safety, the wild turkey meets more than his match in certain individuals of the outdoor fraternity known as turkey hunters.

Beautiful Wings

One November day, in the golden heart of a pine forest magic with autumnal colors and fragrances, I was waiting for the possible sight of a wild turkey that a friend had declared he would drive my way as he rode toward me through the radiant woods. What I expected to see was a tall, snake-like neck and a bronzed, broad back come sedulously, glisteningly, and silently forward through the broomsedge and the huckleberry bushes. Instead of that I saw a vain but thrilling race—indeed, as extraordinary an affair as a man ever witnesses.

My friend, riding a swift and sure-footed marsh-pony, came out of a thicket of young pines about four hundred yards directly in front of me. Between us lay a level stretch of forest, with a few big pines here and there and a soft growth of tawny broomgrass on the wildwood floor. Just as he cleared the thicket, the horseman rode up a wild gobbler, which, probably having heard him coming for some time, had squatted under some brush, from the shelter of which he was finally roused.

What first attracted my attention to the picturesque performance now beginning was the sudden violent start that the horse made in my direction: he came at a wild, driven gallop. Then I saw the great bird above him, superbly beating his way toward me. At the start of this remarkable race the gobbler was thirty feet above the horse and about as many yards ahead. Clearly my friend's game was to try to beat the wild turkey to me and incidently, perhaps, to prove his pony's speed, about which he had been amiably regaling me with some tall tales.

On came this singular and harmless hurricane. And most thrilling it was to watch. The pony having fully entered into the spirit of the adventure, and the wild gobbler being aware of the presence of some sort of strange menace to be escaped only by the most rigorous valor of flight, there was a real race between the two.

The flight of a wild turkey is always impressive, but peculiarly so when, having gathered momentum by beating his powerful wings, he sets his

---

From *Wild Life of the South* (1935).

pinions and sails at cyclone speed—head far extended, feet far extended—swift without exerted motion, onrushing silently, a living airplane, sentient, electric, and touched with that wild glamour which invests like magic light the mystery and beauty of the things of baseless fairyland.

The length of time that a wild turkey can sail seems to depend chiefly on the original height obtained. Many observations of the flight of this magnificent voyageur of the sky confirm my opinion that a wild turkey, upon taking wing, usually attempts to attain height first of all; then he gives attention to the details of direction and speed.

Because my friend and his pony had been close upon him ere he took wing, this gobbler I was watching was not able, evidently, to waste time in mounting, thinking it discreet immediately to put all the direct distance he could between himself and his pursuer. The turkey therefore was never more than forty feet above the ground.

With the luxurious autumn sunlight softly glinting iridescently on his bronze feathers, with the tall yellow pines, and the blue sky, and the glimmering, far swamp of tree-bays and loblollies and sweet myrtles making a perfect and appealing background for the approach of winged majesty, on came the illustrious fugitive, while beneath him, but every moment falling behind, thundered the excited pony. Above me now the great bird gleamed, splendid and swift, gliding high among the clean pine-boles on level, dark wings. He passed, the light on him brightening, fading, flaring softly again. Far through the joyous forest my eye followed him, until he was lost in the quiet, mysterious merging of faint sky and golden leaves and that retired, distant loveliness where beats the forest's heart.

A few seconds after the gobbler had disappeared, my friend arrived on his breathless mount. In the race of about a quarter of a mile the turkey had gained, as nearly as I could estimate, about a hundred yards; but his gaining was continuous, so that there was no doubt of the fact that the pony was outclassed. The matter can be reduced to simplicity when we say that a wild turkey can easily fly on the level at sixty miles an hour, which is a speed no horse can maintain—nor perhaps even attain. In flights downhill a wild turkey achieves an almost incredible velocity; and though, as a bird, he makes comparatively small use of his wings, when he does perform, the spectacle is memorable. He always makes me think of a modest champion—unwilling to make a show of himself, but superb when once in action.

WILD WATCHERS

Of all the watches set by wild game that of the wild turkey is one of the very best. A turkey's senses are preternaturally keen; and since he is as sensitive to sound as he is to sight, his wariness is one of the hair-trigger variety. Often, in mountain glades, in wheat stubbles near woodlands, in rice stubble near forests of oak and of pine, I have observed wild turkeys feeding; and invariably, though apparently undisturbed, they would have a watchman out. He would usually stand on the borders of the feeding flock, a trim, alert, erect sentry, his almost serpentine neck and head singularly rigid. This same guard or outpost is usually to be seen with a flock of turkeys traveling through the woods, sometimes two or three taking it upon themselves to act as warders.

On a good many occasions in the autumn and early winter, I watched wild turkeys feeding, on the open plantation lawn under live-oaks, on the sweet acorns of which these birds are excessively fond. Always there would be the warder. Not infrequently small groups of wild birds would join the tame flock, but remaining somewhat aloof. At a distance of almost two hundred yards the wild birds—of almost the same plumage as their bronze domestic brethren—could be easily distinguished by their alien air—a certain erectness of posture, a certain elegance, a certain wild glamour and grace, a certain air of birth and breeding.

From *Wild Life of the South* (1935). Reprinted here is the second section of the story. The first section deals with deer.

RECONNOITRING

It appears to me that if any D.S.O. decorations are to be given for reconnoitring, the wild turkey will get his. His whole existence is one long reconnoiter, just a continuous scouting party. Outrageous fortune has dowered him richly; his size, his splendor, and the ravishing flavor of his flesh have made man covet him with a mighty longing. He therefore, though he carries no big stick, walks very softly. The chances that he will see you before you see him are about 1,000 to 1. And his hearing is probably keener than his sight.

I remember being in the wildwoods one day near the head of a big lake. As there were much pine-mast about, and scarlet swamp-brier berries, and the sweet seeds of the lotus on the shores of the lagoon, and as the place held much virgin timber, I was on the lookout for turkeys; it goes without saying that the turkeys were on the lookout for me and for the likes of me. A flock came within a hundred yards without my suspecting their presence. Then I saw a snakelike head lift itself out of a patch of gallberries. The head and neck were as stiff as a rod; they glittered in the sunlight. Those marvelous eyes had detected a slight movement that I had made. The gleaming head was withdrawn beneath the bushes, a few moments later it reappeared nearer the edge of the copse. He was periscoping me. Of course, I tried to pretend that I wasn't there at all. But the eyes of a wild turkey are subject to few optical illusions. One long, glittering gaze the old bird gave me, then he dodged under cover, and when next I saw him he was leading the whole flock at a handsome trot directly away from me across the open woods. I saw those birds no more.

On another occasion, early one warm November day, I was on the side of a big wooded gully in the mountains of southern Pennsylvania. It was good turkey country. The original timber had been cut away some thirty-five years before, and the second growth had attained fine size. Many of

---

From *Children of Swamp and Wood* (1927). Only the portion of this story which deals with turkeys is reprinted here.

the ancient trees that the lumberman had rejected offered ideal sites for turkeys to roost. Wild grapes were plentiful that year; there were some chestnuts; and the bottoms of all the gullies had growths of greenbrier, teaberries, and the like, bearing food in which turkeys delight. I was lying on the ground in the sunshine, basking in the warmth of it and marveling at the lingering beauty of the tattered woodland. The world was so still that I could hear the fall of a damp leaf on the far side of the gully. Stalking game is not always strenuous work; there's the kind of stalking here described: to loaf at ease and "invite your soul," and at the same time to feel that very likely you are doing the very best thing to afford you the sight of a bearded gobbler. The real way to stalk a wild turkey is to let him stalk you.

After a half hour or so I heard a step just over the brow of the ridge beyond the gully. It might be a man I knew, it might be a gray squirrel (yet the squirrel can soon be distinguished by the jumps he makes in the leaves), it might be a ruffed grouse, or it might be the visitor I was prepared to welcome. In a few moments I saw the sun suddenly catch a shimmering object on the crest of the ridge. It was a wild turkey. He was coming over the top, headed straight for me. In the full sunlight, on a hillside comparatively bare, he would make his approach. It was an unusual opportunity to discover just how a wild turkey when alone behaves when he is without special apprehension.

The great bird's extraordinary deliberateness was incredible. He appeared as much at his ease as a wild turkey is capable of becoming. I noticed that his feathers were all fluffed out and his wings and tail were much relaxed. He came down the slope at an angle, so that he had visibly to foreshorten the leg that was uphill. The downhill leg was lifted and placed with considerable gingerly care, as if he did not want to dislodge anything. Once or twice I saw him try one footing, withdraw his leg, and then set his No. 10 on a firmer place. All this was so much like the behavior of a somewhat timid human walker on a slope that it was very appealing and interesting. At the same time I had a large silver watch in my pocket that emitted a most stentorian tick. I timed the turkey's walking by the ticks of the watch. The slope was approximately seventy yards long, and, since he undertook it at an angle, he covered probably eighty-five yards. As nearly as I could tell, it took him seven minutes. At that rate, he would take eleven hours to go a mile. But it is not always that a turkey puts on four-wheel brakes. I think he can do a mile in three minutes, running, and in little more than a minute when flying.

The Ways of the Wild Gobbler

One winter day, with my three sons, I was shooting Wilson's snipe in an old ricefield that had been burnt off to attract the birds. Snipe prefer cover that is not too thick, and one of the surest ways to attract them is to burn over a marsh. As the day was cold and windy, and as there were plenty of birds, the shooting for more than an hour was fast. If you have shot snipe, you know the difficulty of that enigmatic target, dodging at dazzling speed on an unpredictable course.

While the sport was still hot, we ran comletely out of shells. I believe that each of us had a box of twenty-five. Together we began slogging through the mud toward our boat.

The burning had been imperfect, so that here and there stood some black tussocks that had been scorched but unconsumed. As we made our way across the bog a magnificent wild gobbler suddenly ran from under one of these tussocks, then took wing only a few feet from where the four of us were sloshing along, laughing and talking, and with not one shell left among us.

The nearest shelter was on the river bank, 200 yards away, where our boat was. Would that wild turkey stop there? Not he. As the line of trees was thin, and for the most part without leaves, we could follow his flight. It took him over the trees and clear across the river—there at least a quarter of a mile wide. To say that it was a complete and superb escape is a masterly understatement.

But the main thing that impressed me was that this great bird, with no shelter other than the sketchy one afforded by the burned tussock, had withstood our bombardment for more than an hour, had lain close and crafty while we must have passed very near him time and time again. If he had made a move, almost certainly one of the four of us would have killed him—even with the 8's we were using on the snipe. Despite all

---

From *Field & Stream*, June 1970.

provocations to do otherwise, he had stayed still, outsmarting us by doing nothing.

I hope this incident suggests that the wild turkey is not the dumb cluck that many would judge him to be on account of the apparent stupidity of the domestic turkey. In more than sixty years of hunting this great King of the Wilderness—along with other game—I have found that I could kill four or five bucks for every wild gobbler. If properly understood, and therefore appreciated, the genuine sport of hunting such a bird is unlike, and I believe superior to, the quest of any other American game.

Near my Carolina plantation, deep in the wilderness, lives a backwoodsman, a prince among true sportsmen, named Tyler Somerset. When he and I were only boys, I asked him one day how it was that while year after year his fellow woodsmen and hunters never even saw a wild turkey, he always seemed to get his limit of five gobblers a season.

"I outquiets them," he answered laconically.

That assuredly is one of the chief requirements of a good wild turkey hunter: he must have infinite patience, caution, and the ability to remain alertly motionless for long periods of time. I have sat with Tyler in the darksome depths of a swamp for at least two hours without his ever moving, or ever uttering a syllable. It seems to me that a good turkey hunter must be capable of blending himself cheerfully with his surroundings for almost indefinite periods of time.

The real reason, of course, why a hunter must be still to be successful in this premier pastime of the lonely woods is that the wild turkey has eyes as keen as any in nature, and hearing as acute. Now, it is one thing to see and to hear, and it is an entirely different matter to identify instantly what is seen and heard. My long years in the woods would lead me to believe that in this ability the wild turkey is far superior to the whitetail deer. If you do not move, and a deer does not wind you, he is liable to run over you and trample you; that is, unlike the wild turkey's, his eyesight depends upon motion for identification. While sitting motionless on a stump in the open woods, I have had a wild turkey recognize me while he was still far out of gunshot.

Where deer and turkeys are native to the same woods, in the course of a deer drive the turkeys invariably come out ahead. At the first human footfall in the autumn leaves, at the first shout of a driver, the wild turkeys will immediately come out running or flying. They are more nervous than deer, and their hearing is keener—or at least they react more quickly to noise. As every experienced deer hunter knows, an old buck may keep his bed until he is almost kicked out of it. This does not prove that he is deaf. He may not identify the nature of the sounds he hears; or, if he does, he may decide that his best strategy is to lie close.

Of course, after a long night of feeding, a deer, being a ruminant, is naturally reluctant to leave his bed. To escape hunters is important; but the business of digestion is important too.

In addition to quite matchless sight and hearing, the flying ability of the wild turkey is more in a class with ducks and geese than with quail and grouse. When I asked Tyler Somerset how far he thought a wild gobbler could fly, he said, "As far as he has to." A quail or a grouse will rarely fly more than 200 yards. Once, in time of flood in the great delta of the Santee, I roused a wild gobbler from the shrouded crest of a giant cypress. I watched him fly more than a mile to the mainland woods. Nor did he alight on the riverbank, which was the nearest land. His flight carried him over the giant pines that fringed the river edge; and he did not come to ground until he was far back in the wildwoods. A wild turkey can fly not only as far as he has to, but farther than he needs to.

In my long years of hunting, during which I have killed 339 gobblers, all in season, and all fairly taken, I have found that the hens and the young gobblers are much more likely to resort to flight than are the old bearded men. They get so heavy (22½ pounds was the weight of the heaviest gobbler I ever killed) that they are much more inclined to slip away by running. An old gobbler always has to taxi before he can rise; for that reason if a hunter breaks one of a gobbler's legs, the bird cannot get off the ground.

All my life I have been associated with hunters, and nothing shows more clearly the distinct quality of a wild turkey hunter than the fact that a turkey hunter is in a class entirely by himself. That is because this sport always requires a little extra edge. Wild turkey hunters are set apart from all other hunters. I trained my three sons to be woodsmen and hunters. Only one became a real hunter of wild turkeys.

Once I visited some friends in central Alabama, near the great Alabama River. The hunting fraternity there adopted me; and almost at once I heard, "Now, Bill, he's a turkey hunter." The others went after ducks, quail, whitetail deer, even fallow deer (the forebears of which escaped from a preserve fifty years ago, and have miraculously become native); but Bill—he was in a class by himself.

In the mountains of Pennsylvania I stopped at a lonely cabin whose owner I knew. His pretty wife came to the door. When I asked for her husband, she said, "Norman, he's gone hunting. I don't rightly know when he will be back. You see," she added with pride, "Norman, he's a turkey hunter."

Ordinary hunters may often behave like human beings; but a turkey hunter is a noble fanatic; he's the zealot of the wildwood. Nor cold nor distance, nor time nor loneliness, nor anything makes any difference to him except to get his gobbler. Coming on the track of a wild turkey, or even on a feather, he goes into a kind of ecstasy. He'll get down on his knee and study the sign. I have even seen a real devotee of this exacting sport try to *smell* a wild turkey track in order to ascertain how long the old bird had been gone from there. It is not generally known, but a wild turkey leaves a very heavy scent—so much so that foxhounds follow it readily. And you have not seen real frustration until you have seen a fine old hound, in full cry on the trail of a wild turkey, come to the place where the great bird has taken wing. He will cast about wildly and vainly and at last give up completely, either with a look of utter dejection, or with an uneasy, furtive air, as if he felt he had been swindled by a ghost. On one occasion, one of my grandest hounds, Roland, who had the aristocratic aspect of Alfred Lord Tennyson, coming to the kind of mystery I have described, simply sat down and howled dolefully.

Ordinary bird dogs, the setters and pointers, will work on wild turkeys, but since these birds will not lie for dog or man, the use of these dogs is not effective unless the dog is trained especially to hunt wild turkeys. But better than an ordinary bird dog for this purpose is a cocker spaniel. He works closer, has an adequate nose, and seems to be more easily broken in the way he has to be broken for this special sport.

One of the very best ways of hunting wild turkeys is to use a dog, preferably a cocker. Of course, a man should have a good idea that there are turkeys about. Their tracks, their droppings, their dusting places, and their scratchings in the leaves and the pinestraw—these are the signs he looks for. Of course, a so-called "flock" of turkeys usually consists of the old mother and her brood of that year. The old men, until the mating season, are solitary or travel in small groups. I once saw eleven big gobblers together. Never at any season will gobblers do as much scratching as poults and hens. However, what they do is heavier, so that it is often possible to tell a gobbler's scratching by the long toenail marks he leaves in the earth, from which he has raked the leaves.

I would not take anything for the great days I have had hunting wild turkeys with my cocker spaniel, Star. We played the game this way: I would take my eager little dog into good turkey country. Signs, of course, meant nothing to him. What he was after was scent. When conditions were good—that is, when the air was still and the ground was damp—Star could usually pick up a trail two or three hours old (I believe the record for a bloodhound on a human being is fifty-eight hours). Star would follow that trail fast, but not too fast. I had trained him to keep me in sight always. The big idea was to have Star trail, find, and then rush in and flush the turkeys. His wild antics and barking would usually scatter them. In their excitement, taking my dog for a fox or some other kind of predator, the turkeys would take wing. But under such circumstances they usually did not fly far. Often some of them would alight in trees. Occasionally, a gobbler's flight would bring him back my way, giving me a chance for a shot as he passed.

But the regular procedure was this: as soon as Star had flushed the birds, he would return to me. Then, since scattered birds gather near where they have taken wing, I would find sufficient cover and sit flat on the ground. Little Star, realizing the necessity for absolute quiet, would lie between my legs, palpitating with alertness and excitement, but otherwise silent and motionless.

After about half an hour I would touch my wild turkey call. There's a special art in this, the chief danger being too much calling. If I ever got an answer, I called no more.

It is much easier to get a young bird up like this than it is to get an old gobbler. However, on one occasion, Star ran into and flushed about eight gobblers. After I began to call, I got two answers from different directions. I decided to let these two old boys call each other. I laid down my call and put up my gun. Within a few minutes there appeared within range two old monarchs of the river swamps. As they were walking almost directly for each other, I waited until their tall necks and indigo heads crossed. Then I touched the trigger and both gobblers fell. Those were the days!

Mention of my turkey call leads me to say that I evolved my own, after many years of experimenting with at least thirty different kinds of wood and combinations of woods. My call, "Miss Seduction," seems to have what Hollywood calls "It." It seems to represent Temptation to a wild gobbler; and he can resist anything but that. It just makes him collapse emotionally.

For the box of this call I use either basswood or yellow willow, and for the cover, black locust. As a proof of its quality, I might say that I have sold, under a guarantee, more than 900; and while there have been many repeat orders, not one was ever returned.

Not long ago I read the remarkable biography of Juan Belmonte, likely the greatest matador the world has ever known. Repeatedly he emphasizes the fact that bull fighting is a mental, even a spiritual, sport rather than a physical one. Such is hunting the wild turkey. It's a chess game in the wildwoods, exacting, diverting, and never tiresome if you have the spirit for it. My reflections and feelings about wild turkey hunting are such that I believe that, once enamoured of the pursuit of this stately, beautiful, and wildly intelligent game bird, a man will come to prefer it to any other wholesome sport of a similar nature. Sports are, roughly, of two kinds: those we watch, and those in which we are engaged. In this one the wild turkey hunter is the chief performer, and although he has no audience, and is not paid in money for his wild-wood skill, yet he deserves to rank with America's premier sportsmen, akin to the pioneers who made the wilderness their home.

And they knew, as the wild turkey hunter of today knows, that sometimes for no more apparent reason than the love of travel, wild turkeys will fly across rivers and lakes, and will traverse huge tracks of country. I have seen an old gobbler swim in preference to flying; and Audubon reported whole flocks swimming across the Arkansas River.

Then, too, wild turkeys get notions. They are subject to vagaries. Undisturbed, and with food plentiful, the great birds will unaccountably decide to move out. While an old buck has a regular and a rather limited range (he loves home), wild turkeys will be here today, and tomorrow they may be many miles away. . . .

I admire a good turkey hunter chiefly because such a man displays patience, enthusiasm, acute woodscraft, game sense, and a quiet hardihood undaunted by rain, by cold, by long tough miles, by disappointment; not turned from his fine grim purpose even by feminine sarcasms from his Lady, who may pour it on him for neglecting her and all else in life for what she, in her resentment, terms "a poor miserable bird in a god-forsaken mountain." But if he happens to bring home one of these bronzed kings of the wilderness, she has ways to make his long and arduous campaign seem worthwhile.

WINGÉD MOUNTAINEERS

I was in the wildest of lone valleys. It was the mystic hour before dawn, and as I stepped out of the car, brought to a halt in the lee of a deserted barn, I was aware of myriads of splendid stars, of the long expanse of the narrow valley sparkling with frost, and of the ancient calmness of the sleeping hills. A wild moon was homing toward the haunted west. I stood in enchanted retirement, intimately sequestered by the solitary night.

Before I had slouched out of my overcoat, stripped thus for mountain climbing, I heard from a lost glen a wild greeting—or warning. Utterly savage, gloriously primeval, as elemental as the candid mountains, came the rasping bark, hacked forth negligently.

"Red fox," I said; and it thrilled me to think that I should find one so comparatively near to civilization—for I could hear roaring away across the mountain a B. & O. freight, agonizing up a grade, blowing like a behemoth.

Weirdly, from the inviolate dusk of certain hemlocks ominously draping the creek bank, a great horned owl intoned to the fox an answer which was suitably mysterious. Far through the valley sounded his soft and melancholy note; and if there's a sound in this world more eerie than the voice of this great night harrier, I have never heard it. Now silence fell: intense, starry, lustrous. I seemed to be in virginal Eden—a place all sparkling, glimmering, and tenderly breathed over by the hale odors of dewy pines, damp hickory leaves, and ripened fox grapes. Immense yet intimate, all the world was chill and sweet, wistful and maidenly.

Leaving my faithful car beside the dark road, I slithered down a bank on which lay a little of woods—earth and loose stones. Amiably I avalanched about thirty yards to the level of the creek. This I waded, crossed an ancient meadow, deep in natural hay, now glossy with rime, and entered the woods on the lowest slope of the mountains.

High above me, fringing the tall ridges rosily, the lights of dawn were showing. All the forest was mystically passing from the beauty of starlight

From *Children of Swamp and Wood* (1927).

to the beauty of dawn. On all sides I seemed to see faint welcomes and sad-gleaming farewells. Up an old mountain road I passed, traversed what had been a mountaineer's orchard, dipped into the hushed fragrance of a pine thicket, and emerged at the mouth of a wild sweet glen down which came stealing, with shy music made among the rocks under the drifted leaves, a tiny rill. From this point forward I walked carefully, for I knew that this was wild turkey country. Only three hours from Baltimore, Washington, Philadelphia, or Pittsburgh I was, yet in the very heart of a region where the great American bird has superbly reestablished himself, to the infinite delight of every lover of wild life and to the pride and joy of the Pennsylvania sportsmen. The splendid native has returned and his reentry into his ancient domain is one of the most enchanting stories of conversation, bordering on the romantic, and almost on the miraculous.

Four hundred yards from the pine thicket I paused in a thicket of second-growth sprouts to reconnoiter. Not far off I heard a piece of bark fall. I knew that a squirrel must have dislodged it, or else that a turkey had become restless on his roost and had kicked it loose. In the woods every sound is likely to mean something. Looking up through the trees, I saw the flaring dawn, a faint and fading star, and, assuredly, certain great black shapes in the tall oaks and chestnuts. They were turkeys, still on the roost. Counting them, I numbered fourteen; but I knew that there must be others a little farther up the glen that I could not see. In the faint fog rising from the stream, the birds looked huge. One became querulous and gave a soft call. This was the old mother. Now they began to ruffle their feathers and to crane their necks. They would soon be flying down. I stole a few yards closer, and from ambush behind a mighty poplar I watched an old gobbler go through a lazy awakening. He shifted his weight, seemed to shuffle his No. 10 shoes, thrust forth his head prodigiously, wobbled his tail to shake off the dew, and then settled back in heavy contentment.

But the younger birds were more restless. One sailed down, and I was surprised at the little noise it made. Others joined it. Soon the whole flock was on the ground. They were so close to me that I could see every movement. They were of course foraging; but they were not yet scratching in earnest. In the leaves on the slopes of the glen the turkeys made as much noise as a troop of cavalry. A single bird seemed to make as much disturbance as a man walking carelessly. But there was a certain constant vigilance. There were alert pauses, crafty listenings, liftings of snaky blue heads in acute wariness. Once I saw an old gobbler pause while he had a great footful of leaves drawn back only half as far as he intended to pull it. He thought he detected a sound that he did not like, or else he was aware of the noise he was making. This scene was to me as arresting almost as would be one in Sherwood with Maid Marian and the others stealing through the glimmering forest.

Taking the back track, I climbed the ridge to the north of where the turkeys were feeding, intending to keep above them so as to study them better. I had gained the crest of the ridge when a weird sound literally burst over me. Comparable to the howling of a shell, it had something like wild, mad music in it. Looking up, I saw two gobblers coming. They had roosted high up on the mountain, a mile above me, and were now sailing down to feed.

This sailing of wild turkeys down the long slope of a mountain is one of the sights of nature which affects me deeply. Launching forth on their great wings, these proud and stately birds volplane roaring down over the tree-tops at cyclone speed. A teal duck flying on a straight stretch of river has been accurately timed as making a hundred and twenty miles an hour. Turkeys, during this superb aerial coasting maneuver, assuredly make not less than a mile and a half a minute. These two that I saw joined the flock feeding below me.

And on what were they feeding? As the time was November, they got little animal food save a few indiscreet beetles and grubs which had either not hibernated at all or had done so in slovenly fashion. These turkeys were revelling in fox grapes, with which these particular mountain slopes were riotously draped. Ridge after ridge, mile after mile, mountain after mountain, extended this wild vineyard. Never anywhere else have I seen so many wild grapes. On these the turkeys were feeding; and on chestnuts, acorns, berries of greenbrier, teaberries, sumac, hips of wild rose, mast from the mountain pines. Indeed, this mast is a favorite food. The ruffed grouse and the turkey thrive on the same kind of food; but the turkey will, whenever occasion offers, stray into cultivated fields after gleanings of grain. When hard winter settles over the hills, the turkey will eat some buds, which then constitute the chief fare of the grouse. But throughout the winter the turkeys depend largely on what they can scratch up from beneath the dead leaves. In Pennsylvania, however, the foresters regularly feed the turkeys, as do also many sportsmen.

After watching this first flock for some hours, I went northward along the rolling ridges, through this wild vineyard. I started a covey of six ruffed grouse—an unusual experience anywhere to-day outside of a preserve. Other turkeys I saw, several single birds, once a flock of five, again a flock of seven. From behind a stump on the sunny side of a ravine I started the red fox. I haven't decided which of us was the more surprised at seeing the other. Then two miles from where I saw the first turkeys I ran into a flock even larger. The woods were literally full of these magnificent game birds. And for fifteen miles on either side of the narrow valley this same kind of country extended. Into this region the great native has returned—perhaps not in all his original glory, but with sufficient splendor.

How has this result been obtained? Well, the sentiment in the region is favorable to the project. Game laws amount to nothing when sportsmen make up their minds to be lawless. But here sportsmen have a good association; no man hunts out of season (at least there is the strongest sentiment against it), the bag limit of one turkey a season is kept, and any infraction of the law is dealt with summarily and rigorously. The wild turkeys have come back, therefore, because the local sportsmen almost unanimously insist that they be dealt with fairly.

Again, a competent Game Department has taken care of the restocking. It has been found that for propagating purposes ordinary bronze turkey hens mate quite readily with wild gobblers; and the turkeys so reared are as wild as the most exacting sportsman could wish. Mountaineers have told me that they have stopped trying to raise tame turkeys because just as soon as the mating time comes and the wild birds begin to call, the tame ones will literally take to the woods and will be seen no more. I remember that on our plantation in South Carolina the finest turkeys we ever had were raised from tame hens and a wild gobbler. In Pennsylvania this restocking of the mountains with turkeys has been systematic, and it has proved most effective. There is no reason why there should not be wild turkeys in every state in the Union, unless the proper sentiment cannot be created. It seems to me that in this case, as in a great many others, sentiment is our only salvation against a materialism that would ruin us. A materialist sees in a wild turkey only so many pounds of meat. This great native can return only to those regions where the materialists are in the minority.

In Pennsylvania there is a strict law against calling turkeys. I think the law should insist that everyone who hunts turkeys should call them. Everyone does, at any rate. During the season the woods are noisy with squawky boxes and squeaky bones. And these are great warnings to turkeys. The genuine calling of a turkey is really a high art, and not one hunter in a hundred can perform the feat. Besides, turkeys come to a call only after they have been scattered; at least, that rule is generally true. But at present the calling of turkeys certainly does the birds no harm, whereas it affords many an amateur woodsman a stern and thrilling satisfaction. He can tell the family when he returns home empty-handed that he never heard his old call working better, but that somehow the birds wouldn't come. And the wise birds, while he is explaining this, will be safely roosted far back in the lonely mountains.

Catching a Wild Turkey

All hunters know that the wild turkey is one of the wariest of birds, and to shoot one is a feat of which even a veteran sportsman may well be proud. Yet this noble bird can be caught alive, and the matter of his capture is not nearly so difficult as might be supposed. Nor do I mean that he can be caught in the egg only, though many a woodsman brings home for setting under his domestic turkeys eggs of the wild turkey. And such a hatching is often successful. Nor do I mean catching the young. I have done this, and it is a tedious business. Many a time I have come upon a flock of young wild turkeys with their mother in the wild pinelands of the South. These birds are, perhaps, most difficult to capture when they are very young, for they are like quail in their ability to hide; and though you may sit and watch for an hour to have them come forth, not a stir will they make until the old mother gives her querulous call. Then, answering her with sweet flutelike pipings, the little ones will troop out of their hiding places like little sprites and elves. I know no sound in nature so appealing as the call of the young wild turkey. When they are a little larger, yet have not as yet acquired full use of their wings, they cannot so readily efface themselves in tufts of grass and beside old logs. I have caught turkeys of this size, but it is almost impossible to raise one unless a tame hen turkey with a brood of just the age of the little wild stranger will take kindly to the newcomer. The only young wild turkey I ever succeeded in raising was cared for in the manner described.

To capture a mature bird of this magnificent species might seem an impossible feat; yet if one understands the turkey's nature, the thing can be done. The time best suited is in the late winter, when a wild turkey will come readily to bait; for by then the supply of the natural winter foods such as acorns, mast, and berries has become exhausted. When a turkey will take bait, he can be led into a trap. One method of capture is the ditch-and-pen device, which is most effective.

Turkeys are baited on an open space which is made to slant gradually

---

From *Wild Life of the South* (1935).

into a narrow ditch some two feet deep. This ditch leads under the wire of a covered pen (sometimes the pen is made of old logs, through the apertures of which much light streams). The ditch ends at the far side of the pen. When the turkeys reach it, they will jump out of the ditch. And though they remain many hours in the enclosure, they will not find their way out again by jumping down into the ditch. All their efforts will be directed toward flying out of, or struggling through the sides of, the pen. It simply appears to be a turkey's nature to try to escape by going forward or up, but never down. On account of this singular trait, wise as the birds are in other respects, they are by the method described, often captured. Occasionally a whole flock will be thus taken.

Prince Alston once caught a wild gobbler for me; and this is what he told me of the way he did it.

"I fed the turkey at the blind regularly for a week. The gobbler would make his visits in the early morning and in the late evening. About noon one day I went to the blind and hollowed out a place next to an old log that lay in front of the blind. This was deep enough and long enough to hold me lying down. Then nearby I laid a lot of sphagnum moss. I covered the hole with brush and leaves, scattered bait over the moss, and came away. The next day I found that the gobbler had not noticed the trap I had made; he had eaten all the rice on the moss.

"Before day next morning I was at the blind, and soon I had hidden myself in the shallow hole. My right arm I stretched out under the moss; the palm was up, and the hand wide open. In this position I dozed for an hour or more. Then broad daylight came, and soon after the big gobbler arrived.

"He fed all over the place in very busy fashion, and at last he came over so close that I might have jumped out and caught him. But I waited until, having walked over my arm, he stepped in my hand. Then I caught him by the ankle and held him fast."

THE GREAT BIRD COMES BACK

If any one had seen John and me at our antics in the woods of that wild valley, he surely would have been forced to the conclusion that the year was about 1809 and that we were scouting for Indians, for we were lying flat among the fallen chestnuts and our wariness made showing ourselves appear a life-and-death matter.

But the observer need have had no illusions. John and I were only out on the mountain, scouting for turkeys a week before the season opened. Moreover, we had had signs and signals to warn us that the game for which we were searching was close at hand. For half a day we had tramped the fragrant autumn leaves, and had seen where a fine flock of turkeys had been scratching for chestnuts and other food. We had seen where the flock had roosted. And now we had at last come within hearing distance of the great birds themselves.

Side by side and flat on the ground we stretched, awaiting the approach of the flock. It was after sunset. In the big timber where we were, the light was already glimmering. To east and west towered the tall wooded ranges, while northward and southward the deep and narrow valley extended in misty silence.

The turkeys made a big noise coming to roost. They evidently forgot some of their daytime wariness. They called querulously, like the variety of the barnyard, and there were a good many little squabbles in the large family.

At last they came into sight. It was hard to count them. They were moving about restlessly, and it was difficult to keep one's eyes on the same bird for even a moment. It was distracting to see so fine a show of wild life come so close to us. Some of the turkeys came within ten steps of us; the most distant of the flock was within easy gunshot.

The majority were sleek and plump hens, though there were many rangy young gobblers, and two magnificent old birds, evidently the

---

From *Field & Stream*, December 1926. Later included in *An American Hunter* (1937).

leaders of the flock. Every turkey was craning its neck curiously, peering up into the bare branches clearly outlined now against the bright afterglow. Soon the soft but distinct *swish-swish-swish* began. Each turkey took a miniature run and rose easily to his chosen perch. It was not hard then to count the flock. Within fifteen minutes all of them were in the big chestnuts, and both John and I were busily counting.

"Did you ever see such a flock?" he whispered. "I make it forty-two."

"Forty-three," I answered quietly. "You must have missed the old boy down the hill yonder."

It was true. Within range of even a short brush-gun, forty-three wild turkeys had gone to roost! But that was by no means the most remarkable feature. What impressed itself upon me was not merely that I had seen such a sight but that the thing had actually happened in one of the most populous states of the Union, for I made this observation only a few years ago in southern Pennsylvania. It was not in a game preserve, nor anywhere near one; but just in the wild mountains, where every man seems to have the right to hunt.

I have said that this observation was made a few days before the hunting season. The reader will wonder whether, after the season closed, any of the fine flock remained. It is really a wonder that any were left, for during the thirteen hunting days of the season (there were supposed to be fifteen days, but two were Sundays) the cannonading along those mountains was almost continuous. Scores upon scores of hunters repaired to that wild wooded valley, but very few came out with a turkey.

The reason was twofold: the great American bird can take care of himself, even when pursued by an army of hunters; and the average man who is lured into the woods by the vision of a forty-pound gobblers' gobbling at him violently from a distance of ten yards has many things to learn about the nature and the hunting of this grand bird. The sportsman who takes the wild turkey fairly has a right to be congratulated, for he has outwitted one of the most alert creatures, mentally and physically, in existence.

On the first day I went into the mountains at daybreak. Three friends were with me. Before we had sufficient light to shoot, we heard a flock coming off the roost. This was a smaller flock than the one John and I had counted. The old gobbler in this flock must have been making a night of it, for he appeared all on edge, and gobbled in the most persistent and irritated manner.

We separated, climbing up to the first bench of the hill in pairs. John was with me. Before we had gone a hundred yards we heard our comrades shoot four times. They were in a deep gorge, and their shots sounded muffled. Yet it might be supposed that the reports of the guns would have startled all the turkeys within hearing distance. But it was not so, for suddenly John laid a hand on my arm.

"Look yonder," he whispered, poining to a large hickory 120 yards up the mountain.

Outlined against the brightening east we clearly saw a fine gobbler in the big shell-bark tree. The shots of our comrades had made him uneasy, for he was standing up on his perch, and his head and neck were craned with curiosity. Once or twice he teetered, and he had to spread his tail and partly open his wings to steady himself.

There was no use to try him from where we stood, and it was as hopeless to try to stalk him. The man who, under any but the most extraordinarily favorable circumstances, attempts to stalk a wild turkey does not understand the bird. Old mountaineers tell me that, even at night, when the moon is up, it is no easy matter to get within range of a roosted turkey.

I have killed them off the roost in the South; but there conditions are very different, since the turkeys love to roost in pines and live-oaks, which are evergreens, or in big trees hung with gray moss. They therefore do not feel themselves so exposed as do the turkeys of a mountainous country, which customarily roost in bare trees.

"I see a hemlock behind him," John whispered to me. "You stay here, and I'll try to get to him behind that tree. If he flies off, you may get a chance at him.

I did not think much of the plan, but no other seemed visible on the landscape; and I must confess that John slunk away in a most admirably effacing manner. But the noise he made! The keen air of the silent, chill November morning was just tingling to transfer sounds. John appeared to me to imitate a wounded hippo tearing his way through dry papyrus.

By watching the gobbler closely I could see that the great bird had located my friend, and had in all probability quite nicely judged the plan whereby the hunter dreamed he could approach. While John was patiently continuing his stalk, and was still far from being within range, the gobbler spread his wings and sailed to earth. He came no nearer to me in flight than he had been on the tree. His escape was easy and effectual.

My comrade had not seen the turkey fly down, and his stalk continued with futile care until I reached him and explained matters. By this time day was broadening, and up and down the long ridges of the mountains a regular cannonade had begun. The turkeys were off the roost, and the army of hunters after them were getting shots at them—or at least glimpses—it seeming to be the rule nowadays that it is good policy for a man to shoot at a turkey if he comes within sight, regardless of the distance.

Such a policy accounts for the cannonade, yet for very few turkeys. Even a 12-gauge 32-inch-barrel gun of the best make, charged with No. 2's or with BB's, will hardly stop a turkey beyond seventy-five yards. The feat is possible, but it is not likely.

The average hunter, having made up his mind not to miss his chance, will blithely blaze away at 150 yards. Then his mind will start to granulate alibis, for he will have to explain to his friends how he missed. I think these men who misjudge the killing distance of their guns are great game preservers; they not only do not hunt the game but they scare it so badly that no one else will get a chance at it.

Few indeed of all the men who hunt wild turkey have that greatest essential quality, a game sense. It is the great requirement. Of course, any hunter, however much of a tyro, may blunder on a chance for a turkey and secure his bird. But the true equipment for hunting, the one thing that will not fail when put to the test, is a game sense, the instinct to know what to do and where to go when following a certain type of game.

The man who knows how to be silent in the woods, who, for an hour or so, can make himself an excellent imitation of a stump, is in a fair way toward getting turkeys. I have a friend whose success in the business world has been phenomenal, and it has been achieved by the hardest kind of driving methods. If he ever meets an obstacle, he "butts the bull off the bridge." This same spirit, unfortunately, he carries into hunting of the wild turkey.

Well do I remember the day when he promised to join me in the mountain at noon. It was toward one o'clock when, far away through the woods, I heard a mighty shouting begin. It was my friend. Then he began to approach; and despite the fact that he knew well enough that he was in good turkey country, he came like an avalanche. I recalled an old line of poetry: "The thunder of his striding was reverberant on the shore."

The leaves rustled wildly about his feet; the dead brush crashed alarmingly; every now and then he would dislodge a boulder that would go hurtling noisily down the mountainside. The shouting also continued. In due time he came up to me.

"Hello," he said. "Where are all these turkeys? I've hunted for an hour, and I haven't found one."

To explain to him the difficulty seemed to me a delicate matter, especially since his manful exertions had made him drip with perspiration. He honestly felt that he had played more than his share of the game, and that turkeys, if they were at all decent, would simply have to let him shoot them. If I were to suggest to this friend that his methods might not be right, he would not understand me, for his ways have made him fatally successful in his dealings with men.

It is an easy matter to contrast him with a good turkey-hunter: a man who studies the signs that the great birds have left, who follows on noiseless feet, who keenly hears their coming and awaits with the immobility of a statue, his gun leveled on the line of their approach. He never forgets that a sound or a movement may betray him.

A wild turkey's static eyesight is not good; that is, he does not readily recognize a motionless man. But there are no eyes in the world more skilful to see movement, and no ears more alert to catch a sound.

Besides the average hunter's inability to cope with the wild turkey's intelligence, the great bird has many other advantages in its favor. One is assuredly its ability to carry shot, for there is no game which can proportionately get away with more. The head, the neck and the butt of the wing—these are the fatal places; but it is not an easy thing for a man to get his aim certainly on any of these.

It would be safe to say that the average turkey which is shot at is missed (unless the shooting be from a blind), and the average one that is hit gets away. I have a friend who wounded eleven turkeys in one short season, and only succeeded in getting the twelfth, a small hen. Indeed, the majority of wild turkeys killed are hens. They seem both tamer and tenderer than the gobblers.

One day in late November I was sitting beside an old logging road on the mountain, waiting on a slim chance for turkeys to come along. I had seen them there before. Some farmers had been hauling wheat over the road, and a little of the grain had spilled out of the wagons. The turkeys had been coming to this as they would come to a bait.

The day was warm and misty, and a very fine rain was falling. After taking this rain for an hour or so, I got up to stretch and to look the situation over. Far up the road, looming mighty big in the mist, were two black shapes. They were turkeys, and they were feeding straight down the road to me. Unless the mist had made them extraordinarily large hens, they were gobblers.

I was behind a little screen of dry oak-leaves. They came straight on, picking in the road. All I had to do was to put up my gun and wait for the turkeys to walk into it. On they came, their beards dragging the ground when they pecked, their big bodies swaying and rocking as they walked down the slope. They were old gobblers, the very kind which every hunter longs to encounter.

I waited until the birds were within forty yards. Then my trigger finger began to tingle. The time seemed right for the speaking of the message. I was loaded with 4's, and had a heavy charge of powder under the shot.

Still I waited, until the gobblers were within thirty yards; until they were within twenty. I might have waited until they had come within two or three. But I was certain of my chance. Laying my sight on the bigger one of the two (the law allowed only one to a man a season), I let drive.

To my chagrin and astonishment, both turkeys rose, and the one at which I had shot appeared to rise more strongly and quickly than the other. They started down the mountain, then took a half-circle above me, passing directly overhead at a height of about fifty feet. I gave the left barrel to the same turkey. It seemed to me that every shot struck. His feathers were sadly disheveled. But he did not stop; indeed, he did not pause. He had urgent business calling him elsewhere. My second barrel, however, turned the birds, and they took a long slant down the mountain. I could see them going for a matter of two miles or more—clear across a wooded valley where the mist was thin, and far up on the ridge opposite. If my eyesight did not deceive me, the turkey at which I had emptied both barrels was ahead of the other one when they came to ground. As the old fellow said about the runaway horse he was trying to sell: "The further she goes, the faster she goes."

I do not mean to say that a wild turkey will on every occasion stage a getaway of this kind; yet the selfsame thing often happens, as every turkey-hunter can testify, and there is no way of accounting for it save by saying that the wild turkey can take care of a good deal more than his fair share of lead.

A further advantage which he has is the fact that he is proof against a winter which will kill quail and small game of that type. It has only lately been discovered that the wild turkey is a true budder, like the ruffled grouse, and that when the snow covers the ground he is by no means shut off from his food. I have often helped to winter wild birds; the best method seems to be to cut off a small sapling about a foot above the snow, sharpen its point and stick an ear of corn on it.

But the turkeys are not dependent on this artificial supply. They are usually so plump that they can go for days without any food with no apparent discomfort. After a hard snowstorm, wild turkeys have a habit of staying in trees for two days or more at a time. I have observed this same habit among turkeys in the South.

When swamps which they frequent are flooded, the saying among hunters is, "After the third day of high water the turkeys will fly out." I have watched a wild turkey fly for more than three miles across a flooded section of delta land, and there's no telling how much farther he could have gone.

I was talking not long ago with a game warden who has charge of the mountainous section I have been describing. He said that the turkeys of a year ago had remarkably withstood all the assaults of the hunters and that one mountaineer had been feeding a flock of forty-nine. The warden himself went to the mountain-man's cabin to see the great sight of forty-nine wild turkeys coming to the evening feed. They came in at about three o'clock.

He said that the first turkeys to take the feed were a pair; these brought others; and in late March, when he visited the scene, there was a remarkable gathering. The only disappointing feature was the fact that the gobblers far outnumbered the hens. If there could be a gobbler law, as there is a buck law in many states, there would be no doubt but that the wild turkey will return to stay.

At present, in many of our most populous regions of the East, he appears to be staging what is little short of a spectacular comeback. In the Southern States he may still be considered to be holding his own, if not positively increasing.

Of course, we can not expect the return of the days of the naturalist Bartram, who in his travels through the South a hundred years ago reported that every morning while in the woods he would be awakened by the "furious gobbling of the wild turkeys, for hundreds of miles around." But it is reasonable to hope that, with a little further protection by man, the great bird will actually come back to give a matchless glamour to the woodlands, the solitary mountains, the wild valleys.

The Way of The Turkey Hunter
~ Part II ~

Turkey hunters are rightly recognized as a breed apart. Tom Kelly, one of the most entertaining of modern writers on the subject, likened them, in a book of that title, to The Tenth Legion, the most famous of all the mighty Roman legions and a veritable cult distinguished by its history, uniqueness, and superior courage over the centuries. Old Flintlock not only belonged to the ranks of devoted turkey hunters, he was intensely proud of his place on the rolls of the obsessed. Rutledge's outlook in that regard was reminiscent of lines written by the poet of the Yukon, Robert Service. Referring to those hardy, sometimes forlorn souls who roam the vast expanses of the Arctic, Service wrote: "There's a race of men who don't fit in, / A race that can't stand still."

Rutledge reveled in the eccentricities associated with turkey hunting, and he wore them as badges of honor. To him, there was something manly, deeply meaningful, and, most of all, redeeming about the sport. "I admire a good turkey hunter chiefly because such a man displays qualities that we usually associate with pioneer America—patience, enthusiasm, woodcraft, game sense, and a quiet hardihood undaunted by rain, by cold, by long tough miles, by disappointment."

Rutledge not only displayed rare introspection in recognizing the way in which the sport of turkey hunting held him in thrall; he also had the storyteller's knack for describing to the uninitiated his addiction. The seven selections which follow give insight into the select company Rutledge kept. In reading them those who are not dedicated turkey hunters will no doubt gradually come to appreciate how rising day after day well before dawn, spending arduous hours afield, and returning home empty-handed can be an exercise in pure joy. And those with personal experience will sagely nod, smiling softly as they do so, in agreement. We turkey hunters will also recognize that beneath his humorous, and by today's standards chauvinistic, statement that "an incurable turkey hunter must either discipline his wife to his vagaries, or else suffer a good many domestic shocks," there runs an undercurrent of truth.

Turkey hunting is great fun, but it is also a fixation. To "talk turkey" with Rutledge is to be immersed in the sport's magic and mystique. We are carried afield with him as vicarious hunting partners, and we are afforded some measure of the boundless pleasure that the sport's devotees derive. Few have been better at putting that elusive pleasure into words and at depicting the turkey hunter's way.

ANY ONE'S TURKEY

The turkey-blind was a simple affair, made of green boughs leaning against two pines which stood almost together. Beyond the blind was a thin trail of peas and rice tailings on a strip of open ground, skillfully sprinkled with pine trash. All around the blind was a knee-high growth of dark-green gallberry bushes; then came the sweet myrtles with their cool and fragrant foliage; then the deep swamp where the turkeys roosted, with its tall gum trees, its shadowy tupelos, its towering elms, and its whispering poplars; beyond the swamp lay the wide, mysterious pinewoods, lonely, baffling. This spot was on Colonel Jocelyn's plantation, not far from the Great House and almost too near the Negro cabins. But the Colonel's code of honor was rigid, even to the point that he stooped not to suspecting even the lowest of his fellow creatures. And he was more than this. He carried his trust to the point of temptation. He proved this when he got Scipio to build the turkey-blind for him, in spite of the fact that rumors with regard to Scipio's persistent poaching and unreliability had come to his ears. Colonel Jocelyn did not believe it. He had known Scipio too long; there was not a better Negro on his plantation or any other. The Colonel expressed this judgment with some explosive emphasis to his frail, quiet-eyed little wife; and so, when on his way home from a deer hunt, he saw the turkeys go to roost one twilight, he sent for Scipio the next day and told him with great secrecy, in a sportsman's whisper, of the turkeys. Inasmuch as Scipio had found the nest in the summer, he had every turkey in the brood marked from the time when they came out of the speckled eggs; and inasmuch as, out of the twenty, he had already killed and sold seven, it required not a little diplomacy to express surprise at their discovery. Yet Scipio's praise and admiration of the Colonel's acuteness was in no wise failing. He listened with great attentiveness, and gravely assented to the Colonel's plan. Yes, he would build it right away; and he would get the rice tailings from the barnyard that very morning; oh, yes, he knew the very spot where his

From *Old Plantation Days* (1921).

boss wanted the blind put. Did he think the turkeys would take the feed? There was no doubt of it. Had Scipio seen them before? Not Scipio; he had not seen a wild turkey on the plantation for years; it was a miracle to him how his boss was so keen as to mark them down; his boss seemed a younger and a better woodsman every day. And, yes, Scipio would surely let him know the first time the turkeys took the feed.

After this conversation the Colonel walked briskly into the house, kissed his little wife affectionately, whistled a catch of an old love song, popular long before the War, and then went out to see the rice-thrashing in the barnyard. And wherever he went, Secret was written on every feature and found expression in every movement.

Meanwhile Scipio had, in all faith, built and baited the blind. He knew very well that the Colonel would forget all about it; that all his enthusiasm and spirit were as transient as a flash of sunlight through some dark door; that the turkeys were his if he could but keep up his cunning and his courage.

The very next day after the blind had been completed, Wash Green, returning from an intimate and friendly visit to some one else's potato bank on the neighboring plantation, and having in his possession that which was not intended for public inspection, took a short cut through the swamp and almost walked into the turkey-blind. He saw that it was freshly made and that no hogs had touched the bait; he noticed its location and guessed its purpose with self-applauding cunning. When he got home he brought his old smooth-bore musket down from the loft over his parlor and, drawing the buckshot, poured half a handful of No. 3's into the barrel and wadded it down with some black moss. Now, he thought, he would steal a march on that sly Scipio who had, time and again, thwarted him, and made him a subject of jest and laughter. Now if he, Wash Green, could slip into that turkey-blind early the next morning and bring home a fine gobbler, the chagrin of Scipio, who was always so proud about his hunting, would be acute and his defeat most mortifying. Wash always relished his victories before they came; he was wise in this where it was a question of getting the better of Scipio, for such victories never actually arrived.

And Scipio, while down in his heart he hated to deceive the Colonel, who had always been so fair and just to him, was fully prepared to make the blind a success. He, too, loaded his musket with big buckshot, and went to bed with his mind on the "moondown" as the time for him to be stirring. And when the moon, almost full—which all night long had sailed in lonely splendor over the purple pine woods, flooding the plantation fields and the great river, which moved slowly seaward, with her mysterious light—began to sink on the bosom of the pine forest, Scipio awoke and, stretching his arms, shuffled to the door. Yes, it was time for him to start. At "day-clean" turkeys flew down. He would be on hand if they came to the blind, but he hardly thought they would take the feed the first morning.

All night Scipio had been dozing in front of the fire with his clothes on; so, by merely reaching for his cap and musket he was ready to start. When he got outside of the cabin the morning air was chill and he buttoned his coat more closely about him. In doing so he felt in the pocket for his box of percussion caps. They were not there. He felt himself with growing and anxious excitement, but the caps were not to be found. Scipio swore softly. There was no use for him to go without the caps. He leaned his musket against the palings of his little garden and went back into the cabin. He must have been gone twenty minutes, and when he reappeared he had the caps but had lost his temper. He plunged out of the door, grasped his musket and disappeared in a foxtrot down the narrow path which led through the broomgrass from his cabin to the pinewoods. But the day had already come; in the east the pale colors were brightening and the sky overhead had its day-blue. The blind was half a mile away, and he would be fortunate if he got there before the turkeys flew down.

His gait took him through the woods swiftly. He was unconscious of their cool and dewy sweetness, their delicious freshness, their serene beauty and tranquillity; he knew only that before him, beyond a certain blind, a dozen wild turkeys might be at their breakfast, and that he might be too late to surprise them. As he got near the place, his anger was replaced by caution; his vehement pace slackened, and he bent low as he crept behind the blind. He slunk from pine to pine, keeping his sight on the clump of green bushes before him; as he came nearer and nearer he disappeared almost entirely in the gallberry bushes. And then, when he was thirty feet away, he was transfixed by something which caught his eye suddenly. He saw a movement in the blind before him. Scipio fell flat in the bushes, bewildered and amazed. Could it be Colonel Jocelyn? If so, he was keener than Scipio had imagined. If it was the Colonel, the presence of Scipio's musket would be embarrassing. Slowly, and with infinite caution, Scipio, without bending his knees, raised himself on his hands and peered over the bushes. He could see nothing. A loose branch had fallen over the entrance of the blind and hidden its occupant. Even while Scipio peered there came a mighty roar from the blind, and every aperture seemed to belch forth smoke. Then Scipio sprang up and, flattening himself behind a big pine, peered forth. What he saw filled him with surprise, anger, and the spirit of vengeance. He saw Wash Green plunge out of the blind, hat in hand, and rush out on the open space where the bait lay. He saw him run down toward the edge of the swamp, stoop down, and rise with a magnificent bronze gobbler held in his hand. Scipio gulped hard, and his thoughts crowded fast. His mind was already made up when Wash, twenty yards away, turned his back and again looked toward the swamp. He had swung the gobbler over his shoulder and had replaced his old, creased black-felt hat jauntily on the side of his head. And so he stood for a moment, a picture of satisfaction and of debonair content.

Scipio had sometimes had occasion to call to him many wild animals which had thereby fallen before his musket. He knew, too, how to imitate the voices of men. With sudden decision he jerked his musket to his shoulder:

"Ha, nigger!" cried Colonel Jocelyn's irate voice, and as it reached the ears of Wash, Scipio's musket roared forth. Wash's black-felt hat flew off and lodged in a myrtle bush; Wash himself sprang into the air as if preparatory to aerial flight; the gobbler fell to the earth, and the terrified Negro crashed through the bushes, screaming and rubbing his head with both hands. He did not look back, but ran on and on, screaming louder and louder as he found the shot had not hurt him. And so he disappeared.

After a few minutes Scipio came out from the shelter of his pine. He fixed up the blind and then walked down to the gobbler and the felt hat. He took the latter out of the bush and grinned as he looked at it. There were five tiny holes through the top of it, front and back. He stuffed it into his pocket, picked up the gobbler and, stopping at the blind to get Wash's musket, was soon on the path homeward.

It was some time before Wash returned home, and as Scipio's cabin was near his, Scipio sat on his steps and watched for the return of the wanderer. They were far enough apart to make it safe for Scipio to grin, as he had ample reason to when he saw the dejected form of Wash Green emerge from the pines and slink along to his cabin. The next morning Scipio's rival found his musket with his cap on the end of it leaning up against his door. And to this day he has not had the courage to thank Colonel Jocelyn for returning them.

Calling a Wild Gobbler

The first thing for the caller to do is to locate his gobbler, which will be, of course, at dawn, still in a tree. The easy way to locate a gobbler is to imitate the whoop of an owl, a sound with which the turkey is so familiar that it rouses him to answer in a challenging fashion without creating in him any suspicion. During the springtime a wild gobbler will answer almost any natural noise of the forest, even the rapping of a woodpecker. He answers most readily from his roost at dawn. But the one call that will bring him flying or running to you is the voice of the hen.

Going into a plantation swamp before daylight one morning, before touching my call, I hooted like a barred owl. To my surprise and delight I was answered, not by one, but by *five* gobblers, roosting at various distances from me—from two hundred yards to a quarter of a mile.

Making sure that I was near enough to this particular gobbler to enable him to hear and to locate me, across the misty swamp I sounded the call: "Keow! Keow! Keow! Keow!"

"Gil-obble-obble-obble!" came the virile answer immediately from the moss-shrouded tupelos up the ridge from where I was seated. A second gobbler answered farther off. This fact was fortunate; for here were rivals. A few moments later, a Cooper's hawk, early awing, gave a scream above the silent river. Again both gobblers answered vigorously, but I kept silent.

While I was playing my waiting game, the wild sweet woodland was awakening all about me. In this solitude the primeval prevails, and it seems to sleep and to wake under the aspect of eternity. Day broadened fast; and the pink and pearly light tenderly revealed the quiet beauty of the trees and bushes, now in their first delicate emerald mist of greenery. The cypresses are the most impressive trees of the swamp, patriarchs older than our Nation,—huge old Titans, ten feet through at the base. Here the holly grows to magnificent proportions, towering seventy feet. Here the water-oak, the tupelo, the sweet gum, the black gum, and the

From *Wild Life of the South* (1935).

yellow pine throng in friendly concourse. Over the bushes and the low trees climbs the yellow jasmine; banding the larger growths huge muscadines clamber. Among the humbler flora are the homelike blackberry, the wild blue flag, the wampee, long purple carpets of blue and white violets, and ferns of magical delicacy and design.

Of the wild things awake and moving in the swamp I saw an old raccoon, pacing sedately down an animal path that ran through a thin growth of dwarf canes. Cardinals I heard, and red-winged blackbirds, vireos and woodpeckers, gray squirrels in positive abundance, brown thrashers, wood ducks.

While I was enjoying the beauty of the swamp about me, the two gobblers had been calling more vehemently, until the whole dewy forest rang with their importunate clamor. It had been twenty minutes since I had given my call a touch. Now I sound it again, softly, seductively. I then heard what only one who haunts the wilderness will hear: the peculiar pompous sounds that a gobbler makes while strutting on the limb on which he has roosted. The performance is exactly like that of a tame bird, except that the monarch's stance is a very teetery one, so that his attempt to make himself overwhelmingly imposing is interrupted by the nervous necessity of keeping his balance.

After a few minutes I heard one of the great birds fly to the ground; then the other came splendidly hurtling with ponderous grace to the earth. I gave two faint notes on the call, and then put it in my pocket. They would come to me. "There ain't a surveyor," I once heard an old woodsman say, "who can run a straighter line than a gobbler will make for a hen."

Peering through the tangled screen of vines and twigs, I watched the long slope of the ridge for the approach of the two monarchs. Coming from slightly different directions, they would probably meet within sight of me. Then, unless I interfered, a battle would ensue.

From the time I started to call until the first gobbler came within sight, the elapsed time was fifty-five minutes. Broad daylight had penetrated even the most remote fastnesses of the swamp.

Almost simultaneously the gobblers appeared: one on the crest of the ridge and one on the side. With obvious yet wary majesty they came, their plumage gleaming, their heads held high. They knew that they should now be within sight of the object of their desire. All this while, faintly and far away, I could hear the three others sounding their challenges from the trees from which they had not yet come down.

While the deer's sense of smell is most acute, the wild turkey's is almost negligible. But his eyes are telescopic in their power. What he detects most easily is movement; and if one remains perfectly still, especially behind some kind of natural cover, the monarch may come very close. Hidden in a turkey-blind, I have had two gobblers come within twelve inches of where I lay.

The two birds were aware that they had come to the rendezvous, and that the hen must now be in sight. They therefore recommenced their strutting, each trying to outdo the other in creating an illusion of grandeur in the presence of the supposed ladylove. The first rays of the sun were now striking long golden lances through the dewy glade, throwing a natural spotlight on these two magnificent birds, as with rigid wings spread until they touched the ground, they pirouetted in their stately woodland minuet.

These knights of the deep swamp, while not strutting prodigiously and menacingly, would suddenly turn normal, and would peer with searching beady eyes for the true object of all their self-display. Yet it was quite evident that they intended to fight; and as that seemed a shame, for I hate to see a fight (which usually means beauty and peace disheveled, and no advantage gained), I rose from my hiding place and stepped quietly forward.

Those who have no faith in magic should see what I then saw. Two great birds, thirty feet from me on the open forest floor, suddenly vanished. The getaway of a startled wild turkey is one of the most artistic performances in nature. These two disappeared in a second; but I had had the satisfaction of having called America's noblest game bird up to me.

TALKING TURKEY

On that day on which we managed to secure the Christmas Eve buck, we had seen turkeys; and whenever I see these traveling the woods in unmolested fashion, I am sure that they are making the rounds of their daily range. Indeed, on more than one occasion, I have taken up a stand on an old road or trail at a certain time of day, knowing that wild turkeys were practically sure of crossing at that point at a definite hour. Their habits are as orderly, and they love home as dearly, as quail; but of course they have a much farther range; and from it they are temporarily driven by even a little molestation.

Though I have killed many wild turkeys in the mountains of Pennsylvania and of Western Maryland, true turkey gobbler land is not found until one has reached the deep South.

Five hundred miles south of Richmond, on the line that a crow would follow if he were heading for Cuba, about ten miles in from the coast, deep in a quiet forest, there's an oasis. In a lone stretch of arid pineland it's a placid pond, and there isn't a thing in it to drink save water. I am not sure that you would drink that water, for the pond isn't large and it gives harborage to many frogs, fish, snakes, turtles, alligators and such like "creeters." Besides, a colony of herons has a rookery there.

It isn't much of an oasis for man; but in a dry time I have known deer and turkeys to come six and seven miles to that place to drink, and on its borders I have seen the tracks of a black bear, though I never saw their maker in that whole country. But tracks don't lie. It was near this pond that I began to acquire that huge respect for the wild turkey which is now a part of my nature. I have the same reverence for a turkey that I have for a julep, a dollar, and some of these other delightful, elusive things. But here's the story of how it all happened.

It was in mid-November, when the Southern woods are in their pride of beauty. I was abroad in the pinelands, presumably looking for strayed stock. But take it from me, when a native in the South begins to act

From *An American Hunter* (1937).

restless at home and tells his wife that he has to go out in the woods to hunt for stock, he's after wild stock. He wants to see a hog with antlers on his noble brow, and a lost sheep that calls, "Quow! Quow! Quow!" Besides, when he locates this lost stock of his, he will take a strange attitude toward his domestic creatures that have wandered from home; he will shoot them on the spot. I know about this. It's a kind of autumn fever, and the way to cure it is to take to the woods, and the excuse to offer is that the pigs and cows have run off.

Well, I came to the oasis. It was late in the afternoon, and the day had been warm. The drought had been long and severe, and this water in the pond was a precious thing. It was so dry in the coastal country that deer hunters carried bottles of water for their hounds. At least they told me so, and showed me the bottles; but I'm getting very meanly suspicious these days. Who knows but that "hound water" may not just be a name for something else?

It seemed to me that if I loitered, lingered, hesitated on the borders of this pond at sundown, still looking, of course, for strayed stock, something might heave into sight over the horizon. That surely sounds fine. I tied my horse about a quarter mile back in the woods; then I sauntered down to the edge of the pond.

On its scummy, black surface I saw a small flock of wood ducks. Two alligators, taking a last look-around before scuttling themselves in the mud for the winter, drifted on the pond's surface. I saw some huge frogs sitting in a melancholy council on the smooth bank. They looked most virtuous and solemn.

On the far side of the pond, two animal paths withdrew into the forest, vanishing in knee-high huckleberry bushes. It was on these two paths that my gaze rested languishingly—this is the word to describe the look of the hunter who has searched for game all day and who toward evening is still gameless.

I skirted the pond edge until I came within gunshot of the two paths. Then I hid myself by sitting down and keeping perfectly still. It seems generally true that for a man to be motionless is for him to be hidden from a wild creature—unless it's a buck to leeward of you.

On the pond the 'gators alligatored; the ducks ducked; and on the pond-slope the frogs kept on looking impressive. I could have taken home frogs' legs, but they look paltry when you are really after a venison haunch or a wild turkey. I kept my watch.

In fifteen minutes I saw the huckleberry bushes move. They appeared alive. Something was coming through them. I eased myself up an inch to see; I counted eight gobblers—think of it—eight! They were feeding slowly through the bushes. I had figured that, of course, any wild life which came near the pond at that time of day would surely come to drink. But the turkeys did not notice the pond. They were feeding in that quietly restless manner, and moving certainly in that one direction which shows that they are on their way to roost.

As they were now heading, they would not come within gunshot. If I moved, they might see me. They clearly had it in their minds to cross the sandy road that lay to westward of the pond. There was an old gum-tree swamp beyond, where some original timber was still standing. Here, thought I, they would roost. I would try to intercept them on their way to bed; if I failed in this plan, I would, at least, "roost" them.

Plans like this always seem as simple and as certain as making money on the stock market. But schemes are not certainties; and that's why some men lose money, and others lose chances at wild turkeys; but particularly that's why we have a few wild turkeys left in his land of many hunters.

My immediate business was to efface myself, and at the same time to move quickly. This is no easy thing to do, especially when you are painfully conscious that the keenest eyes and ears in the wild-life world are bringing their periscopes to bear on you. If ever a hunter wants to feel like a blundering boob, let him try to crawl upon a wild turkey, or, worse yet, on a flock of turkeys. In the latter case, he'll likely be a flock of boobs.

However, I tried to make myself small; I lay flat, and began to crawl through the huckleberries. This was a process which had associated with it a haunting thought: here by this pond was a famous rendezvous for diamondback rattlers; and this was the very season of the year when they, roaming about in search of hibernation quarters, would be most likely to encounter a fool man poking his head through the bushes just on a level with their battery's trajectory. I recalled with unpleasant vividness a huge eight-foot creature of this variety that I had seen killed not more than a hundred yards from where I was now crawling. But I kept on.

Just as I thought I had finished the maneuver, I looked back at the turkeys. They were not much over gunshot away, and just taking the rise of a small bushy hill. I counted them again. The number was surely eight. And they were gobblers. One was a magnificent old bird. I watched him literally roll his unwieldy bulk over a fallen log. I began to wonder if I could really get him on the horse, you know, and whether I ought to try to kill the whole flock or just about seven out of the eight. Truly, pride has her fall, and a hunter's pride ends in an avalanche.

I was certain that I could now skulk swiftly through the bushes and intercept the flock before the birds reached the gum-tree swamp. I did all I could in the way of speed and caution. I came to the very spot that I was positive the turkeys would have to cross. Then I got ready to shoot. The chief thing that worried me was how to get so many home on horseback. But the birds did not appear. I looked the pinelands over from my position behind some palmetto fans on the swamp edge. I rose higher, still looking. I edged over to a tall pine, and now I was at full height, still looking. That was several years ago, and I'm still looking!

Those turkeys simply vanished. They were not out of my sight three minutes, but they blankly disappeared. After a long while I said to myself laboriously, as if the thing really couldn't be, "They're gone." I was telling the truth. And when a man says a turkey is gone, that's the past participle and also the superlative of go. I did not quit my stand until deep dusk. As I walked toward my horse, giving it to the great bird with my deepest powers of awesome respect, I jumped a thundering big buck. I shall never forget his flag, and the wild race he made through the twilight forest. But I was done for that day.

Yet I was not through. While riding disconsolately homeward, I heard a soft step in the sandy road. A dark figure loomed ahead. It greeted me, and I was glad to tell the story of my misfortune to Gannett Cumbee, an ancient hunter of the pinelands. I will not describe him other than to repeat a story of him told by some fun-loving acquaintances of mine.

"Gannett," they will say, "is the toughest man in this country. We don't mean bad or ugly, but just hard. Mosquitoes blunt their bills on him; and it's a fact that when Gannett was working the roads in Hell Hole Swamp not long ago a diamondback about three yards long bit him twice. And the diamondback died!"

Cumbee listened to my tale of woe. I caught him smiling in the darkness.

"I used to have two ketch-dogs," he said, with more relevancy than seemed at first apparent, "and I named them 'Slip' and 'Stealaway.' Them's right good turkey names, too. They describe the whole race. And lemme tell you," he went on. "Never you wait for a wild turkey to say 'put,' the second time. If ever he says 'put,' you say 'bang!'"

"But, Gannett," I remonstrated, "that's all right if you're within range. I've sense enough not to let a scared turkey go through all the preliminaries of a getaway without a salute from me. But I wasn't within range of these at all."

"They seen you by the pond," came the answer. "A turkey will always see you if you move."

Gannett may be hard and he may be rough, but he's taught me some true things about wild turkey nature.

I remember another evening's adventure. A freshet was in the river, and all the lowlands were deeply flooded. At such a time in the delta country a man can have all sorts of sport just following the freshet edges. I had come to a wild thicket, inviolate even to Negro trappers because it was an ancient plantation graveyard. On the dark borders of this I sat down and began to call. Before me was an old field grown to young pines, but they stood sparingly and they had no low branches. I could clearly see what was coming. To my right, fifty yards away, a steep bank fell off and met the creeping freshet tide.

In the dreamy afterglow I called pleadingly. I was using a willow box with a locust top. This combination gives a sure and mellow tone. Suddenly, a movement at the right attracted my attention. I saw a turkey take a step on the brink of the bank. It was a stately bird, and only fifty yards off; but that's not a sure distance for a gobbler. I grasped my gun. As I did so, I heard a startled "put!"

I remembered Cumbee's warning. Quickly I fired, though I had it in my mind to do some certain-looking but fool thing like trying to get ahead of the turkey down in the thicket—and the gobbler disappeared. But I found him lying just at the edge of the thicket. I, in a different sense, "gave it" to that great bird.

While hunting deer, always expect a turkey to walk out or to fly out at the first shout of the driver, the first bark of a hound, the first crack of a stick. A fox may amble out later. An old buck may steal out ahead of the hounds, or he may lie close until they get into the very bed with him. But a wild turkey hates noise, and he has a very nice ear to distinguish what each noise means. I have seen turkeys, taking the bait before a blind, literally melt away as I, in peering at them, inadvertently snapped a tiny pine twig in the texture of the blind. But sometimes a man can come up close on a turkey, and he can be making a lot of noise, too. Strangely, a wild turkey fears not an automobile, nor a buggy, nor a man mounted.

Well I remember an old gobbler up to which I rode. My father and I were hunting deer in the pinelands, and the hounds were trailing ahead of us. It is great sport to ride up deer and shoot them from horseback. I know one man who uses a rifle for this sport, and he has killed some twenty bucks thus riding them out of their daytime lairs. I thought the hounds were after a fox, for the trail seemed mazy.

Suddenly, two hundred yards ahead of us, from the top of a tall pine a big turkey launched himself forth. He had probably flow up there when the dogs began to trail, and he had watched our coming. We rode on slowly, thinking that a bird would fly up out of the dense cover of mixed broomgrass and gallberries which we were traversing. One did. A gobbler of truly lordly size, literally to avoid getting stepped on, flapped ponderously up beneath my horse's very nose. The turkey had evidently been squatting under a bush, and he had stayed tight until the horse's lifted foot above him made him take wing. Had I been on the ground, I could have killed the big bird with a stick.

His getaway was curiously ponderous and awkward. But I was mounted, and worse than mounted, for my startled horse threw his head back and took me in the face. Then he stood up on his heels and turned about. I jerked him down and tried to get my gun to my face. But I was half blinded.

Meanwhile the gobbler was getting away; and the farther he went, the faster he went. I finally let drive after him with turkey-shot at about eighty yards, and I saw one wing-feather fall. But as far as I could see, the escape was complete. The great bird got the better of me; but I've always said that my low-bred marsh pony was in collusion with that turkey.

There's a place not far from home called Wambaw Corner. The big timber was cut out about ten years ago; since then it has become a wilderness of tie-tie vines, young pines, hollies, myrtles, and a thousand other riotous growing things. Also, it is a great corner for turkeys.

I was walking down an old path there late one afternoon, at the bright close of a day of showers. A trusty Nego hunter was about a hundred yards off to my right. I was looking for signs in the path, and of deer tracks there were plenty. But the white sand was beaten too hard for a turkey to leave a track.

My attention was attracted to a piece of old bark that something had evidently just turned up. I stooped to examine it. I just felt that a turkey had not long since wandered down that path and had stopped to pick at that bark and to turn it over. While stooping, I heard a soft warning whistle from the Negro. I rose cautiously. A bronzed gobbler, the sheen of the late afternoon sun glinting on his plumage, was literally flying over my head. He was just clearing the tall myrtles which bordered the pathway. He was, perhaps, twenty-five feet up. He was so close that I was afraid the turkey-shot would blow him to feathers. My left barrel carried 4's. This load I drove home, as I thought.

The bird certainly was hit, for many feathers drifted down between me and the setting sun. But the turkey did no downward drifting. What he did so impressed me remarkably; I have to give it to him that, when wounded, he executed an able maneuver. He began to tower—not as a quail does that is shot in the head, but as a duck does after your ineffective greeting of him. The turkey kept this rise almost as far as I could see him; and as he rose he turned until, instead of being headed toward the settlement, he was headed for a deep river-swamp. When I last saw him, he was above the tops of the tallest pines, and his going was like that of an airplane.

When my Negro hunter joined me, he was grinning. He had seen the whole performance.

"You walked him up," I said.

"He been flyin' when I fust see him," he answered. "But," he added, "he ain't done start to fly right till you shoot."

"Well, if he keeps on, he'll roost on the moon tonight."

"Some of these wild creeters," my hunter said with what seemed to me sound philosophy, "jest ain't meant to die. Gun can't talk no kind of talk to dem!"

I couldn't excuse myself in that way; but I could feel that I had added just one more experience which makes me always willing to give it to the great bird—with honest lead if I can; if not, with candid acknowledgment on my part of general inferiority.

DAYBREAK IN THE OCEAN

Detecting the approach of game by footsteps is always interesting; listening to the voices of game is even more fascinating. Of course, some game is singularly silent: the wild deer, the ruffed grouse, and certain species of ducks are remarkable for their reticence. But the wild turkey is both a noisy walker and a garrulous soul.

Although I have hunted wild turkeys all my life, and as a result have killed them in many places under varying circumstances, a thing happened to me lately in my quest of these regal birds that had never happened to me before. I pass it on to my fellow sportsmen, believing that all of us can profit by the true experiences of one another. After all has been said about superior marksmanship, and expensive guns and ammunition, the degree of one's sport and the degree of one's success as a hunter will chiefly be determined by his skill as a woodsman. The man who doesn't know the nature of his game stands a small chance of forming a table-acquaintance with it.

Now, the business came about in this way: driving down an old sandy road on my Carolina plantation late one afternoon, I saw seven gobblers walk calmly across in front of me. Unarmed, I was defenseless, so to speak. All I could do was stop the car and watch them steal along through the golden broomsedge, with the last long rays of the setting sun glinting on their bronzed backs. Silently they vanished over a little hill in the lonely pinelands. The sun set. A vast stillness lay over the dreaming woods.

As the surrounding country has been intimately known to me since boyhood, I had a pretty good idea of where those gobblers were going to roost. After sundown, if undisturbed, wild turkeys will not wander far before going to roost; so if one sees them very late in the afternoon, and knows the country, he can tell pretty well where they will take the trees.

Moreover, like quail, turkeys have a definite range—far more extensive, of course, yet limited with fair definiteness. If one is familiar with this

---

From *An American Hunter* (1937).

range, he can often intercept the great birds at a particular place at a certain time of day. In fact, I have often killed turkeys by merely taking up a stand beside an old road that I knew they were accustomed to cross at that point at about the same hour each day. The more I hunt, the more I realize that the one great prerequisite for success is the careful study of the habits of the game which is being pursued.

Now, adjacent to my rambling old plantation there are at least two great natural sanctuaries for wild game. One is the wild Santee delta, to which deer, turkeys and even quail resort when they are much disturbed; and as far as I am concerned, I have made it a practice to keep the delta inviolate. The other haven is the so-called Ocean—a vast tract of wilderness; a dense area of bays, myrtles, thickets of high-bush huckleberry, deep copses overgrown with smothers of wild grape, smilax and swamp briers. When game gets into the Ocean, we usually consider that it has made good its escape, and never attempt to molest it there.

Those seven gobblers that I saw late that afternoon crossing the road were heading toward the Ocean. As there is no big timber in the Ocean itself, but only a wide sea of low greenery, I was satisfied that these birds would roost somewhere between the road and the Ocean; and the line of their course I rather accurately determined. To attempt to follow them then might spoil all the sport of the following morning; hence I just drove on home, deciding to make a start before daylight.

Regarding the roosting of turkeys in that country, I want to say a word, for all matters of this kind are of interest to true sportsmen. It is commonly taken for granted that the wild turkey will select for his roost the biggest tree he can find. While it is true that they like big timber on their range, I have not often found them roosting very high or in the largest trees. On my place they nearly always sleep in the thickest parts of the crests of yellow pines of medium height.

Once I saw a big gobbler fly up on a great pine, the top of which naturally sprawled out a good deal. He evidently felt exposed, and before dark he sailed down forty feet into the heavy crest of a much younger and much thicker pine.

Turkeys often roost in the cypresses, sweet-gums and tupelos of a swamp or watercourse. Since these trees are leafless in the winter, it would be supposed that the birds would easily be seen in these bare trees. But the swamp trees of the South are generally hung with great gray banners of Spanish moss, and festooned with huge bunches of mistletoe, and decorated with many squirrel nests, so that wild turkeys, even when roosting in leafless trees, have a lot of natural camouflage to protect them.

Many a hunter has craned his neck and strained his eyes to try to distinguish a turkey from a big bunch of mistletoe; and as often as not he has shot at the wrong object. I usually try to discover what object in the tree does not belong there; and it is generally possible, even in the dim dusk, to make out the head and neck of the bird moving, and to see the long tail, with its square end, hanging down.

As to the height at which these wild turkeys roost, I have seen them as low as twenty feet, and have stood under a whole flock in the starlight, not more than thirty feet above my head. I would say that the wild turkey always roosts within easy gunshot range of the ground.

When disturbed on the roost in the morning, they nearly always fly to the ground; but when disturbed in the evening or at any time during the night, they nearly always fly to other trees. In fact, I have never known one then to come to ground.

In flying to other trees, it is astonishing how short is the distance that they travel. I have rarely known them to go more than two hundred yards, and sometimes to fly not more than fifty. Indeed, I have repeatedly been able to see turkeys alight in other trees when they had been run off their roosts. When thus routed, they will more likely alight in bare than in evergreen trees—possibly because they can more clearly see convenient perches. If the birds are flushed in the late afternoon, and take to trees, they may stay where they are throughout the night.

Before daylight next morning I was back at the place where I had seen the gobblers cross the road. It was a good morning for a turkey hunt: damp, misty, still. Game seems less wary under those conditions, and the hunter is enabled to make progress without much sound. Atmospheric conditions for calling are also perfect then.

By the time the day had begun to dawn wanly, I was a half-mile from the car, and was fairly certain that I must be within calling distance of the birds. On a dark morning, turkeys are slow to leave the roost; in fact, I have seen a whole flock in the trees on a very dismal rainy morning at nine o'clock. I wandered on warily, looking and listening, and enjoying the primeval beauty of that great forest. Southward, now, there stretched away the mysterious Ocean, glimmering in nameless wonder and ancient privacy. I knew that its border would mark the limit of my advance.

Over me were the great yellow pines, and those of lesser growth. Here and there on the rises were great hickories and water-oaks. In the watercourses towered hollies, gums, cypresses. So still was the air that I could distinctly hear sounds from a Negro settlement full three miles away and the rushing of cars on the highway just as distant. At the moment I was in a young thicket of gall-berries, young pines and bays, about waist-high. Between this copse and the Ocean there was the open pine forest, its floor bare but for the brown carpet of needles.

Suddenly, in the very thicket in which I stood, I heard a turkey call; then another; then another. The flock had come to ground without my being aware of their having left the roost. Some people think that wild turkeys call guardedly. Perhaps they sometimes do. But these called with amazing vigor and clearness. They were all about me, yet I couldn't see one because of the density of the thicket. They were much too close for me to try any calling myself. The best I could do for the moment was to stand motionless—helpless, if you please—while my game, within easy range yet invisible, made the morning woods echo with their wild, strident calls. It all seemed like a game called "I Have You, I Have You Not." And in this case, the emphasis was most decidedly on the "not."

Almost as suddenly as it had begun, the calling ceased. Then, about two hundred yards away, in the pinelands adjacent to the Ocean, I heard the turkeys talking. They were not calling, but were just conversing over their quiet little family reunion.

When a hunter more than six feet tall tries to efface himself in the woods, he is embarrassed. Long since I have resorted to crawling on the ground; yet in a country where rattlers may be abroad in the winter, there is some danger in that maneuver. But I wish I had a dollar for every hundred yards I have serpented myself through the woods.

Within five minutes I had cleared the copse, and was well out in the pinelands. Peering from behind a fallen log, I saw the seven gobblers about a hundred and twenty yards away, feeding slowly from me. Unsuspicious, they were as completely relaxed as truly wild turkeys ever become. They fed on the pine-mast, they frolicked a little, they picked at one another, all the time keeping up a querulous minor conversation.

And there I was—helpless. I knew well that it would be utterly vain for me to attempt to stalk them. They were out of range. They were feeding toward the gross thickets of the Ocean, into which it would be useless to attempt to follow them. Magnificent they were—all old birds, any one of which would be a noble prize. Yet what was a poor hunter to do? Go home, I supposed, with a grand hard-luck story; but you can't put a hard-luck story on the table.

True, I enjoyed watching these gobblers; but merely watching them did not exactly fulfill my dreams of what a turkey hunt should be. It was as if I were writing a love story in which I never permitted the hero and the heroine to meet.

While I was in the depths, a new sound came to my ears. Far to the eastward, perhaps a quarter of a mile away, I heard a lone turkey give a yelp. This call was immediately answered by a member of the retreating flock. As you know, a turkey can be called by a flock, but a flock will not go to a lone bird. Members of a flock will answer a call, but that answer means, "Well, here we are. Come on over," not "I'm coming."

As soon as that solitary note sounded through the lonely forest my plan was made. I might get the single bird to come to me, but I didn't like the competition I was up against. No hunter should flatter himself that he can call a wild turkey as well as another wild turkey can. Could I get one bird to call the other up to me?

Stifling the momentary feeling that such trickery might be mean, unworthy business, I continued my crawl so that I could station myself exactly on a line between the flock and the lonesome bird. At last I reached the place, and out of the tail of my eye could see that the seven lordly idlers were still unaware of my proximity. With a big pine between me and them, I eased myself to a sitting position, put my gun up, and waited. Gentlemen, what a wait! That lone bird acted as if he had lead in his shoes; certainly he was in no hurry at all to get shot.

To add to the excitement, a single bird detached itself from the "We are seven" assortment and began to approach me from the rear, calling all the time. To disconcert me still more, this calling was not at all what I expected to hear. It was not the standard "keow! keow! keow!" at all. The turkey behind me kept saying "put!" And the turkey in front kept answering in the same fashion. Nor did the nature of the note or the tone vary during the whole performance.

Closer and closer came the bird from behind, and I was afraid to bat my eyes. It approached within twenty-five yards. But I knew the other one was coming straight for me, and I had my gun leveled in his direction. Would he never heave in sight?

Yes, there he is, amazingly big, tall, shimmering; his long beard is arched out over his ample bosom. Now he is within sixty yards. Shall I shoot? He stops. His neck and head are very high. He's darned suspicious. Will he come closer? Has he made me out? He turns to the right, as if he is going to circle me. He turns his back. He's going to walk out on me. Now or never! The best place to shoot a wild turkey is in the back. I drive him with the choke barrel loaded with 2's. He's down!

I jump up and whirl to shoot the other bird. It is already in the air, and is a hen. I let her go. She must have joined the seven gobblers without my knowing it. I am satisfied with one. I retrieve my prize. Holy smoke, what spurs he has! The sun gleams through the morning mist, lighting up his plumage. He is a regal prize, and with a heart fully content I turn homeward.

Sometimes you can call a wild turkey to you; but for a real thrill and the infallibility of his coming, I strongly recommend letting one wild turkey call another one up to you.

Ain't a God's Turkey

Throughout that unpleasant episode known as the American Civil War, Jim Alston was my father's Negro body-servant. It was Jim who saved my father's life when, wounded and in a raging fever, he fell from his horse in the Potomac River during the Confederate retreat from Antietam. And the rescue was effected under the hot fire of Federal sharpshooters posted on the high rocky bluffs above the river.

After the war Jim was with us on the plantation for many years. Being a Romeo of parts, he married or consorted with one dusky damsel after another. The last one took him to her home, many miles from where Jim really belonged. My father never forgot Jim. Whenever they got together, they were like old cronies. I am afraid that I, being of a younger generation, forgot him. At least he had passed out of my mind for some years when one winter's day, hobbling along with the help of a gnarled dogwood stick, he came to visit me. He had walked sixteen miles, "all the way from Jeemstown."

I knew very well that he had not come all that distance merely to see me (you know about ulterior motives), but I made him happy and comfortable, and we had a good talk. Of course, I was expecting The Touch. But he had more legitimate business with me. The State of South Carolina, it seems, after discreetly waiting for the vast majority of her old soldiers to die off, had begun to pay pensions of $14 a month. I knew nothing of this, but Jim told me that the law had been in effect for about three years and that he had not yet seen any of the money due him. He wanted me to get his pension, and to use some speed in the matter, as he did not have exactly a stranglehold on life. I promised the old man to go to work immediately, and I intended to do so. But I forgot.

Six months later, to my embarrassment, old Jim appeared, driving in an ox-wagon this time. I told him the truth, and offered to lend him some money, promising at the same time to write the vital letter then.

From *American Rifleman*, August 1948. With minor revisions this story was later published as "My Favorite Hunting Story," in *Those Were the Days*.

He accepted the situation with that massive equanimity that a Negro alone possesses. He had no word of blame or protest. But a light dawned in his fine old eyes, and he said, "Lemme tell you a thing."

Before Jim had gone to war, and for some years thereafter, he had been the plantation hunter and fisherman. His sole duty was to supply the Great House with fish and game.

"Soon one mornin' in de fall, your Pa ride to my house. And when he used to come all the way to my house, I done already know I might as well hitch-up.

" 'Jim,' he say, 'Miss Elise comin' up from Cha'son, and Mr. Reginal', and Mr. Edmun', and they is bringin' friends. This is Thursday. We got to have two wild turkey for Sunday dinner. I would've let you know befo', but the word just come.'

"I tell him not to worry. I done already know where a heaby gang of turkey is, and if I can't kill two, he ought to get another plantation gunnerman. I done tell him put his min' at rest. And I tell him he might as well tell that good-for-nothing Sallie gal what he got in the kitchen to mash up the peanuts for the dressin'. I been dat sho about the thing!

"Now, I been long time baitin' them turkey, but I say I better go right off and see if any feed left. I get my hamper-sack, I fill him with rice-tailin' and some broom-corn and some little rice. So I gone to the place. You know that high hill where Susie's cabin used to be, but the house burn down long ago? From there you hold for that long savanna where the Three Sisters used to be—them three big pines what been cut down when I was a boy. Well, sah, that pine slope is the place."

I mildly suggested to Jim that Susie's cabin and the Three Sisters were unknown to me, and that I doubted if I ever could follow his directions. He eyed me quizzically.

"Cap'n," he said, "you don't know enough for me to tell you anything. Howsomeever," he continued, "when I done get there, the pinestraw all rake up. They been there, but maybe two days before. All the feed been gone. I scatter all I had, and I say I will come again tomorrow and see if they find what I bring. Soon in the morning I gone there, and I wait. I gone in the blind and wait till sunrise, and here they come, 'bout forty eleven dozen wild turkeys. I been there a long time, until they done leave. So I say, 'All right, I know you comin' tomorrow same time. If my hand be steady, the Big House will be full of turkeys!'

"That night, which was Friday night, I get ready. I get my ole musket down off the buckhorn rack. You know, Cap'n, you all is done got britches-loader. You just open the gun, slip in the shell, close the breech, and you all ready. But me, I got musket, and it takes time to load a musket the way I load him. 'Bout sundown it begin a jewin' rain. I say,

'All right. Ain't no rain gwine stop me!' I get my black powder and I pour a heaby big load in a saucer on the table. Then I pour out the shot in a saucer same fashion. Then I 'xamine my caps, and lay two of them by the fire to dry out good. I gone outside and get some black moss, and I hang it by the fire to dry. I always used to wad my load with a strip I tear off my shirttail. But Ca'line—you know that wife I used to have what name Ca'line, that no-good 'oman—she say she tired sewing up what I done tear, and she say a man will tear up he clothes like no 'oman will do. That's why I use the moss for waddin'. Well, sah, I wipe off my ole musket, and I blow down the barrel, and the air come clear out of the nipple. I pour in the powder, a debbil of a big load. Then I wad him down with the moss what had done dried off by the fire. 'Bout that time Ca'line tell me it rainin', and we ain't got no wood in the house. So I put on my coat and gone after the wood. I get wet up, too, and I ask how come she did not set her mind on wood till night and rain done come down. But you better not start no argument with no 'oman. All is trickety, and when one begins to talk, a man have to stand back.

"When I rack the wood by the fire, I put the dry caps on the table. Ca'line ax me how come I ain't coming to bed. So I gone to bed and drop asleep. But I can wake up all times of night. 'Bout the time all them hants and plateyes is creeping back to hide for the day, I been up. The rain been slack off, and ain't a wind stirrin'. I put one cap on the nipple, and one in my pocket, and I heist my foot for the turkey-blind. When I get there, day ain't clean yet. So I settle myself, and I make a peephole in the blind, and I wait, knowin' I ain't have to do a thing but take a straight aim at the whole flock and pull the trigger. Now, I been scatter that bait in a line what ran away from the blind. I like to shoot wild turkeys in the head. If you make a trail, all their heads will be together when they is feedin'.

"After a while I hear something. Great God, here they come! Nothin' but turkeys, and they come from every side, and every turkey run on the bait. They begin to eat from both sides of the trail. Their heads been as thick as black pepper. I know I can't miss. But I say I will have to go get the wagon for haul them home. Now, when turkeys is on the bait, you must wait no more. I ease my musket in the peephole. I lay the sight on the line of all them heads.

"*Wham-o-o-r-r!* The black powder make so much smoke I can't tell how much I kill. But I ain't worry. I know I kill plenty. The air been full of turkeys flying away, but I sartain sure 'bout a dozen can't fly. I take my time and climb out of the blind. I begin to look 'bout. Ain't a God's turkey! Ain't a fedder! Salvation Day, what is this? Can't be I miss all that gang of wild turkey. But, same like I tell you, ain't a drop of blood, ain't a scale off a leg! And I wonder what yo' Pa gwine say. Wusser still, I wonder what that mean Ca'line gwine say. I think maybe I bline and can't see the turkeys lyin' all around. But no. Ain't one. Please God, ain't a smell of one. I 'fraid to go home. I say maybe somethin' done happen to my min', and ain't been no turkeys. But the place been sandy, and I see all the fresh tracks.

"Well, sah, I know they ain't comin' back for maybe two or three days. I been in a fix. So I gone home. Now, I been tell Ca'line all 'bout my plan, and when I get near the house she been standin' in the door. Ever since we been married, she been tellin' me I no-account. She look as if she been satisfied she been right all along. I feel so too.

" 'I done hear you shoot,' she say. 'Where the white man dinner?' I tell her the musket gone off accident-like.

" 'You miss, then you lie,' she say. And I feel that way too.

"I walk by her and gone in the house. Cap'n, befo' God, the very fust thing I see is two saucer on the table. One been empty. The powder been in that. One been heap-up with shot. In the tarrigation with Ca'line 'bout the wood, I forgot to put the shot in my musket! I make that big fine plan. I ain't sleep much. I make high promise. I say I gwine show Ca'line what a man I is. I get in the blind, and the turkeys come right up to me, forty 'leven dozen of them. I get the dead bead on them. I pull the trigger. And ain't a God's shot been in the musket!"

Quite thrilled by this narrative, I asked old Jim about the upset Sunday dinner.

"I gone out late that day and killed a little buck, but your Pa was disappoint'. I tell him the same thing I done tole you, and all he say was, 'It isn't like you to do that, Jim.' I don't think he be'lieve me. I know it ain't like me, but still so I done do it. And it all come 'bout 'cause I forgot. You know why I tell you 'bout them turkeys?"

"It's a good story," I answered somewhat vaguely.

"No, sah, that ain't the reason why I tell you. You done understand now what happened to me because I forgot. A man must always remember. A long time ago, Cap'n, you promised me you gwine get my army money. You forgot. Ever since your Pa suspicion me 'bout that thing, and ever since that Ca'line give me that sass 'bout it, I ain't forgot nothin'. And you must not forgot poor old Jim Alston."

Oh, These Hunters!

I have long roamed the wilds with a remarkable man and yearly on deer and turkeys he practices his authentic legerdemain. This is Phineas McConnor, a slight, stooping Negro, who speaks with a lisping drawl. He is half Indian, and lives in the deep abysmal wilds westward from my plantation. Phineas appears to have an especial insight into the ways of wild creatures; he seems to think their thoughts along with them (or a little ahead of them). And he knows his woods. Yet he and I have sometimes been in places where it is not really safe to go unless the sun is shining. That is because in certain of the vast and gloomy cypress swamps of coastal South Carolina, so uniform is the timber, so huge the reaches of that primeval country, unless the hunter can properly locate the sun in the sky, he will be compelled to spend the night in that eerie wilderness, accepting for restless bedfellows wild boars, cottonmouth moccasins, and canebrake rattlers. Yet if you want an old bronzed gobbler, it is into such a place that you must go.

Whenever I want to know definitely about game, whether of the moldering delta or of the swamps or of the pinelands, I consult Phineas. Among the Negro woodsmen of my acquaintance, he is the authority. Except when discussing secrets of the wilds, he is a silent, almost shy, man, with a touch of that uncanny spirit of vivid alertness that often is found in one who has spent his life in outwitting the best intelligence of the game world.

Phineas calls wild turkeys with his mouth; he never uses an artificial lure; and he is one hunter who believes in calling the individual turkey. Looking at me, his wizened face alight, his eyes gleaming, he will say:

"Now I will call Old Ben for you; or, if you want to see her, I can call up Lizzie."

So familiar is he with the individuals composing a flock of wild turkeys that he has their number and their names; and apparently he can put one's number up whenever he wishes to. A part of his success comes

From *Hunter's Choice* (1946).

from his ability to make himself the least conspicuous thing for miles around. When I want to hide, the way Phineas conceals himself makes me appear spectacular. Crouched by a pine stump, he seems a part of it; a little bush will hide him. I have seen him, when cover is sparse, so flatten himself on the ground that he looks like a harmless little pile of trash or like a shadow on the ground.

"Turkreys," Phineas lisps to me, "is very curious. If they don't rightly understand what it is they see, they will come closer to see better. Now, when I see a flock that is not coming my way, and that I can't get ahead of, I hides myself. Then I takes out my red handkerchief and waves it at them. They will say, 'Kut! Kut!' and that means that they is wondering what that red thing is. After a little while, some will start for me. Then I shake the handkerchief again. Pretty soon all will be coming straight for me, and likely on a little fox-trot. They just have to find out what that curious red thing is. And they will come right up to me if I am hidden right."

"But, Phineas," I once asked him, "why don't you use a white handkerchief?"

He laughed slyly, amused over his own fathoming of the wild turkey's mind.

"If they see a white one," he answered, "they will just say, 'Look at that old buck switching his tail off yonder.' They know him. They is not curious about him. They will not come."

While Phineas actually performs this maneuver, there is a certain necromancy about it that has prevented my trying it. I have often seen a flock of wild turkeys under the circumstances he has described to me as the correct ones for the use of the red handkerchief; but I never had the nerve to try it.

"Another thing," Phineas tells me: "turkreys is stubborn, especially gobblers. I often call one until he gets about a hundred and twenty yards from me; then he will stop. He is too far to shoot; and it is not safe to call him much when he is so close. I have had many a one to stop out of gunshot, and fool around there a half-hour before he would walk off. But there is one way to bring him to you. You must be hid so close that he can't make you out at all. It works best if you have on an old felt hat and boots—especially rubber boots. When he is in that stubborn mood, you ease off your hat and you hit it against your boot three or four times, real hard. If you do it right, it will sound just like two gobblers fighting. Then the one you are after gets curious; he has to find out who is fighting. He will come. But you must have your gun ready; for when he starts, he will likely come running; and if he sees you getting your gun up he will quit the country—he will quit the world," he adds spaciously. "Always get your gun up before he starts for you."

Oh, these hunters! Many a mother will praise Daniel Boone to her children, yet will think hunters cruel, and will hesitate to let her boys become hunters. Few things would be more likely to make men of them. The hunters of our country carry out a long, honorable, and glorious tradition; and they contribute greatly to the fearlessness, the endurance, and the ruggedness of our national spirit.

Memorable Hunts
~Part III~

Any sportsman who spends appreciable time afield will enjoy experiences that he will cherish for a lifetime. Such red-letter days involve exceptional success or some unanticipated development which makes them stand out. However, it may be an odd twist of fate, or perhaps a failure so singular in nature as to be unforgettable, that etches recollections of the hunt in the mind of the hunter.

Archibald Rutledge was a participant in many memorable hunts. He also readily recognized that, of all the shooting sports, turkey hunting particularly lends itself to unforgettable quests. Merely managing to take a mature gobbler is a momentous feat.

In my opinion, for all his love and knowledge of deer, it was when it came to telling tales of turkey hunting that Old Flintlock was at his very best. He could take the bare threads of a day afield and weave tales of wonder or woe. He was masterful at the art of embellishing without losing credibility, and certainly he would have been among the first to proclaim the truth inherent in the old adage " 'Tis a poor piece of cloth that can stand no embroidery."

That is not to suggest that the pieces which follow are fiction, or even that the events they report have become distorted in the retelling. It is, rather, that these stories pay special tribute to the poet's ability to craft turkey-hunting pieces in such a fashion that they truly become "tales well told."

Blacks, whom Rutledge was fond of calling his "dusky henchmen," figure prominently in several of the stories. At first glance those who don't know Rutledge might be offended. In that regard, I would simply note that what is today sometimes termed "political correctness" was not always so. Rutledge cherished his relationships with the working men and women of the plantation. Further, one of the appealing aspects of the hunt is that the sportsman can choose his companions. Rest assured that Rutledge preferred being afield with individuals near and dear to his heart. His depictions of the roles his "henchmen" played in the hunting field describe things as they really were in Lowcountry South Carolina of his day.

Such considerations aside, these tales collectively convey most of the elements which make turkey hunting a great one sport—gladness and sadness, delicious irony, abject failure, sudden surprises after agonizing periods of waiting, and the eventual rewards which persistence and perserverance produce. Rutledge shares with us the joy of taking the "regal bird" that was his 339th gobbler. The fact that he had kept count reminds us that to him each hunt was memorable.

THE BISHOP
EARNS A GOBBLER

I had this adventure shortly after I had returned to my plantation home.

This performance began when I shot a huge bull alligator some years ago in comparatively shallow water, in a place with the sinister name of Satan Swamp. I was close to the big saurian; I heard the bullet strike; and I saw the great reptile sink, with the water reddening above him as he went down. I did a little probing with a long pole; but as these grim babies have a disconcerting way of coming to life when they are supposed to be decently dead, I was none too enthusiastic about going into that black water after him. I was alone at the time; my wife was constantly begging me to be careful; and I knew the nature of the game that had been shot. I knew also that whenever a hunter is alone in the woods at any time, and anywhere, he should be especially cautious about taking care of himself. If he has a friend with him, he has some insurance; but if he is alone, as I then was, and anything goes wrong, he is liable to be in real difficulty.

My decision was to go home, rig up some kind of grappling hook on an especially long pole, and, returning to the scene, see if I could not hook the old boy and drag him to the shore. I had intended to bring Prince with me. But Prince, as he usually did when most urgently needed, had mysteriously vanished. He was probably assisting one of my wildwood neighbors in the secret and delicate alchemy of distilling.

My grappling hook was nothing but a big shark hook. This I tied to the end of a long red cedar pole. Then I thrust this contraption through the window of my car. Its middle rested on top of the back seat, and the heavy hook was far up on top of the back seat, directly behind my head when I was behind the wheel.

Equipped for retrieving my big bull, I drove out of the avenue at a fast clip, the end of the pole projecting from the front window. I did not

---

From *Sports Afield*, February 1956. Later included in *The Woods and Wild Things I Remember* (1970).

know it, but the point of the shark hook had become embedded in the upholstery on top of the back seat. Before I realized what was happening, the pole had caught in a pine tree close to the road. In an instant the pole was bent almost double; the hook held for a second, then tore out viciously. I saw all the starry heavens as it struck me full force on the back of the head; then merciful darkness descended on me.

Black Prince found me. When I woke up, I was in bed at home, my head swathed in bandages. For several days I remained prone and groggy. My good foreman meanwhile had retrieved the bull alligator. A monster he was, all of fourteen feet.

This little plantation incident happened in late February, toward the end of the wild turkey season. Already I had killed four gobblers (the season's limit being five). It irked me to be so laid up that my chance of getting another did not seem to be in the books.

It should be understood that turkey hunters are a strange breed. A real turkey hunter follows his sport as if it were a religious rite; he is a man of infinite caution, woodcraft and patience. He will desert home, wife, job, and babies for long periods of time, just for a chance at one of these old bearded men of the wilderness. He is a consecrated, a dedicated man; admirable, too, in the sense that his virtues are those the pioneers had. He will even leave his bed long before daylight and go after a wild turkey—if his wife will let him. Sometimes she has to hide his clothes to make him behave.

But my battered head was not the only thing the matter with me. The bishop of our diocese was about to make what is known as his "annual visitation"; and to my wife this was by far the greatest occasion of the year. Quite near the bounds of my ancient plantation is the old St. James Parish Church, built in 1768. One service only is held there each year; and, being in the nature of a reunion, it is more a social than a religious gathering. Old parishioners come from far and near, bringing their dinner baskets and their gossip hampers with them. Undisturbed by this gay annual gathering, the men and women of an earlier day sleep in the churchyard; the bloods of racetrack, card table and dueling; the beauties of many a reception, many a dance, many a love affair. Now all have fallen asleep—their loves, hopes, fears and ambitions in a little dust quiescent.

I was not well enough to go wild turkey hunting, but my wife suggested that it certainly would do me no harm to go to church with her on this Sunday of all Sundays. She refrained from saying that I positively needed it, but she looked as if she thought I did.

"The bishop's coming, you know," she reminded me.

In defense I held strongly to the notion that by Sunday I would be well enough to try for one last gobbler, whereas church might give me a considerable physical and spiritual setback. A woodsman in church is often uncomfortably reminded of his sins, whereas his city brother is not likely to be so troubled. My lack of immediate and unbounded enthusiasm for the bishop's visit grieved my wife. She began to show signs that she meant to have her way.

"You will have to get Prince to drive you to Georgetown on Saturday," she told me firmly, as if she had it all planned, "so that Dr. Barber can change your bandages. When people see you at church, I don't want them to think that we have had a disagreement." Then she added, "You look as if someone hit you with a rolling pin."

"I tell you what," I said decisively, "I don't want to disgrace you before all your friends and relatives by the way I look, and I just don't see how I can help looking the way I do. Let me drive you to church. A lot of people will be coming here after the service, and any one of them would be glad to bring you home. As soon as I get home, I'll get Prince to take me to the doctor's. Then by the time you get back, I will be presentable enough to keep any fastidious guests from fainting at the sight of me."

My wife eyed me speculatively. She has a disconcerting way of thinking my thoughts and of discerning my most secret plans.

"You aren't thinking of going turkey hunting while I am at church, are you?" she asked. "What would the bishop think?"

The Great Day arrived, mild and still, as if especially prepared for a saintly visitation. I drove my wife the two miles through wild pinelands to the ancient church in the unchanging woods. If anything, the whole region is more remote and lonely than it was a hundred years ago. Formerly rice and turpentine were prosperous industries in this area. Afterward it greatly reverted into that primeval wilderness from which it had been originally wrested. By the old church and even into the churchyard, deer and wild turkeys freely wander; as a permanent feature of the landscape, they have no dread of it; and in the mouldering brick tombs the lordly diamondback rattlesnake has found a congenial habitation. Nature has recaptured her own.

When we reached the church, we were greeted by an embarrassing lot of friends. It seemed as if everybody there was interested in how I looked. I drove away as soon as I could, but not before overhearing an old maid, noted for her strident voice, say positively:

"I was afraid it might come to that."

While I was driving about a mile from the old church, and a mile from my home, on the quiet sandy road running through the pinelands something very special caught my attention. On the left-hand grassy shoulder of the road stood a regal wild gobbler, looking tall as Goliath of

Gath. Lying on the back seat of my car was a twenty-two rifle. I had meant to take it out before driving to church; but now I was glad I had not. Before me was this sudden apparition of glory, literally waiting for me beside the road, almost pleading with me to shoot him. There was no mistaking that streamlined body, that air of wild majesty; I could even see, silhouetted against the snowy sand of the road, the black beard jutting out from the gobbler's breast. While still driving along slowly, with a desperately long reach, I secured the rifle. As I had on my ordinary clothes I thought I might have a rifle cartridge in some pocket.

To keep the shot from tearing the delicate cloth of the linings, my wife always carefully removed from my pockets any bills or coins she could find. It was thoughtful of her. But there her thoughtfulness ended; for she always left the nails, pipes, rocks, shotgun and rifle shells that a rural husband's pockets usually carried.

By the time I had found the cartridge and had managed to get it in the rifle while still driving, I was almost up to the stately bird, standing so strangely still by the roadside. But now, with the car drawing near, he suddenly became uneasy. He ducked back, and began to trot off among some young pines. By the time I stopped the car and stepped out, the gobbler was running through some tall broomsedge that hid everything but his head and his long neck, sheeny with iridescent feathers. The great black beard I had seen, I could see no longer. The wild turkey was well out of range of an ordinary shotgun, but a rifle bullet might reach him, might deliver a final message.

My head throbbing, I rested my rifle in the forked limbs of a small pine and tried to aim for where I thought the gobbler's head joined his body. To my astonishment, and perhaps even more so to the wild turkey's, I broke the gobbler's neck with that single bullet, aiming for a target I could not see. Whilst it must have been more or less an accident, I was a proud man; and the fact that I was exceedingly lucky did not make me feel any the worse.

My exertion in running over to where my great bird had fallen, and my stooping over to retrieve my twenty pound prize, had loosened some of the bandages on my wounded head. Also I could feel some fresh warm blood oozing out of the deep cuts that had not wholly healed. I must have presented a rather bedraggled, even a ghastly spectacle as I made my way back to the car. The excitement and exertion had made me rather dizzy and faint, and I was breathing so hard that I was glad I did not have to speak to any one just then. I had triumphed; but it was well that I could enjoy it in secrecy and silence.

But could I?

Another car was parked so squarely beside mine in the broad road that

I did not see it until I was actually beside mine. Quite evidently I had been seen; for I heard a murmur of excited voices that did not exactly blend with the music of the wind in the pines. When I rounded my car I was greeted by a chorus of feminine voices from the back of the car. Behind the wheel was a member of the vestry. Beside him, looking at the same time benign and surprised, sat the bishop himself!

"Well," said the driver of the car. He was an old friend, but a much more rigorous churchman than was this wild turkey hunter. "Had you forgotten that this is Church Sunday?"

The ladies seemed to be gathering gossip at a joyously rapid rate. Only the bishop appeared cheerful, and willing to accept the whole episode as perfectly natural.

"Your head," said the bishop with real concern, "you've hurt yourself. And what a magnificent gobbler! How I wish I had been with you on the hunt!"

I could have hugged him for his tolerance and his understanding heart. The whole business was so complex that I gave but a sketchy explanation of how the thing had happened, and of why I was not headed churchward on this day of days. I felt some very incredulous looks upon me, and I thought I overheard Mrs. Ravenel whisper, "I warned his wife." But the bishop was urbane and believing.

"Bishop," I said, "if you will come over to the plantation house after the service, I shall be glad to give you this wild turkey to take home with you. I'm sorry to miss the service on account of having to go to the doctor."

"I'd rather go hunting, too," he said with a chuckle. With that the car drove off.

With mingled feeling, the strongest of which was gratitude to the bishop, I turned to my own car. Laying my little rifle and my big gobbler in the back, I climbed in and drove home, where with returning pride, I hung up my regal prize in the game room of the plantation house. I was thinking of how delighted my wife would be. But would she?

Fortunately intercepting Prince on his way from someone's liquor still, I had him to drive me to Georgetown. In answer to my knock at the door of the doctor's home, my way was completely barred by a vast colored woman, whose specifications must have been drawn up in Amazon days. Her name was Daisy Fairy May, and she and I were old friends.

"Is Doc in?" I inquired.

Daisy's reply was a singular one. She put a finger to her lips, cautioning me.

"He done tole de missis he gwine on a maternity case, but Doc, he done gone wild turkey huntin'."

There seemed nothing for me to do but to return home with the same old bandages on my head. Now I would really have a hard time trying to convince my wife that while she had dutifully gone to church, and had welcomed the bishop as a true Christian should, I had taken to the wildwoods like a heathen.

Not long after I reached home my wife and a crowd of friends, including the bishop, arrived at my plantation. While they seemed in gay spirits, I was definitely apprehensive. This was partly because my wife, who had appeared to be in a festive mood, suddenly became oblivious of everything but the same old soiled and bloody bandages on her husband's head.

"You didn't go to Georgetown?" she asked, with edginess of accusation in her tone.

"Yes I did, but Doctor Barber had gone out on a case."

I liked my description of the nature of the doctor's business.

As the good bishop had said nothing about the wild turkey, and of his fantastic encounter in the woods with me, it was apparent that he had sensed some domestic difficulty and had kept his counsel. I therefore decided to tell my story. This I did. I got along all right except that my wife certainly did not seem to believe a word I said.

"A man ought to be able to prove a thing like that," I ended. "Come with me into the game room."

There I displayed my grand trophy.

There was a chorus of exclamations, including the bishop's. "A memorable shot!" he cried. "Most remarkable! As wonderful as I ever heard of! Who needs a better proof of miracles?"

But my wife said not a word. She did look things, though.

"You know, Bishop," I said, "I want you to have this gobbler. I'll have him dressed and ready for you before you feel you must go."

At this my wife's eyes brightened somewhat—but very little. Although she appreciated her husband's generosity, quite evidently she was convinced that I had told a whole series of huge and awkward lies.

After deep night had settled over the plantation, I was restlessly asleep, dreaming of huge gobblers and good bishops and lovely wives who simply refused to understand their honest husbands.

Was I dreaming, or did two arms tenderly encircle me in the darkness? I must have been awake, for I heard a precious voice say with a kind of reluctant sweet repentance:

"My darling wild turkey hunter! I'm so proud of you!"

"But I thought you didn't believe me," I murmured drowsily in protest.

"Oh, I didn't believe *you!* Prince told me that he really did drive you to Georgetown, and he's afraid to lie to me. I catch him every time. Not only that, the bishop told me it happened just as you said; and, of course, a bishop just can't tell a story."

GIL-OBBLE-OBBLE-OBBLE

"Steve," I asked my dusky henchman, "are there any deputy sheriffs after you this week, or can we try for a gobbler in the swamp?"

" 'Fo' God, I hopes to die, boss, but no man can put no cuffs on me dis week, and no man can grab his han' in my coat for no kind o' nuthin'."

But Steve's protests of lily-white innocence are never very convincing. He's a . . . rapscallion, that's the truth of the business; but I love him well. I don't think you can care much for a person who has no redeeming vices.

"You say you saw six gobblers at the head of Flag Creek last Sunday?"

"Yes, sah, I hopes to die, but dar dey wuz."

I didn't ask him what he was doing eight miles from home in the utter swamp wilderness on Sunday; but Steve is almost as good at firing a still as he is at stalking a turkey.

"Suppose we try it tomorrow morning?" I asked. "It's calm, and we are going to have a little moonlight."

Steve licked his lips, his customary reaction to any reference to food, even so remote as a live and roaming wild turkey, two rivers and three swamps away.

"God A'mighty, yes, boss," he answered. Steve isn't irreverent; he's just emphatic in his own way.

He and I have original arrangements about this matter of getting up before daylight. I go to bed and sleep serenely, knowing that he will sit up all night by the kitchen fire. He tells time by the moon and the stars, by the crowing of roosters, and by the conscious passing of the dark hours. And he's infallible in his primitive way, being very close to nature.

I was dreaming of gobblers ten feet high when a soft hand on my shoulder awoke me.

"Cap'n," Steve informed me, "first fowl done crow, and you-all coffee is done ready, sah."

From *Outdoor Life*, March 1942. Later included in *Those Were the Days* (1955).

At 3:30 of that starry morning in early March Steve and I headed up the glimmering Santee for the great swamp where dwell the turkeys. Myriad stars glittered in the placid waters, and a setting moon shed her glamour over the sleeping world. But for the occasional hoot of an owl, the only sound was the murmur of Steve's paddle as he drove our boat up and across the river. At 4 o'clock we entered Flag Creek, a waterway that meanders deep into the heart of the moldering swamp. Giant pines, cypresses, and tupelos overarch the stream, and as we passed quietly beneath them, I scanned their branches carefully, for already we were in turkey country. However, in that eerie light it's a mighty hard thing to distinguish a roosted bird from a big bunch of mistletoe. Perhaps two miles we went, and by then the stars had begun to fade, and the east was flushing. As we could go no farther in the boat, we had to make a landing.

"Ain't far from here where I done seed dem," Steve whispered.

"And where's the still?" I asked.

"Ain't far neither," he chuckled.

Most people have a wrong idea of a Southern swamp. Seeing its gloomy and forbidding edges from a train or highway, they imagine that it is a complete morass, where only the web-footed things can maneuver. But in the Carolina swamps with which I am familiar, there are many high sunny ridges where hardwoods grow, and here the footing is certain. True, you have to know your ground, and you do come to quaking morasses about which you have to detour. But I have traveled far through the great Santee Swamp at night without wetting my feet.

We had stopped the boat at the head of one of these ridges; and soon we were making our way along under hickories and oaks. The first birds of the morning in that part of the country, phoebes and cardinal redbirds, were beginning to tune up. Great blue herons squawked raspingly, as if disgusted that their night's hunting was over. I heard the wings of wild ducks whistling overhead. Suddenly, immediately in front of us, two deer snorted, wheeled, and rocked away into the dense canebrakes, their snowy flags high.

Steve stayed me with a hand on my arm.

"Lemme call," he said.

Forthwith he gave a perfect imitation of the hooting of a barred owl. And in answer there instantly came, not one, but four answers from roosted gobblers.

"I done tole you," he said softly. "Two is down the ridge, and two is off in the swamp on the right-hand side."

Of all the different ways of calling the wild turkey, I consider the coaxing of one from his roost to have the greatest thrill in it. In many states calling is banned; yet much of the calling I have heard no more resembles the note of the wild turkey than crow tastes like pheasant. Advice about calling has been given many times; but it must actually be done a good deal before the touch is acquired. The amateur always calls too loudly, too often, and with too much strident urgency. A certain feminine finesse and restraint are required. You've got to coax your gobbler with faint flirtation. All males are more or less alike in that they do not like females that are too obviously eager. When once you have located your gobbler in a tree at dawn, and have enabled him to locate you by the fewest possible notes on your call, the game to play is a waiting one. I have waited fifty-five minutes for one of the great birds to come to me after I had given him my last call—but come he did.

In that hushed and fragrant hour that comes with the breaking of day in the deep wilderness Steve and I stole forward on the ridge. Before taking up a position to wait for him, I like to get within 250 to 300 yards of a roosted turkey. On a still morning, with those conditions of the air prevailing which enable sound to travel far, it is possible to hear a wild turkey gobble on his roost for a half mile or more; but, partly because the caller is not elevated, his call will not carry more than perhaps 400 yards. Of course, there are exceptions. Much depends on what intervenes to stay the sound. I have had a gobbler answer me full 700 yards across a marsh and a river.

Steve, who had evidently done a little turkey scouting while about his other duties in the swamp, laid a soft hand on my arm and whispered, "Cap'n, a big tree done fall just ahead of we, and it got plenty of bramble vine running on it. Dat's a good place to sit."

With steps like those of a stalking panther he led me to the place. There was just light enough now to see our way along. Dim and mysterious and silent lay the swamp about us; yet it was full of secret life. We were six miles from any human habitation; and as the swamp lies between two great rivers, we were isolated by wide waters as well as by distance.

Under a friendly canopy of jasmine and smilax vines, shining with dew, we seated ourselves on the prone cypress. All four gobblers meanwhile were letting us know that they were on the wire. All this gobbling means just what the English mean when they ask over the telephone, "Are you there?" But it means more than that. It means, "My own true love, did I hear you calling me?"

Deciding to give my attention to the nearest bird, which was roosted on the ridge, I waited for him to gobble. And soon he did nothing else but.

"*Gil-obble-obble-obble-obble!*" he called in his throaty, manful fashion. I waited just a moment or two. Then I answered.

"*Keow-keow-keow!*" the call sounded plaintively.

Instantly he gobbled again.

"Dat's got him!" said Steve. "He jes' like a man gwine to a frolic: he done call he gal, and she done say, 'I'se right hyar, big boy.' "

I slipped the call in my pocket.

There is a nice psychology about this business that is readily comprehended by any one who understands human nature, especially its behavior under the impulse of the mating instinct. The female must allure by being mysterious, secretive. nonchalant. No male likes an easy conquest, for that indicates no great triumph for him. I have observed the working of this interesting law in practically all wildlife.

Steve and I sat silent while the great swamp wakened about us; while gray squirrels began to chatter, while marshbirds called and the far reaches of the virgin forest, that had been indistinct, took form and color. While the three gobblers kept up their voluble calling, ours was clearly the one most interested. At one time we heard him strutting on the limb; for while still roosted, one of these great birds, stirred by the all-mastering mating instinct, tries to make himself look impressive even when he has to do some tightrope balancing to do so.

"When he strut, he mean business," muttered Steve. "He tryin' to show off befo' his lady."

"Just like a man," I suggested.

"Yes, boss, and he gwine git into heavy trouble yes' like a man, too, when he start to carry on wid a 'oman. 'Oman is de debil," he concluded feelingly, evidently moved by personal memories.

After a few minutes we heard one of the gobblers roosted above the morass fly down. But he did not head our way. Five minutes later his companion followed him. That left two on the high hardwoods of the ridge, and one of these we intended for our own.

A silence fell on the swamp, though it was now wide awake. I slipped my hand into my pocket and began to fidget with my call.

"Better not, boss," Steve told me. "You done got him teased already."

Presently we heard a low *swish-swish*.

"He's on de groun'," the Negro said softly. "Git yo' gun up, cap'n, so you won't have to move later. If a man move at de critical time," he muttered, half to himself, "he ain't gwine carry home no turkey."

I thrust my gun out through a little aperture in the greenery. I don't know about other hunters, but I always carry No. 4's in my right barrel and No. 2's in my left for these swamp gobblers. If you don't break down one of these big birds, you'll never see him again. And that reminds me that I was once talking about turkey hunting to a fair lady who appeared much interested in the sport. I had spoken of using big shot, but added, "Of course, if your turkey comes close enough, you can kill him with a stick."

"And do they often come as close as that?" she asked. There's no ready answer to such a question from such a source.

Steve's keen eyes were searching the ridge ahead of us for the coming of his lordship. At least we heard a bush crack. Unless they are scratching, or approaching through beds of dry leaves, turkeys make little noise. But both of us thought our game was near. I got my gun well into position. In a moment, dead in front of my sights, there appeared a huge gray form, big as a calf, and shaped like a hyena. He champed his evil jaws and emitted a fetid odor. It was a wandering wild boar of the swampland. At sight of him Steve's mouth watered until he swallowed.

"Bacon is so sweet," I heard him mutter.

I had a fine chance to kill this old brigand, and would have done so but for the noble game that I knew was now not far off. The huge beast, as dangerous as any in those wilds, went on without getting wind of us until he was passing us; then he ripped off with the mad speed and energy of a buck getting out of a corner. Fortunately he dashed away from our gobbler.

"Hog is jes' like a 'oman," muttered Steve, ruminating on how life had treated him.

"How so?" I whispered.

"She bes' when she dead," the Negro answered.

I do not recommend that Steve's sentiments be quoted in mixed company, but he probably has his reasons for them.

Somewhere on the shimmering ridge ahead of us was a lordly gobbler; and we were the reception committee. It was now full thirty minutes since I had given my last call. The sun was coming up, flooding the lonely country with its golden light.

Suddenly I was aware that Steve's hand was on my arm. He pointed far through the gleaming glade. There I saw the sunshine glinting on two majestic forms. Two great gobblers were strutting, trying to outdo each other in a display of masculinity in the presence of the coveted hen. Here were rivals, urgent and unsuspecting. We had a perfect view of them as, with all their feathers ruffled, with wings taut and lowered, they did their stately woodland minuet. Closer they came to us and to each other. One was a massive bird, with a beard that almost trailed the ground. The other was nearly as large, but perhaps two years younger. I laid my sight on the old monarch.

The question naturally arose; should I try for both birds? But I was alone on the plantation, and a full-grown gobbler is enough for any one man's dinner. Besides, there's a peculiar thrill to the hunter in leaving some game. He likes to think of it still wandering free; and to dream of returning to it.

The birds were now only fifteen yards apart, and the big one was within forty yards. Just as I tightened my gun against my shoulder, my finger actually on the trigger, a gray squirrel broke a dead branch above us. Instantly the gobblers froze upright; slim and alert they stood, ready for flight. I thought it was time, and let drive at the old master. He fell at the shot, and hardly moved afterwards. When we reached him he lay in all his glory of iridescent plumage, scarcely a feather of which was ruffled.

Steve slung him over his shoulder.

"I done tole you, cap'n, dey wuz hyar," he said in mild triumph.

We turned back toward the canoe: when we had gone a hundred yards, from a near-by canebrake we heard a telltale grunt.

It was now Steve's turn to freeze.

"Dat's him," said the Negro. "Oh, do please, cap'n!"

Stealing over to the rustling brake, which at that point was not over three feet high, these being dwarf canes, I surprised the old boar at his noisy rooting in the mud, and promptly collected him for my matchless guide.

I now took the gobbler while Steve dragged the heavy boar, humming a cheerful tune as he did so, which ended with his saying:

"Mandy will be glad for see me now. If a man can bring home bacon, his wife will be sat'fy. But ain't 'oman de debil?"

A Stalk
on the Dunes

My acquaintance with Bull's Island dates from earliest boyhood days, for I was born only ten miles away from this most romantic of the famous sea islands of the Carolina coast. It lies some four miles offshore; but open water does not separate it from the mainland. Instead there are bays, winding creeks and a tremendous sea marsh—all forming a barrier sufficient to isolate the island. Occasionally deer will go and come, but the occurrence is rare; and the other game, except, of course, for the migrating wildfowl, stay in their remote and idyllic haunt.

About fifteen years ago, Gen. Francis Burton Harrison, who then owned the island, but whose duties as Governor-General of the Philippines kept him away from this magnificent game preserve, wrote to ask me to visit Bull's in order to estimate the game there. As the island is nine miles long and in places nearly two miles wide; as it is densely shrouded by a tropical forest; and as this business of counting game that is not tagged is always uncertain, you can well imagine that I had my troubles, and that I could come to no definite statistics. However, I estimated the deer at eighteen hundred, and the wild turkeys at six hundred. All these latter had been raised from two wild eggs that had been hatched by a common hen.

During the time when General Harrison held the island, there was practically no hunting, so that the game had every opportunity to increase. Natural fresh ponds supplied abundant water, which attracted in the winter thousands of ducks. Indeed, Bull's Island is the very sort of place about which every sportsman dreams. I believe there is more game there than on any other similar area in North America; and certainly it is the finest private preserve in the States.

From the hands of General Harrison the island passed into the possession, a few years ago, of Mr. Gayer Dominick, of the famous New York

---

From *Field & Stream*, September 1934. Later included in *An American Hunter* (1937).

family of that name. He built upon it a beautiful home; he has protected the game so that it has steadily increased; yet he has in no way attempted to change the primeval loveliness of this earthly paradise. Its woods of oak and pine, myrtle and palmetto, are still virgin; the superb beach is as lonely and as primal as when the Sewee Indians roamed there. The present owner, with admirable good taste, has accepted Nature as his outdoor decorator; and she was never in a happier mood than when she shaped those rolling mysterious dunes, those dusky towering pines, those stately forest aisles which are fragrant and full of bird song during every month in the year.

In December last, Mr. Dominick very kindly asked me to visit the island for a shoot. He could not be there, but he told me to make myself at home. As the turkeys had been hunted a good deal, they were plenty wild enough to afford sport of high excellence. And that is how it happened that at three o'clock that memorable December afternoon I started out alone down Moccasin Trail in an attempt to stalk one of the island's old gobblers. Let no man imagine this an easy task. All I have to say is that while there are a good many turkeys on Bull's, the place is big, the woods are dense, the incessant roar of the surf makes calling almost impossible, and the turkeys are wild turkeys.

Moccasin Trail is a game-path which winds along the top of a very ancient line of the dunes that for centuries has been forested. This singular elevation is some twenty feet above the floor of the woods on either hand, so that it affords the still-hunter the excellent advantage of looking down on both sides far away into the glimmering forest. It runs parallel to the present beach-line, at a distance of about a quarter of a mile. Between the trail and the ocean is a strip of dense forest, mostly palmettos and scrub oaks; then a sea of dunes, topped by beach-grasses, with patches of myrtle bushes and scrub pines in the tiny vales; then the hard sea beach.

On a sea island such as this, because of the proximity of the Gulf Stream, the winter temperature will average from ten to fifteen degrees higher than it is on the mainland near by; and this genial warmth makes for a riotous yet beautiful growth of trees, shrubs and vines. But the jungles are not hopeless, as they are along the Amazon, for example, or along the lower reaches of the Congo. The humidity is equable; the air crystal fine; and, in the winter, there is an absence of the insects that one associates with a semi-tropical wilderness.

There are alligators on the island, which do not seem to take hibernation seriously as do their mailed brethren of the mainland swamps and rivers; there are no rattlers, I am glad to say. The fact that there are neither foxes nor wildcats accounts for the perfect chance that the turkeys have. Raccoons there are in almost ludicrous numbers. . . .

Well, down Moccasin Trail I stole, the sun striking long golden lances through the peaceful forest. There was no wind, but the surf kept up its soft trampling so that it was not possible to hear those furtive steps that warn the still-hunter of the approach of game.

About a mile down the trail I ran right spam into two does that turned as if they had a syncro-mesh transmission joint and rocked away with an ease which no human being could ever imitate. A little farther on I heard a subdued rustling in the underbrush. I sat down to wait.

Presently there came to sight a herd of the island's wild hogs. I had been told to shoot these, as an attempt is being made to rid the island of them. But I didn't have the heart. A genuine wild boar may afford real sport, but not this group of grunting pigs gone wild. When they got my scent, they made a rush that would have done credit to a frantically surprised and scared whitetail stag.

The sun was dripping lower, and with every moment my chances, measured by the flight of time, were diminishing. On I wandered through that idyllic wilderness, marveling at the signs innumerable of deer and turkeys. I came to a very high place on the trail, which afforded me a long look ahead and to either side.

Suddenly, full two hundred yards away, I saw the slanting sunlight flash on a broad iridescent back. The gobbler was in an open space of woods to my right, between me and the beach. At the first moment I saw him, the bird was in full run. He had spied me first, had identified me, and had made up his mind about my intentions. Yet he was coming my way, but bearing toward the beach. In another moment he had disappeared.

As a rule, when once a wild turkey has seen the hunter, why, it's all off. "If he makes you out," an old woodsman once said to me, "he'll quit the country; he'll quit the world."

I dropped back two hundred yards, cut in to the left the same distance, and took up a stand and waited. After fifteen minutes I took out my call and gave a wary yelp or two, though I knew well enough that a man is as likely to be able to call a scared wild gobbler as he is to make a hole-in-one straight for nine holes. For ten minutes more I sat there waiting, hearing only the dim rush of the surf and the crackling rustle of the sere palmetto fronds.

As I felt sure that the gobbler had not passed me in the woods, and rather certain that he had not backtracked, there was just one other thing that he could have done: turned out on the wild rolling dunes. There, of course, my chance would be less; it is hard for a man to make himself inconspicuous on sand-dunes. Yet, failing to stalk my friend, I might rout a buck from the myrtle clumps in the vales of the dunes. Beachward therefore I turned, or, I should say, crawled.

Between the woods and the sand is an extraordinary growth of stunted oak trees. They are dwarfed, gnarled and tough. These sentinels of the island forest have stood all the sea winds that blow. Their lower branches sweep the sand, and a man cannot get through them; he must crawl under them, and part the dense-growing stubby branches as he advances inch by inch.

I lay flat and began my crawl. In darkness almost at first, I could see the wide light of the open beach ahead. Toward this I slowly worked, not forgetting in my advance that this enforced caution was a good thing. On a place like Bull's Island a man may happen on big game at any moment.

At last I began to emerge, so that I could take in the rugged contour of the great dunes. I lay still for a minute and surveyed the situation. A bald eagle, mighty of pride and wing-spread, circled over the surf-line; no other life I saw. But what was that black object two hundred yards ahead and to my left? On the very crest of a high white dune he stood, outlined against the sky above the ocean. The last rays of the setting sun were on him, lighting him up. Straight and tall he stood. Is there anything more trimly alert in nature than a wild gobbler which, having been frightened, runs off and then pauses to reconnoiter?

Had I had a rifle, the chance at the old boy would have been a sporty one; I had him silhouetted against the bright sky-line. He looked perfectly black. But he was far out of gunshot range, and I was afraid to crawl from beneath the tangle for fear that he would make me out. I thought his next move would be back toward the woods, for it was getting on toward roosting-time. I decided to wait for him to lead the first card.

As I lay there, out of the woods about a quarter of a mile away came three deer. Shadowy and graceful they were, trooping across the glimmering sands. The big stag with them was certainly a ten-pointer. Where were they going? Why, to have a romp in the surf! It is a characteristic of all sea-island deer that they love the beach and the water. They love to wander along knee-deep in the warm water, to pace the beach, to play almost like children in the gleaming shallows.

The gobbler saw the deer; and instead of heading toward the forest, he thought he'd go down toward the ocean and take a look at the sad sea waves himself. Over the crest of the gray dune he vanished. My part in the business was clear: I had to follow him as swiftly and as discreetly as possible. The dunes roll like a wild sea, and there's a real chance for stalking among them.

The two hundred yards that had separated us I traversed in time that would have made an onlooker imagine that I was in training for the Olympics. Arriving at the very dune on which the gobbler had been poised only a minute or so before, I lay down and then began pulling myself stealthily up by the tough beach-grass.

When I reached a little notch in the crest of the sand-hill, I peered gingerly over. Nary a turkey. Far up the beach I saw the deer. Between me and the next high ridge of dunes lay a sandy valley, fifty yards wide and as bare as your hand but for a single tiny patch of myrtle bushes. This entire vale was lifeless.

North and south I looked, and even back to westward, toward the dark forest into which I knew the gobbler would steal by sundown. But he had vanished. He could not have reached the outer beach before I had reached the dune on which he had been posing. Where was he?

The patch of myrtles was so small, and the bushes so low, that it appeared unlikely that it could harbor the fugitive; and it must be remembered that a scared turkey remains a real fugitive for some hours. I studied the bushes. After a few moments I detected a stir in the tops of some of them, as if some creature were stealthily brushing their bases. Stealing along the side of the dune, and still concealed, I came to the very place whence he had disappeared. Here were his big tracks in the sand.

Edging up to the top, I saw that the line of the tracks led straight down to the greenery. He must be in there. But the myrtles were a hundred yards away to the northeastward. Seventy yards down in that direction I skulked in the shelter of the immense sand-hill. Then I decided on a bold maneuver. I would walk right over the dune and down to the bushes. From where I crossed, they would be not more than forty yards away. In such a case, the turkey might crouch and hide in the only cover available until I got right up on him.

Over the dune I walked, hurrying toward the strange green copse. The place had an area not larger than that of the average room. Not a thing stirred in it. I got within fifteen yards and then stopped, looking. The great gobbler rushed out of the bushes on his mighty wings. He was heading for the beach. He was going to cross the ocean. He was going abroad.

Forty yards away, as he topped the crest of the next immense sand-hill, he veered crazily to the left—to make for the woods, of course. I let drive, and down he came, dead. When I reached him, not a feather was ruffled. He was all bronze sheen; and when I lifted him, I knew that he was one of the finest I had ever killed. He had a beard six inches long, and he weighed twenty-one pounds.

As I turned homeward the sun sank gloriously behind the tall pines and the ragged palmettos. I thought: the hunter's life is a happy one. Despite the panics and the depressions, he can still have his sport, especially if he has good friends to help him to it. If things keep on as they are, Mahatma Gandhi will soon be the best-dressed man in the world. But not the happiest. A sportsman does not need to envy even a saint.

BIG TOMS IN BIG TIMBER

I have been telling how a man may make his sport in the woods and fields more certain, and increase the degree of it, by taking heed that he does not scare the daylight out of his game. To no kind of game is this sort of caution more essential than to the wild turkey, which is as sensitive to possible danger as anything that lives. Moreover, when a wild turkey once gets going, there is no telling how far he will travel. Your scared quail or grouse may fly three hundred yards; but your terrified turkey is likely to vanish into worlds unknown. Yet because of the exactions that this grand bird imposes on the hunter, the following him is one of the major wildwood sports.

The scientists who have been telling us that light or electricity or some other such substance is the swiftest moving thing in the world are either trying to hide a domestic secret or else they are bachelors. For as every married man knows what it means to be king of a country ruled by a military dictator, so he also comes to know that the swiftest thing in the universe is the manner in which a wife gets on to her husband's curves. She reads him as a Ph.D. reads a primer, and his deepest craftiness is to her absurdly obvious. Isn't it so?

For this reason, when a woods-loving husband begins to be attentive to the vitals of a tintype locomotive that has wheezed and banged all summer, despite a patient woman's pleas that the machine be fixed; when he acquires a touching solicitude for a decrepit alarm clock; when he makes many secret trips into the attic or the den whence issue certain strange, strident calls—she knows for a certainty that the wild turkey season is about to open. With fatally masculine elaborate secrecy he makes no mention of the Great Day. But the night before, his wife

From *An American Hunter* (1937).

inquires quite calmly, "At what time are you starting on your turkey hunt in the morning, Henry?"

He discreetly names a time about two hours after he intends going. But she reminds him that last season he was out at three instead of five, whereupon he eagerly agrees to be as soon as ever on the job. A man's guile is often rendered innocuous by the mere fact that he himself believes in it.

Being one of these guileful turkey hunters, I never miss the first day. But I shouldn't like you to get suspicious and to imagine that what I have said about sportsmen's wives has any application to me. Oh, no. I was just supposing that in some households wives detect their consort's little schemes. In any well regulated home, of course, the man is head of the house, the last word, the final arbiter, the fount of authority, the source of wisdom, and all the rest of that applesauce. Oh, yes.

Though I am not a collector of antiques, I am a retainer of one. Through the dim November night this skittering relic bore me. We were going about nine miles up a lonely mountain valley. We were hell-bent for turkeys. It was the first day of the season. I was happy. Nothing, so far, had gone wrong.

I had my gun and shells. I had managed to start the engine, and so far she was running. Not even the alarm clock had failed me. Had it not succeeded not only in alarming but in jumping from the bureau, doing an Olympic swan-dive? Within me was a good breakfast. I think no huntsman is more joyous than when he is taking the field, with a clear conscience, on the first day—one reason for his state of mind being that he hasn't yet missed a thing that season.

I stopped my car at an old abandoned barn. The fuses on my chariot were fizzing, the engine was boiling merrily, and there were certain other undetermined sounds emanating from the mechanism which made me think of one of those musical attachments to band instruments. But what mattered all this? She had brought me to the place.

I got out in the chill mountain dawn. Ringed by mountains and by stars I stood. Frost glittered on the grasses of an old field beside the barn and on the fallen apples in an old orchard nearby. Tinglingly still and virginal was that white dawn in that lone valley. But deep in a hemlock hollow I heard a red fox give a rasping bark, which was answered from a neighboring hill, and from far away a great horned owl intoned softly his weird melancholy note.

This valley is twenty miles long, some two miles wide, and, as far as human beings are concerned, more in a state of desertion than when the Indians roamed it. But there are some deer here now, and a good many grouse; also, it is one of the few places in which the wild turkey has become firmly reestablished. Here a man, if the breaks are with him, can get his gobbler in one of the hollows where the wild fox-grapes riot, on one of the benches where the dogwood berries and the teaberries hang low, among those gray boulders lavishly strewn yonder on the high slopes of the ridges.

Going down an old trail in the starlight, I slithered over the creek bank and down its gravelly decline. On wading the shallow stream, I found myself in a broad meadow, deep in natural hay, now frost-rimed and glimmering. Across this I passed, entering forthwith the fragrant dewy woods of scarlet oak and mountain ash. Along an old logging road I passed, winding up into the mountain, a road unbelievably gullied by rains. The woods were still, held in the delicate cold hand of the frost. Except those on the scarlet oaks, most of the leaves were down.

I know not of a pleasanter thing than thus to walk at dawn through sweet chill woods, with nature's nameless fragrances awaft in the mountain air. There is a "country where men are men"; but it isn't found in any particular place. Rather it is on the bosom of Nature, for there a man is essentially at home. There he was cradled, and there he shall sleep at last.

Most people who are sick are heartsick and homesick. They ought to go back to the woods and the fields; there they'll find man's ancient home. And just as a man can lay aside his business cares when he gets home, so life's cares can be laid away as we approach Nature's old hearthstone.

After a pull of about a half-mile I paused to rest a little. On a frosty morning, when a man's hunting consists chiefly in watching and waiting, it doesn't pay to get overheated. As I paused I distinctly heard a step in the thicket off to my left. When frosted fallen leaves are tramped on, they give a good deal of sound. This sound was loud enough for a man to have made, or a bear; but I took it to be a grouse.

And right there I had to decide a question that assails almost every hunter: when after one kind of game, of a superior and wary sort, should a man accept humbler chances? Every man answers for himself. I invariably take a grouse when I can get him, even though my real ambition be for a lordly gobbler. At the end of a day it is far, far better to reach home with a handsome ruffneck in your bag than to reach there with a masterpiece in the way of a Great Excuse.

I have gone turkey hunting so very often that I have at last learned that fairly to kill a fine wild gobbler almost anywhere in America today is a rather rare thing. The turkey seems to me somehow equipped so as to make the taking of him excessively uncertain. The oil shares of the stock market are absolutely regular in their behavior compared to the shiftiness of the wild turkey. I remember hearing an old mountain hunter say disgustedly: "Them turkeys is gone. When I say a turkey is 'gone,' I mean he has quit the country, he has done flew the coop, he has quit this valley, he has quit the world! He's clean gone!"

Now that we have accomplished that detour, we shall return to the grouse whose no. nines I heard rudely smashing the innocent leaves. He was in a dense, viny thicket, where certain wild grapes had taken a notion to romp over the scenery, doing a Salome dance with nine veils which they had draped over the low trees and bushes. Beyond the thicket was an old clearing, in which a staggering cabin long deserted was valiantly attempting to stand.

I thought that it might be a good plan to circle the edge of the thicket; then, if the grouse elected to cross the old field, I might have a chance at him. Though a star was still visible above the dark ridge ahead of me, there was almost light enough to shoot, especially at a bird against the sky, which was now pearly and gemlike in color.

Whether the grouse heard me I shall never know. But hurtling out the thicket he came just as I had reached the edge of the clearing. Clearly he was silhouetted against the sky. I fired at him at long range—about sixty yards—using the left barrel and No. 4's. He dropped like a plummet. Later, when I dressed him, I found that one shot had struck him in the head and one in the neck. The first break had come my way.

And now, high up in the mountain ahead of me, I heard a shot. This was followed by several others in rapid succession. Somebody, I knew, had started a flock of turkeys from their roost. They would be flying down the mountain. I stood out in the old field to watch.

High in the morning heavens I saw a dozen black spots, unbelievably high. But these rapidly descended, growing larger every minute. They were turkeys, volplaning down the mountain, far above the tree-tops. Several of them were in a direct line with me. It was not unlikely that they might come to ground in my vicinity. I did not try to hide. Standing still is usually worth more in such a game than this jerky business of hiding and dodging. Movement is the thing to avoid—movement and sound—in the hunting of this great bird.

Three turkeys, one a great gobbler, took a half circle over the tail of a ridge two hundred yards above me and came dropping to earth. I distinctly heard their wings strike branches as they descended somewhat awkwardly through the tree-tops. They were now, I knew, on the ground. And I was faced by a master wildwood problem: what is a man to do if he knows where turkeys are but does not know what direction they have taken? Perhaps the nature of the landscape will help him; for in hilly country, after flying down the mountain, turkeys will usually feed back up.

Of course, a man's foolish to lay down rules for the standard behavior of intelligent wild game. As a general principle, I believe it may be said that the turkey is the kind of a bird that cannot be stalked; he must be ambushed. In such a case as the one in which I found myself, I decided to reconnoiter gingerly, getting, if possible, by a circuitous route, above the birds.

It was an hour later when I reached a place some three hundred yards above the spot on which the turkeys had alighted. And no sooner had I taken my stand than I decided to abandon it, for just below me I heard another hunter calling. Most men, when they call wild turkeys, give the wise birds the best kind of warning because they call as no turkey ever yet spoke.

I yelped a soft answer to my friend's entreaty, whereupon he did what an amateur is always apt to do: he began the most persistent, mechanical, non-stop calling imaginable. That kind of behavior is wild turkey life insurance. I'm not at all sure that the game laws of any state should forbid it.

The wild turkey's note is exceedingly variable, in that it has a considerable range of tones, many of them as soft as a flute; and most of the calling is of a very desultory sort. The youngest birds may yelp rather regularly in childish fashion, and in the mating season the old gobblers and the hens will get amorously garrulous. But in November, when the trees are bare, the woods are open, and the voice of the gun is heard in the land, turkeys are generally silent.

On most occasions a turkey either has a definite reason for calling or else it happens to be in a vocal mood. And so keen are a turkey's sense of hearing and its intelligent discriminating power that it has seemed to me well-nigh impossible to lure a mature bird well within range without having it become suspicious, even of the most perfect imitation. Most expert callers desist when the bird comes within about a hundred to a hundred and fifty yards. Much calling fails because of over-eagerness on the part of the caller.

It is perhaps well to remember that the main thing is not to make a noise that a turkey will hear, but to make a deceiving sound. One soft, appealing note in the right key is worth a hundred vociferous yelps.

The man gabbling below me was no fit company for a hunter to keep, and my next move took me at least a mile northward. By this time the sun had risen behind red clouds. All the frost was melting. The woods were still and dewy. The warmth of the atmosphere made me think rain not unlikely.

Big Toms in Big Timber   105

I took up my watch on an ancient charcoal hearth where, sixty years ago, before the days of coke furnaces, some charcoal burner had toiled at his quaint trade in this lonely mountain fastness. These hearths apparently are never overgrown; and being perfectly level open spaces, usually along old trails, they are frequently visited by wild game. Here a buck will pause to browse on the low-hanging greenery fringing the hearth's edge; here turkeys will dust themselves in the ancient ashes. And to this place will the hopeful hunter repair, to pursue the standard American policy toward Mexico.

Turkey hunting takes more downright patience, more prone silentness than any other game I know. A turkey is the kind of a cavalier who has to be waylaid, and a man must assume the pose and the silence of the Sphynx to waylay him. I have watched many a turkey hunter on a stand, and the average was fidgety. He was eating his lunch, smoking, whittling a stick or giving other signs of restlessness.

A friend of mine, who loves to still-hunt because he is thereby given a chance to doze, fell asleep as usual on his stand. Upon awakening, he hard a rustling off to his left; and his blinking eyes soon told him that the last of a large flock of turkeys, that for some time had been parading all around him, was now disappearing through the woods.

When there is no wind, it is not difficult to hear a turkey coming. It seems to me that in dry dead leaves he makes almost as much noise as a man. Unless he has been startled, his progress is likely to be curiously slow and desultory. About every third step he is likely to pause and look about—listening, appraising the situation.

My stand overlooked a dark hollow where a little steam gurgled, and where certain poplars towered astonishingly out of the rich soil at the base of the depression. For an hour I watched gray squirrels playing; and once a doe that some hunter had started came bounding past me. She halted on the brink of the hollow, palpitating. Then she stole softly into a thicket.

Suddenly, above me on the mountain, there was a great commotion. Evidently a hunter had run head on into a flock of turkeys. I got ready to shoot, for such a collision is likely to give the hunter at a little distance away from the encounter a better chance for a shot than the flusher himself.

Down the gorge and below the tree-tops I saw a bird coming. He looked very big and black. I counted him as mine. A hundred yards from me another hunter shot him. Such was his momentum and such his downhill decline that when he stopped falling and rolling he was almost at my feet. The lucky gunner came dashing down the gulley, and I had the pleasure of handing him his bird. It was the first turkey he had ever killed, and he was justly proud of a fine shot and a fine bird.

But I had nothing of the kind to take home. The morning was getting late. The woods were misty now, and a soft rain had begun to fall. It is at such a time that the luckless hunter begins to make up the story that he plans to tell when he reaches home empty-handed.

I left that stand and wandered down the glade. The rain was whispering down gently on the dead leaves; a sibilant song it was, deadening my footsteps. I was following an old trail beside the little stream. The gulley's bed here was widened so that there were little plateaus of soft soil, built up by the washing of the waters. On these grew tangles of wild raspberry, with here and there a greenbrier brake.

I had my gun cocked, and in the hollow of my left arm, for this was a good place for a grouse. The stream murmured. The rain pattered with quiet insistence. I could not hear the sound of my own footfalls. It was a good chance to get a close flushing shot, if only there was something to flush.

There was.

Suddenly, out of a heavy raspberry clump directly in front of me, there rose, with a mighty commotion, a great bird. It was a wild gobbler. He had not detected my approach until I was almost upon him. But he made a swift rise; and as he elected to fly downhill, I had to shoot rather quickly. I saw him fall heavily through the low sweeping boughs of an old hemlock. I found him on the ground beneath the ancient tree, lying there in all the beauty of his regal plumage. A stately bird he was, the hero, no doubt, of many a thrilling campaign of retreat and escape.

I didn't think it worth while getting sentimental over him. For a wild turkey to fall fairly before a hunter's gun is a better end than to be caught by a fox or a wildcat. I shouldered him gladly and ambled on down the mountain in the rain.

It took only about nineteen twists to crank the car. And though she ran in a panicky way, showing signs of the heaves and of acute mania, she took me home. And I want to add that when a man takes a wild turkey home, there's domestic felicity ahead for a while; and he may even be led to think that of the great ocean of love, his portion, after all, is at least more than a thimbleful.

FIREWORKS IN THE PEAFIELD CORNER

A good many sportsmen find their game by going out and looking for it; others depend to some degree on the intelligence brought them by friendly natives. Some of the best sport I have ever enjoyed has been made possible by hints that the human dwellers in the wilderness have given me. Some plantation Negroes have an almost uncanny finesse in locating game; others are just plain liars, who will tell me of giant stags and huge flocks of wild turkeys that are purely hypothetical. As a result, when tidings concerning game are brought to me, I have to discriminate.

The sun had gone down on the last day of the year when I saw old Gabe Myers riding up the plantation avenue on his white horse. As I had said goodbye to him only an hour before, when I had liquidly wished him a Happy New Year, I could account for his return only by supposing that on his way home to Peafield Corner he had seen game and had come back to report to me. I have hunted deer and turkeys with Gabe for thirty-nine years.

"Well, old hunter," I said, "did you come back for another Happy New Year?"

"I don't never refuse," he admitted, "but what done bring me is big news. My boy George was shootin' squirrel down by de Big Oaks a little while back, and he run on four able bucks—yes, sah, four of 'em. Dat ole gun he got miss fire, and he say dem deer just stand right there in de old field and look at him. Four bucks," he repeated.

"And you think we can catch them right there in the morning?"

I confess that I wished that the report had come from a more reliable source than "my boy George," one of the most no-account Negroes who ever stole my chickens and watermelons. For years I had tolerated him

---

From *Field & Stream*, December 1932. Later included in *An American Hunter* (1937).

merely on account of his matchless father. I had serious doubts whether George could distinguish a deer from a squirrel.

"Plenty of acorns is in dat corner," Gabe told me. "I believe we might pen up dem deer if we start at day-clean."

"We'll meet you by the Old Parsonage at daylight. Now don't drink any moonshine tonight, and don't go gallin'. Let's hang up some horns first."

Promising to be moral and immaculate until the hunt was over, my old woodsman rode into the shadows of the December day.

While the great pine forest that surrounds my Carolina home was still dim and dewy the next morning, we gathered at our rendezvous. Gabe led the Negro drivers: Steve and Sammy and Lewis. My three sons and I were the standers. I have raised them to be hunters, believing that every man should not only know how to handle a gun, but be able to get about in the woods, for a man who is not a sportsman never realizes what harmless and spirited joy he misses. I started each one of my boys to hunt with me when he was six years old. While only one is now of age, each has hung up his gobbler and his antlered stag. Each has learned how to roll his own. Besides, we have countless happy memories of our days together in the woods and fields.

Peafield Corner is a heavily wooded triangle between Montgomery Creek and the Santee River. Once a great and prosperous plantation, it is now the haunt of wild game. Old Gabe, who lives there, has a hard time raising any crops on account of the deer, and his turkeys are forever straying off to mate with wild ones. To drive the place, we send the Negroes back along the river, from which they turn and come out to us on the main road, a mile away.

Sending my eldest son, Arch, to the Tarkiln Stand on the road, I put my youngest at the head of the Doctor's Branch, a famous crossing so named because a physician of old days had let two old bucks slip by him there. My second boy, Middleton, stood in a deep corner next to the Old Parsonage. I stood at the Crippled Creek. We had the corner blocked off; but it has been my experience that the game that is cornered is often the game that gets away.

For twenty minutes, while the drivers were taking the hounds back by the river, I heard no sound in the woods save the dripping of dew from the needles of the long-leaf pines, the drowsy awakening call of birds, and the music of the wings of wild ducks speeding over the forest toward the delta.

Then the Negroes began to drive. I have taught them not merely to whoop but to sing their spirituals as they do at camp meetings; and if there is any sound more melodious than those pagan voices ringing the wildwoods at dawn, I have not heard it. Almost simultaneously with the first voice of a driver came the first voice of a dog. We had two with us, Old Horse and Bing; the former a rangy veteran of the Walker strain, and the latter an English beagle with a high-pitched whimper. Both dogs were soon on a hot trail, and the drivers warmed to their work when they heard the pack begin to give tongue.

Driving out to the hunt that morning, I had told my boys all about the four bucks. All of us seemed equally at a loss to know exactly how to handle such embarrassment of riches. I suggested that two extra shells be taken out of the belt and laid handy. But I had no definite recommendations. I have a friend who killed three deer at one shot, and another who missed a herd of eleven. They were coming straight for him, and he shot both barrels at their twinkling legs, thinking to put the whole crowd out of commission. He didn't cut a hair; and it served him right for trying to kill them all. Of course, I was not sure that "my boy George" had seen four razorbacks or four possums. Yet when the dogs began to chime, hope rose in my heart.

From our stands we could see a long way under the great pines back toward Peafield Corner. There was plenty of light to shoot. It was the first day of the new year. We ought to make history.

Every second I expected to see a forest of horns. That the drivers had seen game was evident from the way they were singing out; it sounded as if they had been converted. But not a thing could I see. On came Old Horse and Bing, the deep-toned musician and the wailing baby. They could not be mistaken. I had a cold chill that the deer had already walked out of the drive and that the dogs were running a trail an hour old. But it was not so.

Suddenly I heard Arch, off to my right, let drive. There was only one barrel; he must have killed his buck. Then, deep down to my left, I heard Middleton salute the dawn with both barrels. The dogs were raving now, and the Negroes had gone quite daffy. To them the sound of the gun suggests a certain dinner, and no other thought stirs them quite so soulfully. But there was something queer about all this. If this bombardment had been at the four bucks, I ought to have seen their telltale flags flashing far off through the misty morning woods; if the bucks had separated, one should have come to me or to my youngest son next to me. But his gun was silent, and nary a deer did I see.

Little Bing, who is white, I made out some two hundred yards ahead of me. She was raging about frantically, but apparently there was nothing ahead of her. I was completely bewildered—so much so that I committed what is in our country one of the cardinal blunders of a deer hunter: I left my stand. Slowly I began edging my way down toward Middleton. Having fired twice, he ought to have two bucks and would therefore need more help than Arch. You know how we think those things out.

Confused as I was, it did not reassure me particularly to hear the voice of "my boy George" join the hunt. It was a discord in the general harmony. Besides, he is the kind of man on whom you can always count to do the wrong thing in the woods. Anybody can drive deer; but a good hunter will drive them to you. George has a system worked out whereby he always drives them away from you.

I had gone perhaps thirty yards from my stand when an intuition made me stop. I leaned against a pine, scanning the open country between the advancing dogs and drivers and myself. In that space there were only a few sparse bushes—hardly enough to hide a rabbit. But you all know that a deer can sometimes make himself mighty small; I do not know a better skulker. That's why I lingered there, not quite convinced that the dogs were playing me false. They were still on a hot trail; and certainly something had gone to the boys.

Suddenly I saw him. But it was not a buck. Why hadn't I guessed ere this critical moment the solution of the mystery of the great outcry of dogs and drivers, the three shots, and nothing seen or heard? My Negroes had run into a flock of turkeys. Here came one now, a noble gobbler. Evidently he was badly scared. He had been running hard, and had all his feathers drawn in so tightly that he hardly looked to be half his natural size. When a wild turkey comes dodging along through bushes, his long, snakelike neck is often the first thing seen. I once told an amateur hunter to look out for this very thing when I left him on a deer stand one day. Not long after I heard his gun blare manfully, after which detonation one of my old hounds set up mournful yowling. He had come out through some huckleberry bushes to the stander, who had promptly decided that his tail, waving high over the brush, was the neck of a wild turkey. That dog's tail never did lose its crazy list after that.

The minute I sighted my gobbler, I must have made some instinctive movement, for he instantly checked, standing there tall and wary, a beautiful and splendid creature, utterly wild. Both barrels of my gun were loaded with buckshot. I had no chance now to shift to 2's or 4's. The turkey was going straight to the stand I had left. Now he was sixty-five yards away, broadside; and he would come no nearer. At that distance a man is far more likely to miss a turkey with buckshot than to kill him.

I brought my gun up, got the sight on the gobbler's bronze shoulder, and let drive. He instantly fluttered out and began to flop heavily. I started to walk toward him. As I did he recovered his feet and began to run in a wobbly fashion toward a bushy watercourse. I carefully marked the exact spot where he entered this cover.

When we left home that morning, I had left the bird dog, Jim. But when we had reached the rendezvous, Jim showed up apologetically behind the car. I had scolded him for coming, but now I thanked my stars that I had him. He was lying out in the road by the car.

About this time the dogs came up on the trail of the gobbler, and I stopped them. Then came the drivers. Then Middleton appeared with a twenty-pound old tom slung over his shoulder. From the other direction came Arch, with a similar trophy. If I could get mine, we'd have three, and the sun was not yet up.

Going out to the road, we ran full into a party of Christmas hunters, twenty-two strong. Most of them apparently were in the big woods for the first time. Their excitement at sight of the two great gobblers slung nonchalantly over my sons' shoulders was interesting to watch. They were full of curiosity and questions.

"Jim," I called to my setter, "come in here with me."

"What are you going to do now?" one of the visitors asked, giving all of us a survey as if he thought we were miracle workers.

"Oh," I said lightly, "I'm just going in these bushes here to kill another gobbler."

"By golly!" said the man. "Now ain't that sumpin'?"

"He's just kiddin' you," another said.

I went in with Jim. He made a beautiful point on the wounded bird, which got up heavily and flew back toward my audience. When I shot him, they had to scatter to get clear of his ponderous fall.

"Holy snap!" one of them cried out. "Is killin' turkeys as easy as that?"

"Them's tame turkeys," one of the crew suggested.

"Huh!" said one of their old grizzled guides. "if them's tame turkeys, I is the Prince o' Wales."

So, after the fireworks in Peafield Corner, we were back home early to a New Year's breakfast.

"How many were in the flock?" I asked Gabe as we planned further fireworks.

" 'Bout sixteen, sah."

"We did well," I said; "but what about those four bucks? I was ready and waiting."

"My boy George," Gabe told me, "he done see them. But he been on the wrong side of them, and he run them across the creek."

George would do that.

My 339th Gobbler

From the title of this story you might suppose that I'd devoted my life exterminating what many sportsmen think is the greatest game bird in the world. But all the 339 birds were fairly killed, in season, and over a period of 60 years.

I've hunted them in Virginia, West Virginia, Maryland, Pennsylvania, and North Carolina, but nearly all my turkey shooting has been done in the Santee River delta region in my home state of South Carolina. There, and in few other places, this superb bird is found in its pure, original strain. Several states wishing to repopulate their barren ranges with wild turkeys have secured stock from this area, and at least one got its stock from my McClellanville plantation.

Considering how long I've been hunting, and the fact that until recently the season's wild-turkey limit in South Carolina was 20, my total bag isn't large. In pioneer days, Meshach Browning of western Maryland is said to have killed more than 2,000 of them, and Jim Brady of Pennsylvania, who was killed by Chief Bald Eagle, nailed something like 1,700.

Wild turkeys usually travel in flocks of 10 to 20, and while their range is wide the schedule they keep is fairly steady. Generally they feed in a great circle and, if not molested, will roost in the same area night after night. They can run as fast as race horses, and though their flights ordinarily are short, I've seen one zoom a mile over a flooded delta. Their hearing and sight are incredibly keen, and they are so swift on the getaway that I've never been able to kill more than one turkey to every five whitetails I've dropped.

How go you about killing a wild turkey? Well, some men are hunters while others are turkey hunters, and there's a big difference. I know some men who'll hunt nothing but wild turkeys, and for them the sport is like a religious or ceremonial rite. I also know hunters who think that stalking wild turkeys is tiresome. They'd rather shoot rabbits scurrying ahead of beagles.

From *Outdoor Life*, January 1956.

It's true, of course, that it takes a little extra edge to kill a wild turkey—unless you just run into a piece of good luck. That happens sometimes. For example, I knew a quail hunter who once had a wild gobbler step right in front of him. It was just out of gunshot range, and the hunter expected any second to see the bird take wing or run dodgingly away. It didn't move. The man simply walked up to it and nailed it with his No. 7 quail shot. His elation abated somewhat when he discovered that the gobbler had only one eye, and that he'd approached it on the blind side.

I knew another man who, hunting a field at the foot of a mountain, saw a gobbler ambling away from him to gain shelter in the brush. It ran into an old wire fence half-hidden by honeysuckle vines. Before the gobbler realized what was happening, the hunter caught it alive. He carried it home and tried to tame it, but the bird never lost its wildness and fastidiousness regarding food.

While hunting turkeys at daylight one morning, I heard a duck hunter shoot close to the river bank about half a mile from where I was sitting under a huge pine. A few minutes later a fine gobbler, flying from the direction of the shot, alighted on a branch right over my head. While I was maneuvering to get my gun up, he lost his hold and dropped dead in my lap. That duck hunter had filled him with 5's or 6's, and the old boy had just enough strength to make it to that tree. I gratefully picked him up and carried him home. But when you hunt wild turkeys, you mustn't expect a thing like that to happen. Incidentally, this gift turkey isn't included in my 339.

A great deal of my good fortune as a turkey hunter has been due to some Negroes who work on my plantation. They are matchless woodsmen. They can think as game does, move through forests like shadows, and fade away like ghosts. They don't hunt, but they teach me how. Once I asked Prince, my foreman, why a buck we were watching just stood out in the open while a wild clamor of drivers and dogs pushed up behind him.

Prince considered the situation, then said, "He's readin' his book."

That reading probably saved his life, for instead of coming to me, standing on a well-used deer crossing, the buck whirled and jetted through drivers and dogs. From the moment he turned I knew he was heading for the river, beyond which, in the wild morasses of the delta, he would be safe.

Some men suppose, probably judging by the domestic variety, that wild turkeys are dumb, and they don't understand why others consider hunting them such fine sport. It's because of its difficulty and uncertainty. It offers a challenge that only those naturally gifted with woods sense and great patience can master.

An ordinary hunter will regard a wild gobbler's track without emotion, but a turkey hunter wouldn't hesitate to abandon wife, children, job, and home just for a chance at one of these old bearded men of the wilderness. And he will play that chance with infinite care. I've sat in the woods with Tyler Somerset, a good turkey hunter, for fully two hours and during that time he never uttered a syllable or batted an eye. He just looked, sometimes turning his head slightly to listen better, and all the time ready for instant action.

Of all wild game, the turkey is perhaps the most difficult to stay with. If he ever discovers that you're after him, he will literally quit the country. For that reason, while I can always promise a man a shot at a buck, I make no such promises about a gobbler. He's here today but tomorrow—if he gets wise to your designs on him—he may be 10 miles away. Often he will fly across rivers and lakes, pass from one mountain to another, and traverse huge tracts of country. And he's a walker, too. Compared to wild turkeys, grouse, quail, pheasants, and wild ducks hardly go anywhere on their feet. Even when he's just ranging for food, a wild turkey may travel several miles a day, and when he's quitting suspicious country he may go even farther.

Turkeys also get notions, and for no discoverable reason will suddenly leave good, quiet territory and wander for miles. They sometimes act as if they had something on their minds that they can't figure out. Sometimes they act as if they were just plain goofy.

When I lived in Pennsylvania's beautiful Cumberland Valley I cultivated the acquaintance of a turkey hunter named Seth. I hunted with him in the wilds of Path Valley clear up to the Juniata, in Bear Valley, on Sideling Hill, in the Big Cove, and on Two-Top Mountain. We even got into West Virginia on a hint from a friendly mountaineer that there were turkeys at a place called Seldom Seen.

As I had regular work, I always had to get home by night. But Seth's regular work was to kill gobblers. I've known him to spend the night alone in those wild mountains just because he'd come upon some scratchings that looked not over a day old.

"To kill a gobbler," he used to tell me, "you got to see him first, and you mustn't let him see you at all. A wild turkey that sees a man is a turkey that gets away."

Seth knew more than I did about hunting wild turkeys and, following his advice, I had some grand sport. His advice was simple: "Stay high on a ridge where you can look down both sides, and let them come up to you. Outwait them."

Times without number I have been completely outsmarted by an old gobbler, but I've never let it worry me. I never regret seeing a wild creature escape, especially if it does so after a bold decision and by a crafty maneuver. I guess it is because I find live things more appealing than dead ones.

"Well," you say, "if that's true, how about those 339 gobblers?"

It's simple: I could have killed a great many more. I've called up gobblers and just watched them. Once I called two, and they came from different directions, each looking for a wildwood princess with a seductive voice. They had a great battle—over me!

Living as I do in the wilderness, my wife sometimes says to me, "We have no meat." Then I take my gun into the woods to try to correct the situation. And those who look askance at my turkey-shooting record should be reminded that the birds always have at least a 75 percent chance to escape.

On Valentine's Day, 1954, I called on Prince Alston, my foreman. "Prince," I said casually, "I need to kill a gobbler. I don't mean one of those little barefoot boys. I want an old bearded man."

"Yes, Cap'n," he said simply. "You remember that dogwood thicket on Hickory Hill next to the Wambaw Swamp?"

"I know where you mean."

"My mind tells me I can pick up a trail there. When I am ready, you be ready."

Day after day for nearly a week Prince came and went in the jeep. He went at all hours, and on his return he made no report. But I'm used to his ways. He came to me on a Friday night and there were lights in his eyes. I knew what that meant.

"Come with me before daylight tomorrow," he said. "I will take you to seven old gobblers on Hickory Hill, and I know their schedule."

I understood exactly. He'd found scratchings in the leaves and pine straw, had learned from the heaved-up windrows in which direction the birds were feeding, and had found out whence they'd come and whither they'd gone. That's what Prince meant in speaking of their schedule. If you can figure out such a routine, you can probably get a shot by intercepting turkeys. Thus, while I did the shooting, credit for much of what happened later belongs to Prince.

I met him in the back yard in the starlit dimness preceding daylight, and he drove me in the jeep deep into the wilds of a deserted plantation known as Wambaw Corner. I wanted to be in position by full daylight, but it's not necessary to hunt wild turkeys before that. They have a wholesome respect for foxes and wildcats, and usually don't come to ground until the woods are bright and clear. On misty or rainy days, I've known them to stay on their roosts until late morning.

Prince is a man of a few words, but I always listen to what he has to say—especially if it has to do with hunting. He kept issuing brief orders to me as we bumped along. He would stay in the jeep about half a mile from where he expected me to go into action. I was to walk to Hickory Hill, beyond which the great Wambaw Swamp mouldered in all its eeriness.

"You remember where you tumbled that old swamp buck that had horns as flat as a paddle?" he asked.

"I'd never forget that."

"Well, last fall you had a man cut a few of those big shortleaf pines right on this edge of Hickory Hill. Those pine tops on the ground make a good place for you to hide. Right in front of you will be dogwoods, and wild turkeys love dogwood berries. That whole hill is scratched up, but most of the scratching is right under the dogwoods."

I told him I understood his directions, and appreciated his strategy.

"I broke a green-pine limb," he told me, "and laid it down in front of the dead pine top where I want you to be. The only thing is, I believe it might rain. If they come, and it starts to rain, shoot fast, because you know a turkey hates rain. He's going by that swamp and hunt for some brush like an umbrella. I will come when you shoot."

I left Prince in the jeep and made my way to Hickory Hill. It is wild country. Several times deer snorted and dashed away from me, and overhead I heard the thin music of ducks' wings. I felt a few drops of rain, and while the east was brightening I heard thunder in the west, and the storm seemed to be coming my way.

I found the place where I was to wait, but I crawled into the pine-top shelter warily. It was a mild morning. In my country, snakes don't really hibernate, they only doze. I had an uneasy feeling that these pine tops might be housing a diamondback, a copperhead, or even a cottonmouth moccasin. Of the three, I have the keenest dread of the last.

But I got safely settled. In a situation like this, a man must try to remain concealed yet he must be sure he's free to shoot. I arranged that. A little rain was falling, and deep thunder was rolling up from the west. Perhaps the turkeys wouldn't even leave their roost. Maybe they'd shelter under some thick bushes and wouldn't come out on the open hill to feed. I didn't feel too hopeful. But magical things can happen to a man in the woods.

Suddenly, close to me but off to my right and behind a dense screen of pine needles, I heard the strident call of a gobbler. It surprised me, and for a moment I thought it might be another hunter touching his call. But then I heard a short soft note. That was unmistakable. At least one gobbler, possibly more, was within easy range. I couldn't see him, and I dared not move. Would he pass behind me out of range? Would the rain turn him back? Or would he walk out into the open woods in front of me?

I waited. The rain continued and thunder rolled through the misty forest. I was in a position that seemed to call for breaking all hunting rules, and this I decided to do, for sometimes it's the only way to win. Getting my gun ready for instant action, I simply stepped out of my ambush.

The rain hid a good deal from view, but what I saw was enough. A small flock of gobblers was huddled droopingly under some jasmine vines about 30 yards to my right. Apparently they were more interested in trying to keep dry than in breakfasting on the dogwood berries.

The instant I appeared, they were galvanized into action. Some dashed through the thickets, two took wing away from me and through dense timber, but a third rose across the open woods and headed for the swamp. As my gun spoke, he dropped like a plummet. It was my 339th gobbler, killed under circumstances I'd never encountered before. A regal bird he was, weighting, as I found later, 21 pounds. A pure wild turkey gobbler rarely exceeds that.

I'd thought Prince was a half a mile away. But regardless of where he's supposed to be, he always gets to fallen game as soon as I do or even before. It was Prince who proudly lifted this king of the wilderness.

His eyes glistening, and not with rain, he said, "I is so glad." That made it unanimous.

GREAT GOBBLERS
~ Part IV ~

Turkey hunters have a tendency to endow their quarry with almost supernatural powers or to ascribe qualities to the bird which no gobbler really possesses. They do this, more often than not, as a result of their own failure—a humbled hunter's exercise in self-justification. Yet there is an element of accuracy in descriptions regularly encountered in the sport's literature: "hermit gobbler," "call-shy bird," "wary warrior." Terms of this sort offer a measure of insight, for the uninitiated, into just how difficult it can be to bag a mature tom. And visions of devilishly difficult toms that repeatedly outwit hunters, sending them home with empty game bags and dragging footsteps, add to the narrative romance that most readers welcome.

Any old master of the sport, a veteran who has earned his hard-won stripes in long hours spent cramped at the foot of some tree, bedeviled by the cold on chilly days and mosquitoes on warm ones, will have had encounters with gobblers which are richly deserving of the simple yet evocative description "great." For Rutledge each and every turkey taken was special, a prize to be hailed at the moment of triumph as well as respectfully spoken over when it graced the dinner table.

Yet for him, as for all hunters fortunate enough to enjoy repeated success in the sport, there were a few birds that truly stood out. In these seven stories we meet a total of ten such toms, each of which had some trait that set him apart from others of his kind. In nature they range, in Rutledge's descriptions, from "Rajah" to "Rogue," but each was a meaningful part of his life as a turkey hunter. These "bearded men" are likewise intriguing to us, for they stand as enduring examples of great gobblers.

Four Bearded Men

I don't know exactly how it is with the rest of the boys, but as far as I am concerned I love best to read of the hunting I never have had, and probably never shall have. For example, I never have had a shot at a bull moose, a black-tailed buck, a pronghorn antelope, a grizzly bear, a sage grouse, a ptarmigan. Reading the stories of hunters who have had these experiences has all the charm of novelty for me. Of course, when a man writes about ring-necked pheasants, ruffed grouse, bobwhites and white-tailed stags, I get the thrill of recognizing the kind of game and the kind of hunting with which I am familiar.

As the wild turkey is unquestionably the greatest game bird in all the world, as I have hunted him for 50 years in his native wilds, and as his range is now unhappily exceedingly limited, I believe my fellow sportsmen might like to hear of some of my firsthand experiences with this king of the wilderness. I have chosen four rather typical experiences out of a possible 200. These illustrate pretty well the nature of turkey hunting, the wildness and wariness of this great bird, the chances and quirks of fate that occur when any hunter is after game worthy of his best mettle.

Early one morning in late February, two or three years ago, when I was out in a field in front of my plantation house down here in South Carolina, my wife came out on the front porch and rang a little hand bell for breakfast. The day was mild and still; the sun was just coming up; birds were singing from the patriarch live oaks, the tall yellow pines, the shadowy thickets. Some mallards were lazily quacking on the river that runs just behind the house. A short time before the bell rang, I had seen three deer steal out of the field where I was, where they had been eating the oats, and go into the dense thickets near by. You might guess that I live in the wilderness. You are right. I am 20 miles, three rivers, two swamps, and a wild morass from the nearest railroad.

When the little bell sounded from the porch, as if in answer to it, from

---

From *Sports Afield*, May 1946. Later included in *Those Were the Days* (1955).

the river bank behind the house, an old wild gobbler sounded off. You know how it is with a tame gobbler: when he is feeling bucky, any noise will bring forth an answering challenge from him. I have known wild gobblers, especially at daybreak when they are still on the roost, to answer the hoot of an owl, a man's imitation of such a whoop, the scream of a hawk, the distant bark of a dog, the shout of a hunter, and even the sound of a gun! But I never before had known one to answer a bell.

Hurrying to the house, I picked up my turkey call, my gun and shells, and beat it out of the back door. My wife, fully realizing the meaning— and the importance (those red points days!)—of all this, moved hopefully behind me to the back porch, awaiting developments.

Between the house and river are my camellia gardens, under huge oaks and magnolias. The river bank itself is grown to bushes and canes, through which a narrow path winds. As I was edging down to the bank, I heard the old boy again, about a hundred yards away. Immediately I sat down behind a stump. Then I touched my call softly, alluringly, only once. To call too much is fatal. You have to vamp him. Like a man, he does not care for this ripe fruit that falls into his hand. What he gets stirred up over is a siren, an enchantress, a wildwood princess, shy and wonderful, hard to obtain, full of shadowy avoidance, and therefore greatly to be desired.

The gobbler answered my call. I turned my head, saw my wife looking with a turkey-dinner longing at me, and I nodded at her, reassuring her that all looked right. Up the path through the jungle came the huge old bearded man of the wilderness. I could hear him strutting, but I could not yet see him. I had laid down my call and had my gun leveled for the river bank.

In hunting these superb old fellows, I invariably use No. 2 shot. Of course, they can be killed with shot of a smaller size; but as a rule it takes an awful wallop to put one down to stay; and a wild turkey that is merely wounded, especially if he still has his legs, will likely get away. He can outrun a horse; and, unlike other wounded game birds, he does not duck into the nearest cover, hoping to be passed over. He will quit the country; or, as one old woodsman said to me, "He will quit the world."

When this old bird I was luring came in sight, he gave me a shock. I had somehow miscalculated the distance to the little pathway through the canes. It was about 70 yards; and with any kind of shotgun and any kind of shot, that is a risky distance at which to chance this kind of game. At first I saw only his black bulk; then he straightened up, and the sun struck his plumage, making its iridescence gleam and shimmer. He stood at least three feet high, and I could see that he had a long and heavy beard. I had the gun full on him; but I waited. I knew he had heard my call; and I knew that he would come to it: I mean to the very spot from which it had been sounded. Sure enough, after a moment's survey of the premises, he turned and came directly for me. I let him come within 35 yards; then I laid him down—22 pounds of regal game bird; and that is about as heavy as the genuine wild turkey ever grows. As he is streamlined and tailored, most of his weight is in his breast, which is as plump as that of a grouse.

My wife saw me pick up this wild gobbler, and waited for me as I brought him to the house. I guess I reached at that moment a lifetime's high point in her estimation. But it was an honor I had to divide generously with the turkey, a good housekeeper being what she is.

When I tell you about the second gobbler, I am not recommending my story to you as a standard method of hunting the wild turkey. It was just one of those things; for in the deep woods strange things happen to a hunter. I had known of a flock of turkeys about two miles down the river, near the ruin of a once beautiful and stately plantation house.

At daylight one morning between Christmas and New Year, I went down there to see what could be done about correcting the meat shortage. I found a good place, sat down, and waited for some more daylight to come. I was under a huge oak, on a slope overlooking a marsh, beyond which was the river, on the bank of which were some giant cypresses, shrouded in gray moss—a favorite roosting place for turkeys. They like big trees, plenty of camouflage, and prefer trees that are near or over water. I had taken out my call and was about to start something when a mighty shotgun blast from the river bank told me that I had been preceded. Some other hunter had had the same idea about those turkeys.

Under such circumstances, if a flock has been scattered, and a man will hang around for an hour or so, he might call one of the big birds up. But somehow my instinct told me that this had been a lone bird, and that he had been killed. My instinct was only partly right. It was a lone gobbler, but here he came flying across the marsh straight for me. As he had attained considerable elevation, and was really getting under way with his characteristically powerful momentum, I knew the shot would be the kind that permits one, after it is all over, to offer an alibi. I got ready to shoot; but something stopped me. I saw he was going to light in the tree over my head.

Now, you may well ask whether it would not have been more sporting to have tried him on the wing. Yes and no; and no because the chances were really against my killing him; and if there is one thing I hate to do it is to wound a fine wild creature, and have him die a lingering death somewhere back in the wilderness. If I waited until he settled on the tree

I knew I could kill him; and, by the way, that was why I was supposed to be there.

This ponderous live projectile landed right over my head. He came to rest on a limb about 70 feet up. There he was in plain view; and his long beard gave me an idea as to his weight and the breadth of his bosom.

As, if he peered down, I was in full sight of him (and a wild turkey can identify a man even if the man makes no move at all), I at once began to get my gun on him, manuevering for a shot. But while I was doing this, the old boy sat down on the limb; then he began to rock and to weave on his perch. Suddenly, letting go all holds, he fell like a plummet straight into my lap! At least I had to get out of his way as he fell. The other man, of course (probably using 4's or 5's), had really killed the gobbler; but he had had strength enough to make it to that big tree. I just picked him up and walked home with him. But, as I said before, when you go turkey hunting, don't expect this sort of thing to happen to you. Yet it might.

All one January afternoon I had been following a flock of turkeys on the sunny hickory hills that bordered a monstrous swamp. The signs were very fresh; it was a large flock, and there were some big birds among the lot. How did I know these things without seeing them? After some experience, you can estimate the number of birds by the amount of scratching; and you can tell the size by noticing with what masculine vigor the toes of the old toms have raked the ground under the leaves and pine straw. Often, I felt, I was close on the birds; but I never saw them.

Right here, however, let me say that it usually is a mistake to follow a flock of wild turkeys: The eyesight, the hearing, and that strange sixth sense that nature's children have of just feeling danger without touching it, are, in this magnificent game bird, without equal. I should say that a wild turkey can rarely if ever be approached by following him. He may come to you, but you will hardly get to him.

So convinced was I that the flock had roosted in that immediate vicinity that the mist of the morning found me there again. If you are out in turkey country at that time of day, and the woods are still, you can nearly always hear the birds talking on the roost or flying down. Then, if you are properly located, you have a good chance of calling one up.

These woods had been timbered two years before; but because of some defect certain great yellow pines had been left standing. In the dim twilight of daybreak I began to search these for a telltale black bulk. While the light is still uncertain, if you are careful, you can walk right up under a wild turkey. And that is just what I did. Full 90 feet from the ground, near the crest of a giant pine, I saw an old gobbler roosting. You might say, "That's only 30 yards—a dead easy shot." But remember that, in shooting up, the pull of gravity against your shot does not afford you the same chance as if you were shooting horizontally or at an angle. And by the way, I think it is well to point out here that you generally can identify a turkey in a tree by his tail, which hangs down like a shingle. You also may see him crane his head against the sky. Such observations keep you from shooting at bunches of mistletoe and squirrel nests.

With 2's in my long choke barrel, I had a resting shot. The only thing against me was the poor visibility. The gun blared. I heard turkeys flying off at some distance. I even heard a gobbler answer the gun from across the river. But my old bird just sat right where he was. I did not know if I had missed him clean, had shot at something that looked like a turkey, or whether I had killed him, and that in a moment he would come tumbling down.

Deciding that I had missed, I laid it on him again. And this time he fell resoundingly. I can't be sure why he did not fly at the first shot; but I believe wild things do not always identify the sound of a gun. They are used to many noises in the woods. Another explanation of this gobbler's strange behavior was given me by an old backwoods friend, who said, "The first time you shot, you missed a deaf gobbler."

One afternoon I was hunting quail in the pinelands. I was walking down an old sandy road, and my setter was ranging the woods, now on this side and now on that. As so often happens, the unexpected happened. I was looking for quail, and my gun was loaded accordingly; but 100 yards ahead of me out stepped into the road a superb gobbler. He was really one of the old bearded men of the wilderness. The setter at the time was far off to my left, and had no inkling of the turkey. I was pretty sure, however, that that king of the wilds, with his marvelous senses always at razor-edge sharpness, had located both the dog and me.

I put it down as hopeless. I knew that if the turkey had not yet, he would certainly soon discover one or both of us. And that would be all. He might fly; but more likely he would run. A heavy old bird dislikes to rise; if he does, he always has to taxi for a little distance before he can take the air.

I had nothing but bird shot cartridges with me: besides, I knew that even if I had turkey loads, the movement of loading the gun would surely be detected. To my amazement and growing incredulity, the old bearded man just stood there; and he stood at his full height, with all his feathers drawn in. Something had alerted him.

Rather idly and without hope of getting more than a couple of paces nearer, I walked on. Slowly the gap between us was diminished. My footfalls were soundless on the sand. I was now within 50 yards; now 40; now 30. A moment later he turned his head all the way round. In a second he had taken his characteristic little run, and up he rose. But it was too late for him. Even though I had nothing but 8's in my gun, he fell at the shot. He lay there at my feet, but still I was only half convinced it had happened. How could he have stood there all that time and let me approach, in full sight?

I knew he did not do so because he was tame; for we were miles from human habitation; besides, he had all the characteristics of the true native bird: the pink legs, the indigo head, the slender and long legs and neck, the iridescent plumage. I examined him carefully. A little to my chagrin, I discovered he was stoneblind in the left eye; and I had approached him from the left side. Otherwise he was perfect, as fine a specimen as I ever killed. What had brought my luck about was that incredible combination of circumstances: the far-ranging of my setter, the sand on which I could walk noiselessly, the gobbler's stepping out in the road with his blind side toward me!

But I am not advising any hunter who yearns to bring home a wild gobbler to look for one that has lost his sight.

BIG TOM

Patsy's Place is on Tuscarora Summit, six hundred feet above the valley and two thousand feet above sea-level. As it is a typical roadside refreshment stand, you can get all the pop and chewing gum you want; and I take it that the mountain and Patsy's fairly represent our piebald civilization—grand in some way, and tawdry in others. What makes Patsy's grand to me is the fact that, just over the eyebrow of the hill, almost within a good stone's throw—especially if you're heaving it downhill—there are gigantic and garrulous gobblers.

Now I'll quit fooling and tell you one.

Leaving my car at Patsy's in the chill mist of dim dawn at that high altitude, I turned into an old mountain road running south along the bench of the mighty hill. The wood was foggy and tattered; all the winds were asleep. Far in the valley I could hear those noises from the farms which show that the day's work is beginning. One of the charms of hunting turkeys in the Tuscarora Mountains comes from the fact that, in a strip of woods between the Pittsburgh-Baltimore pike and a big modern farm, a lordly wild gobbler is likely to stalk athwart your path. And then it's your duty to see to it that he stalks no more.

The highway was not a quarter of a mile behind me when, from the dim woods below, I heard a big bird give one of those drowsy, complaining calls. You know what I mean. The flock had been scattered the afternoon before. This old fellow had roosted alone. Now that he was on the ground once more and was getting awake, he wanted to join the family for breakfast. He was just like a husband clowning around the house before the biscuits and coffee are ready.

Such a bird at such a time is really an ideal one to call. I do not ever think it unfair to call a wild turkey; if you can really do it, you deserve all you get. The calling of most hunters is the very best life insurance that the big birds ever get, for most of this calling might be the notes of a

---

From *Field & Stream*, November 1931. Later published as "Bronzed Mountaineers" in *An American Hunter* (1937).

nightingale or of a tree-frog or of a braying mule as well as of a wild turkey. In Pennsylvania it is supposed to be unlawful to call turkeys; but the reverse might save more game. It takes a touch of woodland genius to argue a turkey into coming your way.

Obeying that law, I decided that my best chance was to get ahead and then in front of the talkative wanderer. You know as well as I that there's simply no such thing as following a wild turkey successfully. "I shall go to him, but he shall not return to me," said King David about his departed son; and without meaning any irreverence, we can say of a wary gobbler, "He shall come to me, but I shall not go to him." No, never. For every step you take, he'll take three; and for every rod you look, he's looking five. And he can hear you heave a sigh.

To walk on dry leaves that cover a wild chaos of rocks, and to do the thing noiselessly, is a feat of which even a wildcat might be proud. I didn't do it, but managed as best I could. Determining the direction that the turkey was taking, I went straight ahead for a quarter of a mile, then down the mountain two hundred yards, flushing in my course three fine grouse, which seemed to let me come much nearer than if I had been hunting them. Looking about for a place to wait, I saw a chestnut stump low to the ground. The spot was fairly open. I sat down listening.

Not two hundred yards ahead my old friend called complainingly. He was coming straight for me. He had not heard me avalanching all over the mountainside. If I did not move, it did not seem possible that he would not walk right up to me. And that's like getting an unexpected legacy.

At such a time, when the hunter has to wait his chance, he has a good opportunity to get excited. Some men keep getting more and more excited until they run that high temperature known as buck-fever. Others get hot and then cool off nicely. On a good many occasions I have had to take a sudden, unexpected shot at a buck—walking him up, as a rule. I recall killing an old stager in that way; and after it was all over, why, then I got scared!

As my eyes scanned the khaki-colored woods, apparently so dead yet full of sleeping life and of tense and wary life, the regal gobbler himself stepped into sight. What amazed me was his height. How could a thing so tall and therefore so conspicuous stay around those woods all those years? He was walking slowly, pausing now and then to peck fastidiously at something on the ground. Then he would stand, his head high. Now he gave a deep, throaty call and came on. He was within ninety yards; and if he and I had been holding the two ends of a string, he could not have been coming straighter for me. Apparently he intended to walk right up and investigate me.

I waited until he got his head well behind a big oak; then I put up my gun. The turkey-hunter who jerks his gun up at the last minute will probably miss, or not get a chance to shoot. The instant that wild bird's marvelous eyes catch the movement, he's gone. He says "Put!" but he doesn't stay put. Most of the misses recorded under such circumstances as I describe can be attributed to the fact that the hunter did not get his bead on the bird long before the turkey came within real range. If an old gobbler is walking up to a hunter, that hunter must aim at the turkey when the turkey doesn't see him.

In this part of the country we think that if you get a turkey where you want him, 4's are the shot. Of course, if he comes close enough, you might just reach out and grab him, or whack him over the head with your snickersnee. But generally we have to shoot. I always carry 4's in the open barrel and 2's in the choke. It takes a bludgeon blow to break down one of these old mountain sultans.

Now my gleaming prize was within sixty yards. Was he going to walk right up and ask me to give him some of my lunch, eating it right out of my hand? I have killed turkeys at that distance; but if one is as far as that and is coming closer, I always let him come. There really isn't much danger that he will come too close—so close that there is peril that after your shot you will not be able to pick up anything more than a beard, a No. 10 shoe-print and a gobble.

Where do you shoot a turkey—that is, if you have time for a deliberate aim? Most men of my acquaintance shoot for the neck, just below the head. A few prefer the base of the wing, or just a direct shot into the breast. Within a fair range, the head-and-neck shot is undoubtedly the thing. One shot placed in that vital region may bring down the bird for keeps, while he may beat his way off manfully with a dozen lodged at random in his burly body.

My gobbler—for I had already claimed ownership—stopped behind a fanlike cluster of chestnut sprouts. He suddenly appeared to have shrunk astonishingly. No longer the drowsy bird with fluffed-out feathers, he was now trim, keen, a lance in rest. He had heard before I did what now assailed my ears. O cursed spite! O heart bowed down!

"Charlie! Oh, Charlie! Hey, Charlie! Where are you? I'm up here! I'm lost! Oh, Charlie!"

One of those babes in the woods was shouting his head off just above us on the ridge. I wished I had had his range.

If the gobbler had been out in the clear, I would have saluted him as he stood; but he was behind a regular barricade, and this business of expecting your shot to go through just the right peep-hole doesn't work so well. Generally shot will miss the holes and bury themselves in the obstruction. What to do?

Feeling as if I'd like a good crack at both Charlie and his lost child, I sat motionless. The wild rajah stood motionless. But he was all on edge. At such a time a turkey has a decided advantage over the hunter.

Once more the idiot yelled above me. Then, with a jerking dart, the great bird turned and fled back and down the mountain. I did not shoot. I did not even jump up. As calmly as I could I recognized that one of life's great chances was gone.

I had been made the victim of one of those mishaps to which every hunter had better reconcile himself. Besides, the day might not be wholly lost, despite Charlie. I would take another deep semicircle and try to intercept the old boy again.

But now it had started to rain—one of those fine, persistent, sleety things that makes a lot of harsh whispering on the dead but unfallen oak leaves. You know that continuous, soft racket which makes almost every sound indistinguishable. When you hear something, you can't tell whether you've heard something or not. It is nature's true camouflage against the still-hunter. But at the same time his own maneuverings are rendered thereby silent and obscure.

Far down the mountain I went, tried sitting still in the rain, found it not so hot, and then began to move slowly and disconsolately upward again. This mountainside is laid in the neatest folds you ever saw: a rolling ridge, then a gully, then a ridge and then a gully—just like that. And there's very little difference in the height of the ridges and the depth of the gullies. Each of the latter has a little stream running down it. In the gullies are tangles of grape-vines, wild raspberries, teaberries, a few laurels, and then those little thickety places beloved of game of all kinds. Out of such places I have started deer, turkeys and grouse.

I ambled slowly, my shoes beginning to slosh a little. The lisping drizzle hushed the sound of my own footfalls. Because I had been disappointed, and because I was wet, I got off the alert. Ahead of me was a rather dense wild raspberry patch. The gully here was wide and flat, so that above the little silvery canes there was clear space for shooting. My gun under my arm and the safety on, my hat pulled down, my collar turned up, I looked like Defeat. But ye gods!

With a noise that sounded as if a barn were tumbling down, or as if there were an afternoon tea, out of the drenched raspberries rolled my old gobbler—bigger and better than ever! I had blundered on him in the rain, and it was the rain that had prevented his hearing my approach. He got up like a whole flock. It flashed over me that my carelessness in not being ready would prevent my getting in both barrels handily. One would have to do the execution—if there were any done.

He headed up the gully, then veered to the left, for all the world like a huge grouse. But, of course, no turkey ever leaves the ground with the same lightning and unerring speed as does a grouse. He was some fifty-five yards away before I got the sight dead on him. I let him have the choke barrel with the 2's.

When I had jerked my head up upon his arising, rain from the brim of my hat had cascaded into my eyes, so that they were bleary when I pulled the trigger, and still so after I had shot. I did not see the turkey go on. I did not see him fall. I saw one fluffy feather in the air; that was all. But when I reached the spot, there he was, lying black on the tawny leaves, with hardly a bronzed feather ruffled. A superb specimen was he—a veteran of many thrilling escapes. I picked him up and started my long climb back to the car, and in my heart the intense disgust for Charlie and his stray infant abated considerably.

I don't know if you've ever climbed over slippery rocks hidden by leaves, carrying a gun and toting a 21-pound gobbler. It's hard but not half so hard as if you didn't have a turkey to carry. It must have been near noon and still a-rainin' when I pulled into Patsy's Place. I like Patsy's coffee; besides, I wanted him to get a just estimate of my ability as a hunter. You know how that is.

In the smoky little room were two strangers wearing bedraggled hunting regalia. As I came in they got up from their table and came right over to me.

"Oh, migosh!"

"Ain't I done tole you so, Charlie?" asked the other.

"Oh, cripes!" the first fellow exclaimed, feeling the manly bosom of my prize.

"Did one of you fellows get lost this morning?" I asked. "I thought I heard somebody calling above me."

"Sure. I was calling Charlie," one of the men said. "I seen a turkey, but we was so close to a farm I was skeered it might be a tame one, and I didn't want to shoot no man's old brood tom. Hey, is that a real wild gobbler? Holy snap!"

"Shucks!" said Charlie disconsolately. "I believe that's the very turkey what came runnin' to me when you were callin'. I was down on the edge of that cornfield, and I took it for a farm bird. Well, holy roll! How did you know he was wild, stranger?"

"I asked him," I told Charlie.

"Did you, though?" he queried incredulously. "Ain't you foolin'?"

"Well, I tell you," I explained. "Whenever you see a turkey in the mountain, shoot him; get that done first. Then you can ask him if he belongs there."

"Do tell!" Charlie exclaimed. "Don't a fellow learn a lot in the woods?"

"Yes," I agreed, "but all of us need to learn more."

Yet I parted from this noble pair with a feeling of genuine thankfulness, for if they had not been so dumb, what chance would I have had to take home old Tom of the high Tuscaroras?

TALL MAN OF THE TWILIGHT

I saw him first when the sun had gone down behind the great yellow pines. Driving home with my Negro Prince, after a long and unsuccessful day in the pinelands of my plantation, we had come on a stretch of road that, in Revolutionary days, had been a famous straightaway race-course.

The road is still broad, sandy and level for more than two miles. On either side are the wildwoods, and my home place is the only human habitation for many miles. This road, once important, is now rarely traveled, and for that reason I was surprised to see, some three hundred yards ahead of me, what I took to be the form of a very tall man in the afterglow.

"Now, who could that tall man be?" I asked Prince.

As we seldom see a stranger in my country, I knew that Prince was a little uneasy. This business of seeing tall strangers at dusk didn't appeal to him. But before he answered, we both saw the mistake I had made. A great stag, wandering early out of the dewy haunts to the eastward, had been standing head on in the road. As the car approached he wheeled giving us a chance to appraise his size and the prodigious heights of his horns, and vanished whence he had come.

A hundred yards from the road, on the side from which he had entered, is Montgomery Branch, a famous watercourse, heavily grown to myrtles, sweetbays and young pines. Deer love it. My guess was that the buck had gone no farther than this long thicket of dense greenery. I stopped the car, and Prince and I hurriedly took counsel.

We were agreed that the stately gentleman could not have gone far. It was almost twilight; he was probably hungry after his long day of rest and drowsing; and he had not been badly scared. But the big question was this: when we started him again, what course would he take? As all good deer hunters know, the answer to such a question is not so puzzling as it might appear. Deer have their favorite haunts, their definite ranges, their regular runs.

From *Field & Stream*, March 1939.

The trouble in this case was that at the head of Montgomery Branch there are three choice stands. When Prince got after the buck, he would almost assuredly run one of the three. But which one? That's just the sort of query that makes deer hunting an eternally fascinating sport.

Now, of the three, one was called the Dogwood Head, because there was a big clump of dogwoods that made out at that point from the swamp. It was on the same side of the swamp on which we had seen the deer. But it did not seem likely that he would come back to where he had been frightened.

The second stand was on a hill far across the branch, on a high pineland ridge lying between the swamp and the Big Ocean, a monstrous gloomy place and a natural sanctuary for deer. I was satisfied that this buck, from the course he had taken, had just come out of the Ocean. Now, if it had been daytime, it would have been a good bet that he would return to his fastness, for nothing is more characteristic of deer nature than the habit of retracing steps.

For many years I have observed that if a stag walks into a place he will probably walk or run out over the same course. But in this case I eliminated the possibility of his acting as he would in daylight. The sun was down. He had come out to feed. He yearned to eat up my plantation peas, peanuts, and sweet-potato vines—some ripened dry, but still succulent and alluring.

"Prince," I whispered, "my guess is the Laurel Tree. That old rascal doesn't want to come over this side again just now. He'll hardly run back for the Ocean. He will likely run the other side of the branch, and in toward the plantation. That's where he's headed for, anyhow. Give me ten minutes, and then turn Blue and Red Liquor loose on his track."

Putting Prince and the dogs out of the car, I sped down the road for half a mile. Then I walked across the woods and the swamp, already dewy and misty. But in the South afterglows are long and often radiant: and there was still light enough to shoot when I got to my stand, within gunshot of the swamp, in the middle of a broad savanna, with here and there broomsedge, gallberries and clumps of sweet myrtle. It is a great place for deer to lie, and it is likewise a famous crossing, called the Laurel Tree. Some three hundred yards directly behind the stand, there is a huge magnolia tree—a rather curious phenomenon, as these stately trees are very rarely found in the pineland country.

Silence fell over the immense and lonely forest, though I knew well enough that half a mile away a good Negro's heart was pounding and his mouth watering while he struggled with two hounds straining on the leash. It was so still that I could distinctly hear voices from the plantation, a full mile away. Woodcock began to flit like big bats from one watercourse to another. I heard wild ducks speeding over the pine-tops toward the river. Owls began to hoot.

Sighting my gun against several objects, I found that there was still light enough to shoot. But over the long savanna, down which the buck would come, if he came at all, a fog was rising fast. Mysteriously it veiled the woods. It troubled me. One does not like to have a great stag burst out on him out of the mist. But we can't fight nature.

My misgiving suddenly changed to satisfaction and excitement as the voice of Blue and Red suddenly echoed through the twilight country. They were broadcasting in no mealy-mouthed fashion the fact that they had discovered a deer. I stood up to listen, for in this kind of hunting a man has to be very careful to note, as soon as he can, just what course the dogs are taking. By so doing he can often cut off a deer. In this case I knew that at least I should soon discover whether my guess as to the right stand had been the correct one.

For a moment the dogs bore over the first hill, and then into the branch. There they evidently started the buck anew, to judge from the turmoil that they made. The deer probably had been standing there skulking ever since Prince and I had first seen him. I heard my Negro whoop, which was indication to me that he must have seen a ghostly white flag in the dusk.

For another moment or so the hounds bore toward the Ocean, and my hopes ebbed with the fast-fading light. Suddenly, just where I had hoped the buck would come. I heard a tremendous crashing of brush and splashing of water. Then out burst in full view, monstrous in the twilight, a wild boar! I mean a wild boar, an old brigand of the Big Ocean, come forth from his lair in that impenetrable fastness to root up my property like a steam-shovel.

Ordinarily I would have shot the hulking brute, and gladly; and great would have been Prince's rejoicing. But I had to let him go. Gray he was, as tall as a young calf, and built along the lines of a heavy hyena. As wild as any stag, he plunged off through the forest, and I could hear him going for several hundred yards. Once, when he struck the harsh obstruction of some burnt bushes, he went through the place like a locomotive.

Meanwhile the dogs were silent. Only one of two things could have happened: the big deer had gone in the Ocean (where dogs will not go, especially at dusk), or he had dodged Blue and Red. As I did not know which one of these was the real answer. I sat motionless. Every old hunter knows that a great chance comes just when apparently all chances are over and gone.

But Prince, who is accustomed to whoop as if he had found a still as long as a buck is headed my way, had likewise fallen silent. Two dogs and two men were completely puzzled; and there remained but a few minutes of light. Then out of the silence came a sound that for me never loses its peculiar thrill, though with it I have been familiar for close to fifty years: it was the sound of a wild gobbler leaving the roost.

Montgomery Branch is a favorite roosting place for wild turkeys, and I was not surprised that Prince and the dogs had routed one. He had come my way; but as no wild turkey ever flies very far at twilight, if roused from the roost, he did not come all the way. I heard him alight, and I knew that I would stalk him, for invariably, if driven from one tree at dusk, a wild turkey will alight in a bare tree, where his black bulk looms startlingly against the sky.

One turkey would be better than no deer. I reasoned; and I was on the point of easing forward to try to locate the old tom when the dogs once more opened. This time they were back in the branch, and I wondered if they were on another deer, or if my buck had decided to cross it after all. As there is much water in Montgomery, and plenty of tussocks and tiny islands, it is no hard feat for a deer to dodge even good dogs there. Red's grieving tenor rose through the tall gums and tupelos; old Blue's mellow baritone chimed in manfully. But there was an uncertainty about their performance, as if they had come upon a trail many hours old. Silver in the west now, above the dark momentous pines, I saw the evening star. The sky still showed some color, but the afterglow was about gone. Meanwhile neither Prince nor the hounds seemed to making any progress.

I was so satisfied that the deer had slipped out of the drive that I stood up and took a step forward toward the swamp. But I stopped in my tracks, though nothing I had seen or heard warned me. It was just a hunch. I even cocked my gun on that hunch.

Then I heard a bush crack. And I heard the subdued rustling that a deer makes as he skulkingly works his way through evergreen bushes. I located the sound. It came from a dense patch of sweet myrtles on the edge of the swamp. It must be my buck, but unless he showed himself I might just as well not have heard him. Then I saw something white gleaming, and it wasn't his tail.

Forth into the misty savanna stole a regal stag, his tall white rack gleaming in the twilight. Seeing a deer in that light is enough to make a man believe in ghosts, so silent and imperceptible are its movements.

Now in the mist he faded, now reappeared, coming my way, but then vanishing. I had my gun up; but to judge the distance and to get the sight on him were different matters. At what I took to be forty yards I let drive, the roar of the gun breaking in upon the stillness of the woods as if a war had started in a graveyard. I shot just as the buck was entering a patch of fog, and for the life of me I could not see what I had done. However, I did not hear anything getting away.

Then through the branch I heard some real running. Both the hounds and Prince will always come to a shot. Prince got there before either Red or Blue. But in a few minutes we had all gathered, a little awed, I think, about the prone form of the tall man of the twilight. A stately stag he was, carrying great symmetrical antlers of ten points, and they were almost pure white. Into the side of one horn a buckshot had buried itself (I do not mean flattened), and this one dark spot stood out from the immaculacy of the otherwise snowy antlers.

"Why did you stop whooping?" I asked Prince.

"I done see dat big gobbler on a tree."

"What happened to the dogs? They started on him; then they quit."

Prince did not answer for a moment, but I guessed his thoughts. Near where we were hunting is an ancient church, and beside it a large cemetery. Prince has misgivings about hunting in that country, especially at dusk.

"You thought that maybe we had seen something in the road that wasn't a real deer?" I asked.

"When the dogs wouldn't run him, I say he must be something we should leave alone. Dogs know more than people."

"But here's the buck," I said, "and you'll have to admit that he is no hant."

"No, Cap'n," Prince answered as he stooped over to get the big buck on his mighty shoulders, but there was in his voice something which told me he was still unconvinced that we had not been in a haunted and dangerous country.

I told him about the wild boar, and he sighed regretfully. I reminded him of the gobbler. He said that we ought to try for him at daylight. But that would be tomorrow, and our adventure with the old bronzed king—another story.

The Rajah of Bellefield

I have long believed that in wild nature you will find as many real personalities as you are likely to find in human life. The longer a wild creature lives, especially an intelligent big-game one, and the more he is hunted, the more certain he is to develop an individuality that is distinct. Western hunters have known grizzlies of that kind. I have known several old whitetail bucks that have been unique personages—and I have known the Rajah of Bellefield.

Many otherwise good naturalists object to the theory that members of the same wild species are not equally endowed; but just as all men are created unequal, so many of nature's children are either created, or else become, far superior to their fellows. I have noticed, for example, that some thrushes, catbirds, brown thrashers and mockingbirds sing much better than their fellows. In the case of big game, however, superiority always means higher sagacity, a certain extra awareness and wariness.

In my country along the Carolina coast the greatest game bird we have is the wild turkey; and when pure-blooded, he is the greatest game bird in the whole world. In keenness of intelligence, in size, in brilliance of plumage, in swiftness, on foot or on the wing, he surpasses all others. There are birds, of course, that can and do fly faster than the wild turkey; but when he really gets going in the air, he presents a fancy target for even the most expert wing-shot.

The turkeys in my woods and swamps are of the pure original strain. I have hunted wild turkeys in Virginia, West Virginia, Maryland and Pennsylvania, and have killed some fine birds in those states—in most cases too fine, in the sense that they were too heavy. All of them were impregnated with some domestic blood. But the wild turkeys along the great delta of the Santee River, where our Government has lately established a fine sanctuary to insure their survival, are of the old original strain.

I should put the limit of weight of one of these mature bronze

---

From *Field & Stream*, January 1943.

gobblers at 21 pounds. His head is indigo in color; his legs and feet are pink; his tail is a lustrous chestnut, barred much like that of the ruffed grouse. His neck, shoulders and back show remarkable iridescence. When he moves in the sunlight, he glitters. While I am a great admirer of Audubon, I have always considered that his wild turkeys are too clumsy; they seem to lack that superb tailor-made appearance, that perfect streamlining which all genuine wild turkeys have.

The Rajah of Bellefield was a wild gobbler, but not an ordinary one. He was one of these wild personages. In country where turkeys are hunted hard by experts, he had survived seven seasons. All seven seasons I hunted him; but, as the saying goes, "no soap." The fact that he was a genuine personality was proved by the attitude of my Negroes toward him: they were superstitious about him.

"He is too big," they would tell me in support of their belief that he was what they call a "token," which means an apparition. "He's smarter than man," they said. "It might not be a good thing to kill him," they warned me, their eyes beginning to roll and to show that degree of white which is the infallible sign that they have spooks on their minds.

White hunters, although they did not share this superstition, were puzzled by being continually outwitted. One said to me: "You know, that old gobbler hid from me in the open woods, under a bush no bigger than a fan-dancer's fan. I walked by him within twenty feet, and he never moved. After I was well past him, he stormed away in the opposite direction. He played a regular grouse trick on me."

I do not know how often he had been shot at, or how often he had been wounded. I only know that he kept on living, and that Bellefield was where he hung his hat. His life history appealed to me so much that, over a period of years, I studied his behavior, and finally came to know him about as well as it is possible to know any creature that is wholly wild.

As he appears to represent to a perfect degree his whole glamorous race, I am going to give some of the highlights of his biography. This may not amount to much more than a discussion of his habits. Nevertheless I take it that all who love the woods and want to become better hunters should give a lot more time to the study of the game they are after. Too many men go hunting who don't know a bluejay from a bluebill.

I raise tame turkeys; that is, my old colored cook, Sue, raises them for me. Over a period of three years Sue cursed the Rajah; then, believing him to be a spirit, she let him have his way. And what was that way? Why, he would come boldly into the plantation fields—come, indeed, almost to the front steps of Sue's house—select five or six tame turkey hens, and escort them to the woods with him. They never returned. The old sultan had to have his harem.

One year, just after the season closed on March 1, he came almost in my front yard, gobbling and strutting—apparently knowing as well as a hunter the meaning of that date. One of my tame hens was allured by him. And every morning for two weeks the love-struck hen would hopefully return to the place of their first meeting, calling and calling her Romeo.

And where was the Rajah? He had gone afar with some wild girl friend of his. He was a traveling man. That tame turkey hen almost grieved herself to death. However, she presented me with sixteen half-wild turkeys, some of which were so full of the Rajah's blood that they were strutting like comical little gobblers at two weeks of age! You haven't seen elfin dignity until you have seen a baby wild turkey strut.

Did the Rajah remember his tame inamorata? Had he any fatherly feelings? Judge for yourself. Several times a week, all summer, he would come out of the gross wilderness at sundown to roost right on top of the turkey-yard fence! All Sue's innumerable grandchildren were scared to death of him, and as dusk came on Sue herself took a very tolerant attitude toward him. But I think her tolerance was a mask for subtle dread. How could you explain the fact that the wildest and most hunted thing in that country would spend the night in your own backyard? How did this old gobbler know that the young turkeys in the yard were his own children? How could he suddenly, silently, eerily appear out of nowhere, at a mysterious hour, and at once massively assume domination over everything?

These questions troubled Sue, and she brought some of them to me. My rational view of the situation gave her no comfort at all. I just told her that if the Rajah appeared on the first day of the season, or at any time thereafter, I would kill him. He had carried off a lot of my turkeys; clearly he was planning to carry off more, and he was infecting my Negroes with nameless apprehension.

"He will not come after the season opens," Sue told me, speaking of the Rajah as if he were a man. "He knows."

And in deftly contrasting my intelligence with that of her hero, she made mine look mighty small.

Late one winter afternoon, when the season was in full swing, I was in the fragrant wilds of Bellefield, scouting for the Rajah. It had become a regular habit of mine. This place, some ninety acres in area, lies along the river and is utterly wild, full of cypress ponds, sunny thickets and open ridges. Great yellow pines soar above the evergreen growths of myrtle and bay, cedar and holly. With good cover, ample water and food, and with a semblance of the primeval wilderness, it has always been a fine place for wild turkeys. In such a dusky wildwood twilight comes prematurely, and it was so on this particular day.

I had a kind of plan for getting a shot at the old Rajah. I knew his haunts and his habits. I knew one or two great pines where he was likely to roost. How about waylaying him near them? He would come stalking along and would pause to crane his neck, peering upward for the right tree and the right limb on it. While he was thus presenting himself perfectly for a shot I would crack down on him, and then bear him home triumphantly through the twilight. And let me tell you, if you can go home thus burdened, a lot of your sins are going to be forgiven and forgotten by some one waiting for you there. You see, I had the thing all laid out. But there is a slight difference between having a plan laid out and a wild gobbler like the Rajah laid out.

Yet fortune favored me. Here I was, sitting on an old pine stump, on the edge of a ridge that led down to the river and past the huge pines which looked as if they were made for roosting places. The sun was just going down; but, as I have said, it was getting dim in the dense thickets all about me. Gray squirrels were doing their last shuffling in the leaves. I heard the first flight of wild ducks pass over.

Then came to me the "tramp-tramp" of a wild turkey. You can't ever mistake it if once you have really heard it. You would never confuse that sound with the walking of a deer, for his four feet make a lot of indistinct noise. But you might easily take the walking of a wild turkey for that of a man. This one was coming down the ridge toward me, and I was sure it must be the Rajah.

It was! He came in sight at just about 130 yards. In the dusk he loomed huge. On he came. I now had my gun up; in fact, it had been up before he had appeared. At 120 yards he stopped with a jerk. Here I was on a stump, my back against a big tupelo, and the tupelo backed by a dark thicket. I was motionless. Yet the Rajah saw me; and while he may not positively have identified me, yet he was filled with suspicion. He did not run or fly. He just stood there, drawn up very slim and very high. He stood still so long that I thought I could not hold my gun.

In the woods, this business of the hunter's outquieting game, or the game's outquieting the hunter, is strategy as vital as it is ancient. Now, had the Rajah been a buck, and if he had not winded me, he never would have seen me. But a wild turkey will identify you, no matter how still you keep; and if he once sees you, you might as well kiss your big chance good-bye.

Finally, when I was just about to lay down my gun, the Rajah took a

The Rajah of Bellefield   143

little run, rose lightly and, almost without sound, climbed steeply and headed for the big pines.

"At last," I thought, watching his flight, "he's going just where I thought he would, and just about dark I'll speak to him in those tree-tops yonder."

But it was not to be. High over the giant pines the Rajah hurtled. I saw his black bulk as he went clear across the river, to be lost in the vast and mouldering cypress swamp over there. Just about that time an owl laughed, and I thought there was something especially personal and derisive in his tone.

Early one February morning I got within two hundred yards of the Rajah in that same cypress swamp. He was still on the roost, and I had located him by his gobbling. I know he didn't hear me coming, for I waded toward him through shallow water. I know he didn't see me, for it was too dark and the swamp was too thick. Hiding myself in the tangled top of a fallen tree, I touched my call. The Rajah gobbled.

Ah, at last! What would be more natural now, especially if I intrigued him by calling no more, than for him to sail right down to me? He would sail down, and why shouldn't he come toward a lonesome siren, ladies' man that he was? Why not, indeed? I sat there, just palpitating. Although he had fooled me a hundred times, I felt I had him now. You know how I felt.

Did the Rajah storm out of that moss-shrouded cypress? He did. Did he come to where I had done my best to seduce him to come? He did not. He went clear over the swamp, far out, at least a half a mile, into a huge old field of marsh, hundreds of acres in extent—a place of cover so perfect that it would be utterly vain to attempt to approach him there. In fact, it is only rarely, and by accident, that a man approaches a wild turkey. You have to let him come to you. As the Rajah played this dirty trick on me, leaving me bogged down physically and mentally in that God-forsaken swamp, I did not hear him say "Ha, ha, you old boob!" But that's just what his great maneuver meant.

A short time after the mating season began, when I could hear my big tame gobbler and some wild ones performing at the same time, the Rajah came literally into my yard, challenged my gobbler to a combat, and killed him with startling dispatch. One of my Negroes, who saw this encounter and who was apparently scared of both gobblers, did nothing to prevent it.

"De big wil' one," he reported to me, "just knock dat tame one dead. Yes, sah, one lick done it."

The road from my remote place to the nearest store skirts Bellefield. On several occasions, when I had no gun, I saw the Rajah in the road or near it. Once I drove so close to him that I could almost measure his beard. It looked a foot long. But could such a thing be?

On February 28, 1942, the last day of the wild turkey season, I was out before daylight as usual, but I had no plan to go hunting. The day before, I had brought in from the woods some wild highbush huckleberry bushes, and I wanted to get ready to set them. In the twilight of the morning I was beginning to dig the first hole when, right by the front gate, a quarter of a mile away, I heard a wild gobbler sound off from the shrouded crest of a cypress in a pond in the woods. When possible, a wild turkey loves to roost over water. Rather idly I strolled over to the house where my Negro foreman lives. I got him out of bed and into the yard, telling him to listen.

"*Gil-obble-obble-obble!*" echoed on the damp, still air. The gobble of a wild bird is short, sharp and indefinably wild, very unlike that of the domestic turkey.

"Dat's him," said Prince, still half asleep.

"Still on the roost?"

"Yes, sah."

Somehow neither one of us thought it might be the Rajah. Wild turkeys can occasionally do very foolish things, and I thought that this bird was making the mistake of calling me to him. Without any especial excitement or enthusiasm I got my gun and call and walked down to the gate. There I turned to the left in the woods, going as far as a big live-oak, beyond which gleamed the waters of the pond. I heard and saw nothing. The wet leaves rendered my walking noiseless.

I sat down by the huge oak, loaded my gun, and barely touched my call. The turkey had not gobbled again. It was possible he was already on the ground. I waited. If you want to kill one of these old boys, you have to use all the patience there is. Five, eight, ten minutes I sat there. Then, 150 yards away, a huge black shape hurtled out of a patriarchal cypress. The minute I saw him I knew him.

"Omygosh!" I muttered, getting my gun up. "It's the Rajah himself."

Maneuvering almost like a grouse among the cypresses of the swamp, he set his mighty wings when about half-way to high ground, and sailed to earth, coming down at just about ninety yards from me on a little knoll, right in the open, with only a few big pines standing here and there. He stood at his full height, and in that posture was, I believe, the most impressive wild thing I had ever seen. It was the Rajah—and just out of sure gunshot!

I knew he had heard my call. A wild turkey always hears everything. If he walked straight ahead, the way he was faced, he would escape, as he would, of course, if he walked straight away from me. There he stood, superb, statuesque—a real king of the wilderness.

Suddenly he decided. With a quick duck of his head he started my way. All this time I had the gun on him. Once he went behind one of the big pines, and he stood there, invisible, for a couple of minutes. When he emerged, he was only fifty yards away. I had never before been so close to the Rajah when I had a gun. My arms and eyes ached, more from suspense than effort. On he came in majesty. At thirty-five yards I killed him so cleanly that he probably never knew what happened.

As soon as I tried to lift him I realized that this was no ordinary gobbler. I had never before seen such a bird. All his plumage was either soft chestnut in color or gleamingly iridescent. When I weighed him at the house, the scales gave 21½ pounds, and his beard measured 11¾ inches—which I think must be some kind of record. His spurs, with which he had executed my tame gobbler, were more than an inch long.

Had I misgivings about killing this old wily veteran? Perhaps. The Rajah was a grand old bird. But any such regrets were mitigated by the reflection that I could now raise tame turkeys in peace and have about me Negroes who were not always pop-eyed with superstition about the Rajah.

THE OLD BRONZED MEN
OF THE HILLS

America's greatest game bird, the wild turkey, now is extinct over the greater part of its former extensive range. In only a few states is turkey hunting still worth while. Nowhere is it sufficiently abundant to rob the sport of its adventure.

In these days, if a man can kill a couple of wild gobblers in a week of hunting, he has done well. And that is possible even in Pennsylvania, one of the most populous states in the Union. Some sections of Pennsylvania are still so wild that bear, elk and deer are encountered. For thirty years I have hunted those regions, and among my most thrilling encounters have been those with wild turkeys—the old bronzed men of the hills.

Hunting turkeys in the mountains of Pennsylvania is still-hunting, and, as calling is not permitted, it is a sporting proposition. Concealment is not as necessary to lure your bird in close as the ability to keep still. I have been unable to learn whether the wild turkey uses its sense of smell, as the deer does, to detect its enemies. But the keenness of a turkey's hearing is one of the marvels of nature. Its eyesight, too, is better than the deer's, especially in the matter of detecting movement on the part of the hunter.

To bring to bag one of the old bronzed men of the hills, a man has to study his game with great care, and then apply that knowledge. Of course, a rank amateur may blunder upon a bird. But turkey hunting usually is painstaking and patient business.

Wild turkeys frequent old roads during wet weather. On a misty November day, following a heavy rain, I was sitting beside a road that was the only highway between two wild valleys. It crossed a high ridge, and I was near its crest. In hauling grain over this ancient trail some farmers had spilled a little wheat and corn from their wagons, and I had found that the wild turkeys were coming out of the deep woods after the grain. Here, then, was a double chance; a road on a wet day, and one that was

From *Outdoor Life*, September 1934.

accidentally baited. I took up my watch beside an old chestnut stump that afforded me some cover. My position commanded the approach from both directions. In still-hunting of this kind it is essential that the watcher be a listener as well.

Because of the vital importance of this game of listening, I never hunt turkeys in the mountains on a windy day for, in addition to the confusion of sounds caused by rattling boughs, creaking trees, falling leaves, and the hollow roaring of the wind, the listener is handicapped by the wariness of the game which is greater when the wind is blowing. Another condition which determines the accuracy of listening is the dryness or dampness of the leaves. Very wet leaves deaden all footfalls. Very dry leaves cause footsteps to be clearly heard but so merged and mingled with the rustlings of the dry leaves that the identity of the walker may be lost. The best condition is when the leaves are damp.

On this particular day, conditions were just right. It was one of those soundless, misty days in mid-autumn when all nature seemed to be sleeping. After I had been at my watching station for twenty minutes, a whole family of gray squirrels began scampering in the leaves on the slope below me. A covey of quail trooped past me. Then, after silent waiting and watching, I heard a telltale tramp. An inexperienced listener might easily mistake a wild turkey's walking for that of a man. My game was a hundred yards away and not yet in sight. Because of the irregularity of the tramping, I knew that there must be more than one bird. The approachers were coming from the road. On reaching it, would they turn down or up? I was downhill from them.

As soon as I had fairly located them, I crept back into the brush, making a long, wide detour in order to enter the road above them. The bronzed mountaineers have rather fixed habits, and one is that they prefer not to walk downhill. As a rule they fly down and walk up. Coming to a road that climbs the mountain, they will nearly always take the upward slope.

After a fifteen minute stalk through the damp brush, I was back on the misty trail, and, as I hoped, above my birds. My game was to wait. They might have crossed the road and gone on, but the chances were that they had run into some of the grain, and were following the trail upward.

Fifteen minutes I waited, passing up a cock grouse that walked within twenty feet of me. If you are really hunting turkeys, don't shoot at anything else. At last, through the mist, two great gobblers appeared. Slowly, silently they came up the road, pecking negligently at the spilled grain. Their heavy breasts literally wabbled as they walked, and their beards stabbed the sandy ground. Two old veterans these were, monarchs of the wilderness. They looked almost coal black. Even in the mist I could catch the gleam of subdued iridescent plumage. They were coming to me, and they didn't know I was there.

In hunting wild turkeys I always use my old 12 gauge, 30-inch shotgun, with 4's in the right barrel and 2's in the left. Many fellow sportsmen laugh at me for using 2's. But long experience has taught me that it takes a ponderous wallop to break down one of these old-timers, and the 2's deliver just that punch. I have known so many fine birds to escape wounded when shot with 6's or with 4's at a long distance that I am partial to the heavier shot.

The two gobblers were now within range—that is, within sixty yards. In Pennsylvania we are allowed only one a season. I looked them over carefully to make a choice. As one's beard seemed slightly longer than the other's, he was elected. It did not appear quite sporting to shoot him down from the gray ambush of the fog. I therefore decided to flush them and give them a chance just for sport's sake.

As I stepped boldly into the road the gobblers straightened up. Then they whirled in unison, took a swift little run, and were off into the misty air. I threw one headlong, and it never moved. Later I found it weighed twenty-one pounds, had an eight-inch beard, and spurs nearly three quarters of an inch long. Upon dressing it, I discovered it had been feeding on teaberries, acorns, wintergreen, and greenbrier berries. One of the acorns thus retrieved I planted in a little pot of soil, and now I have a thriving young white oak of royal ancestry!

I have said that wild turkeys fly down the mountain and walk up. One of the most imposing sights in all nature is to see these great birds fly from a mountain ridge down to the valley far beneath. After they have a start, they set their wings and volplane down over the tree tops at cyclone speed.

Sometimes, as they perform a graceful arc to check their flight, then glide earthward silently or skim across to the opposite ridge, they come within view of the habitations of man. In fact, I have killed turkeys within sight of farms. Mountaineers have complained to me that they cannot raise tame turkeys because the birds wander into the hills when the mating season begins.

The inevitable mixture of tame blood, resulting when civilization gets too close to the wilderness, prevents Pennsylvania turkeys from being of a pure wild strain, although they show their sullied ancestry in plumage only. The only pure-blooded wild turkeys I have ever seen are those of the deep-river swamps of the South.

These birds have blue heads, pink legs, long slender bodies, and soft brown and black plumage, shot with iridescent purple sheens. There is no white on them. Occasionally the underside of the primaries will show a dusky gray. Despite their apparent slenderness, they attain great weight, and are as plump-breasted as grouse. I have weighed a Southern wild gobbler that tipped the scales at twenty-two and a half pounds. But hunting the pure bred birds in the South is no more thrilling than pursuing their cousins in Pennsylvania.

One rainy day in the hills I was sloshing along empty-handed, when I had one of those woodland adventures that linger in the mind as long as life lasts.

I was walking up a gully between two wooded ridges. The rain and the drip from the trees muffled my footsteps. The gully was grown to wild raspberries and old grapevines. I had the breech of my gun under my coat to protect it from the wet; into my bleared eyes water was running incessantly.

Suddenly, out of a grapevine tangle not more than twenty feet ahead of me, a great black form rose with a storming of wings. The gobbler started to my right and before I could get my gun clear and wipe my eyes, it had a grand start toward an escape. It was going up and off, and quartering to the right, a shot that compels the hunter to take into account all sorts of angles.

I shot blindly and was dumfounded to see the bird collapse and come crashing down. The good 2's in the choke barrel had done their work.

Once, on the crest of a noble ridge. I slipped behind a tangle of grapevines on the edge of a dense pine thicket. I knew that there were turkeys about, and I knew that they can resist almost any temptation except grapes. For half an hour nothing happened. I was getting stiff and chilly and was about to move on when I heard something coming up the ridge in the shelter of the grapevines. What was it? Grouse? Man? Turkey? Skunk? The walker came within thirty yards of me and stopped. For ten full minutes I heard not a sound. Then I decided to edge in. The suspense had me down. At my third step a fine gobbler launched itself upward. I caught it just before it reached the tree-tops, and the lordly black form pitched down. I had been lucky again.

THAT TWENTY-FIVE-POUND GOBBLER

I suppose that there are other things which make a hunter uneasy, but of one thing I am very sure: that is to locate and to begin to stalk a deer or a turkey, only to find that another hunter is doing precisely the same thing at the same time. The feeling I had was worse than uneasy. It is, in fact, as inaccurate as if a man should say, after listening to a comrade swearing roundly, "Bill is expressing himself uneasily."

To be frank, I was jealous; and all the more so because I knew that Dade Saunders was just as good a turkey-hunter as I am,—and may be a good deal better. At any rate, both of us got after the same whopping gobbler. We knew this turkey and we knew each other; and I am positive that the wise old bird knew both of us far better than we knew him.

But we hunters have ways of improving our acquaintance with creatures that are over-wild and shy. Both Dade and I saw him, I suppose, a dozen times; and twice Dade shot at him. I had never fired at him, for I did not want to cripple, but to kill; and he never came within a hundred yards of me. Yet I felt that the gobbler ought to be mine; and for the simple reason that Dade Saunders was a shameless poacher and a hunter-out-of-season.

I have in mind the day when I came upon him in the pinelands in mid-July, when he had in his wagon *five* bucks in the velvet, all killed that morning. Now, this isn't a fiction story; this is fact. And after I have told you of those bucks, I think you'll want to beat Dade to the great American bird.

This wild turkey had the oddest range that you could imagine. You hear of turkeys ranging "original forests," "timbered wilds," and the like. Make up your mind that if wild turkeys have a chance they are going to come near civilization. The closer they are to man, the farther they are

From *Outing*, March 1919.

away from their other enemies. Near civilization they at least have (but for the likes of Dade Saunders) the protection of the law. But in the wilds what protection do they have from wildcats, from eagles, from weasels (I am thinking of young turkeys as well as old), and from all their other predatory persecutors?

Well, as I say, time and again I have known wild turkeys to come, and to seem to enjoy coming, close to houses. I have stood on the porch of my plantation home and have watched a wild flock feeding under the great live-oaks there. I have repeatedly flushed wild turkeys in an autumn cornfield. I have shot them in rice stubble.

Of course they do not come for sentiment. They are after grain. And if there is any better wild game than a rice-field wild turkey, stuffed with peanuts, circled with browned sweet potatoes, and fragrant with a rich gravy that plantation cooks know how to make, I'll follow you to it.

The gobbler I was after was a haunter of the edges of civilization. He didn't seem to like the wild woods. I think he got hungry there. But on the margins of fields that had been planted he could get all he wanted to eat of the things he most enjoyed. He particularly liked the edges of cultivated fields that bordered either on the pinewoods or else on the marshy ricelands.

One day I spent three hours in the gaunt chimney of a burned rice-mill, watching this gobbler feeding on such edges. Although I was sure that sooner or later he would pass the mouth of the chimney, giving me a chance for a shot, he kept just that distance between us that makes a gun a vain thing in a man's hands. But though he did not give me my chance, he let me watch him all I pleased. This I did through certain dusty crevices between the bricks of the old chimney.

If I had been taking a post-graduate course in caution, this wise old bird would have been my teacher. Whatever he happened to be doing, his eyes and his ears were wide with vigilance. I saw him first standing beside a fallen pine log on the brow of a little hill where peanuts had been planted. I made the shelter of the chimney before he recognized me. But he must have seen the move I made.

I have hunted turkeys long enough to be thoroughly rid of the idea that a human being can make a motion that a wild turkey cannot see. One of my woodsmen friends said to me, "Why, a gobbler can see anything. He can see a business chance that a Jew would miss. He can see a jaybird turn a somersault on the verge of the horizon." He was right.

Watching from my cover I saw this gobbler scratching for peanuts. He was very deliberate about this. Often he would draw back one huge handful (or footful) of viny soil, only to leave it there while he looked and listened. I have seen a turkey do the same thing while scratching in leaves. Now, a buck while feeding will alternately keep his head up and down; but a turkey gobbler keeps his down very little. That bright black eye of his, set in that sharp bluish head, is keeping its vision on every object on the landscape.

My gobbler (I called him *mine* from the first time I saw him) found many peanuts, and he relished them. From that feast he walked over into a patch of autumn-dried crabgrass. The long pendulous heads of this grass, full of seeds, he stripped skillfully. When satisfied with this food, he dusted himself beside an old stump. It was interesting to watch this; and while he was doing it I wondered if it was not my chance to leave the chimney, make a detour, and come up behind the stump. But of course just as I decided to do this, he got up, shook a small cloud of dust from his feathers, stepped off into the open, and there began to preen himself.

A short while thereafter he went down to a marshy edge, there finding a warm sandy hole on the sunnyside of a briar patch, where he continued his dusting and loafing. I believe that he knew the stump, which shut off his view of what was behind it, was no place to choose for a midday rest.

All this time I waited patiently; interested, to be sure, but I would have been vastly more so if the lordly old fellow had turned my way. This I expected him to do when he got tired of loafing. Instead, he deliberately walked into the tall ranks of the marsh, which extended riverward for half a mile. At that I hurried forward, hoping to flush him on the margin; but he had vanished for that day. But though he had escaped me, the sight of him had made me keen to follow him until he expressed a willingness to accompany me home.

Just as I was turning away from the marsh I heard a turkey call from the shelter of a big live-oak beside the old chimney. I knew that it was Dade Saunders, and that he was after my gobbler. I walked over to where he was making his box-call plead. He expressed no surprise on seeing me. We greeted each other as two hunters, who are not over-friendly, greet when they find themselves after the same game.

"I seen his tracks," said Dade. "I believe he limps in the one foot since I shot him last Sunday will be a week."

"He must be a big bird," I said; "you were lucky to have a shot."

Dade's eyes grew hungrily bright.

"He's the biggest in these woods, and I'll git him yet. You jest watch me."

"I suppose you will, Dade. You are the best turkey-hunter of these parts."

I hoped to make him overconfident; and praise is a great corrupter of mankind. It is not unlikely to make a hunter miss a shot. I remember that a friend of mine once said laughingly: "If a man tells me I am a good shot, I will miss my next chance, as sure as guns; but if he cusses me and tells me I'm not worth a darn, then watch me shoot!"

Dade and I parted for the time. I went off toward the marsh, whistling an old song. I wanted to have the gobbler put a little more distance between himself and the poacher. Besides, I felt that it was right of me to do this: for while I was on my own land, my visitor was trespassing. I hung around in the scrub oak thickets for a while; but no gun spoke out, I knew that the old gobbler's intelligence plus my whistling game had "foiled the relentless" Dade. It was a week later that the three of us met again.

Not far from the peanut field there is a plantation corner. Now, most plantation corners are graveyards; that is, cemeteries of the old days, where slaves were buried. Occasionally now Negroes are buried there, but pathways have to be cut through the jungle-like growths to enable the cortege to enter.

Such a place is a wilderness for sure. Here grow towering pines, mournful and moss-draped. Here are hollies, canopied with jasmine vines; here are thickets of myrtle, sweet gum, and young pines. If a covey of quail goes into such a place, you might as well whistle your dog off and go after another lot of birds.

Here deer love to come in the summer, where they can hide from the heat and the gauze-winged flies. Here in the winter is a haunt for woodcock, a good range (for great live-oaks drop their sweet acorns) for wild turkeys, and a harbor for foxes. In those great pines and oaks turkeys love to roost. It was on the borders of just such a corner that I roosted the splendid gobbler.

It was a glowing December sunset. I had left the house an hour before to stroll the plantation roads, counting (as I always do) the number of deer and turkey tracks that had recently been made in the soft damp sand. Coming near the dense corner, I sat against the bole of a monster pine. I love to be a mere watcher in woodlands as well as a hunter.

About two hundred yards away there was a little sunny hill, grown to scrub oaks. They stood sparsely; that enabled me to see well what I now saw. Into my vision, with the rays of the sinking sun gleaming softly on the bronze of his neck and shoulders, the great gobbler stepped with superb beauty. Though he deigned to scratch once or twice in the leaves, and peck indifferently at what he thus uncovered. I knew he was bent on roosting; for not only was it nearly his bedtime, but he seemed to be examining with critical judgment every tall tree in his neighborhood.

He remained in my sight ten minutes; then he stepped into a patch of gallberries. I sat where I was. I tried my best to be as silent and as motionless as the bodies lying in the ancient graves behind me. The big fellow kept me on the anxious bench for five minutes. Then he shot his great bulk into the air, beating his ponderous way into the huge pine that seemed to sentry that whole wild tract of woodland.

I marked him when he came to his limb. He sailed up to it and alighted with much scraping of bark with his No. 10 shoes. There was my gobbler poised against the warm red sky of that winter twilight. It was hard to take my sight from him; but I did so in order to get my bearings in relation to his position. His flight had brought him nearer to me than he had been on the ground. But he was still far out of gun-range.

There was no use for me to look into the graveyard, for a man cannot see a foot into such a place. I glanced down the dim pinewood road. A moving object along its edge attracted my attention. It skulked. It seemed to flit like a ghostly thing from pine to pine. But, though I was near a cemetery, I knew I was looking at no "hant." It was Dade Saunders.

He had roosted the gobbler, and he was trying to get up to him. Moreover, he was at least fifty yards closer to him than I was. I felt like shouting to him to get off my land; but then a better thought came. I pulled out my turkey call.

The first note was good, as was intended. But after that there came some heart-stilling squeaks and shrills. In the dusk I noted two things; I saw Dade make a furious gesture, and at almost the same instant the old gobbler launched out from the pine, winging a lordly way far across the graveyard thicket. I walked down slowly and peeringly to meet Dave.

"Your call's broke," he announced.

"What makes you think so?" I asked.

"Sounds awful funny to me," he said; "more than likely it might scare a turkey. Seen *him* lately?" he asked.

"You are better at seeing that old bird than I am, Dade."

Thus I put him off; and shortly thereafter we parted. He was sure that I had not seen the gobbler; and that suited me all right.

Then came the day of days. I was up at dawn, and when certain red lights between the stems of the pines announced daybreak, I was at the far southern end of the plantation, on a road on either side of which were good turkey woods. I just had a notion that my gobbler might be found here, as he had of late taken to roosting in a tupelo swamp near the river, and adjacent to these woodlands.

Where some lumbermen had cut away the big timber, sawing the huge short-leaf pines close to the ground, I took my stand (or my seat) on one of these big stumps. Before me was a tangle of undergrowth; but it was not very thick or high. It gave me the screen I wanted; but if my turkey came out through it, I could see to shoot.

It was just before sunrise that I began to call. It was a little early in the year (then the end of February) to lure a solitary gobbler by a call; but otherwise the chance looked good. And I am vain enough to say that my willow box was not broken that morning. Yet it was not I but two Cooper's hawks that got the old wily rascal excited.

They were circling high and crying shrilly over a certain stretch of deep woodland; and the gobbler, undoubtedly irritated by the sounds, or at least not to be outdone by two mere marauders on a domain which he felt to be his own, would gobble fiercely every time one of the hawks would cry. The hawks had their eye on a building site; wherefore their excited maneuvering and shrilling continued; and as long as they kept up their screaming, so long did the wild gobbler answer in rivalry or provoked superiority, until his wattles must have been fiery red and near to bursting.

I had an idea that the hawks were directing some of their crying at the turkey, in which case the performance was a genuine scolding match of the wilderness. And before it was over, several gray squirrels had added to the already raucous debate their impatient coughing barks. This business lasted nearly an hour, until the sun had begun to make the thickets "smoke off" their shining burden of morning dew.

I had let up on my calling for a while; but when the hawks had at last been silenced by distance, I began once more to plead. Had I had a gobbler-call, the now enraged turkey would have come to me as straight as a surveyor runs a line. But I did my best with the one I had. I was answered by one short gobble, then by silence.

I laid down my call on the stump and took up my gun. It was in such a position that I could shoot quickly without much further motion. It is a genuine feat to shoot a turkey on the ground *after* he has made you out. I felt that a great moment was coming.

But you know how hunter's luck sometimes turns. Just as I thought it was about time for him to be in the pine thicket ahead of me, when, indeed, I thought I had heard his heavy but cautious step, from across the road, where lay the companion tract of turkey-woods to the one I was in, came a delicately pleading call from a hen turkey. The thing was irresistible to the gobbler; but I knew it to be Dade Saunders. What should I do?

At such a time a man has to use all the headwork he has. And in hunting I had long since learned that that often means not to do a darn thing but to sit tight. All I did was to put my gun to my face. If the gobbler was going to Dade, he might pass me. I had started him coming; if Dade kept him going, he might run within hailing distance. Dade was farther back in the woods than I was. I waited.

No step was heard. No twig was snapped. But suddenly, fifty yards ahead of me, the great bird emerged from the thicket of pines. For an instant the sun gleamed on his royal plumage. My gun was on him, but the glint of the sun along the barrel dazzled me. I stayed my finger on the trigger. At that instant he made me out. What he did was smart. He made himself so small that I believed it to be a second turkey. Then he ran crouching through the vines and huckleberry bushes.

Four times I thought I had my gun on him, but his dodging was that of an expert. He was getting away; moreover, he was making straight for Dade. There was a small gap in the bushes sixty yards from me, off to my left. He had not yet crossed that. I threw my gun in the opening. In a moment he flashed into it, running like a racehorse. I let him have it. And I saw him go down.

Five minutes later, when I had hung him on a scrub oak, and was admiring the entire beauty of him, a knowing, cat-like step sounded behind me.

"Well, sir," said Dade, a generous admiration for the beauty of the great bird overcoming other less kindly emotions, "so you beat me to him."

There was nothing for me to do but to agree. I then asked Dade to walk home with me so that we might weigh him. He carried the scales well down at the 25-pound mark. An extraordinary feature of his manly equipment was the presence of three separate beards, one beneath the other, no two connected. And his spurs were respectable rapiers.

"Dade," I said, "what am I going to do with this gobbler? I am alone here on the plantation."

The pineland poacher did not solve my problem for me.

"I tell you," said I, trying to forget the matter of the five velveted bucks, "some of the boys from down the river are going to come up on Sunday to see how he tastes. Will you join us?"

You know Dade Saunders' answer; for when a hunter refuses an invitation to help eat a wild turkey, he can be sold to a circus.

THE ROGUE OF ORQUIC VALLEY

While a great deal of my hunting has been done with the aid of dogs, I believe that, after all, an especial thrill is reserved for the man who hunts his game all alone in the wilderness. I know that I still tingle when I think of the old rogue of Orquic Valley.

For a whole year before I ever saw him, rumors had been coming to me about him; and when at last I did lay eyes on him, all expectations were justified. And when I say "all expectations," I mean that he met my expectations not only as regards his size and beauty, but more particularly those of wariness and downright smartness. I did not get closer than two hundred yards of him; and from the manner of his escape, I judged that he had been watching my approach long before I ever made him out.

He was known as the Rogue, not because he trampled down native gardens and killed people, as rogue elephants are said to do, but simply because he was smarter than the men who hunted him. Every time they tried to call his hand, he held some tricks that beat them. To hear about the Rogue Gobbler of Orquic Valley, all you had to do was to stand on the street corner or in some hardware store during the season, or, for that matter, long before or long after it.

Some said he would weigh thirty pounds; some said he had a wing-spread of six feet; others averred that he could see farther than a rifle could shoot. I heard one man say that when he heard the Rogue get up in some laurel he thought that a transcontinental airplane was rising out of the brush. Time and again hopeful wives, promised wild turkeys by their husbands, had to repair to the meat market for Sunday's dinner. I heard of one girl of spirited temperament who promised to say "yes" to the first eligible bachelor who would bring the Rogue home. The sort of offer is certainly enough to make hunting a more than usually interesting pastime—like killing two birds with one stone, as it were. But the maiden remained unwed.

Hearing about this great bird got me just where I live. And I now

From *Field & Stream*, July 1936. Later included in *Hunter's Choice* (1946).

propose, boys, to tell just what happens when two old rogues get into the wildwoods together, the one having designs on the life of the other. Turkey hunting has been with me a kind of religion ever since a hatchet was a hammer; and perhaps I have learned a little of the art. Yet even after almost a half-century of hunting the noblest game bird that graces America's wild, I am going to confess that I am still in the kindergarten; and I doubt if any human being ever acquires a complete education in this high art.

In passing, however, let me say that if any man would be a successful hunter, let him do at least two things; let him study painstakingly the character and habits of his game; and then let him be endlessly persistent. To understand your game, and to keep everlastingly at it—these help more than any other things I know.

Having both grouse and turkeys in mind, on the first day of November I hied me a daylight to the wilds of Orquic Valley, one of the wildest of the wild regions of southern Pennsylvania. On one side of the valley, which is completely wooded and is without human habitation, there is a State Game Refuge of 1,700 acres; on the other side is just mountain and then more mountain. On the opening day of the season, both deer and turkeys are likely to forsake their rambling into the outer country and to betake them to the fastness of the sanctuary. Even grouse appear to know just where they will be safe.

Between the refuge and the free mountain opposite there is a huge level swamp, very long and perhaps some sixty acres in extent. Through it runs a trout stream, which beavers have dammed. The backing up of this water into the dense jungle of sphagnum moss, teaberry, laurel, alder, little pines, and spice bushes makes this hard going for the hunter, and for that very reason it is as much of a sanctuary as the refuge set aside for the state.

This year there are in this part of the country no wild grapes in the woods; and, of course, all the chestnut trees have long since been killed. The turkeys are short of food, and as a result are going in for what is normally the food of the grouse: berries of the greenbriar, the scarlet hips of wild roses, berries of the teaberry, and the staghorn sumac. With these foods, the wild swamp is amply supplied; and I had heard that the Rogue had been coming out of the refuge to forage in this morass of the wilderness.

Now, here is a thing about a wild turkey that too few hunters consider carefully: it is that he is the victim of routine. If you know what his range is, and if the food to which he has been accustomed is still to be had, he will be there; moreover, he will be at a certain place at a certain time of day. So much is the lordly wild turkey a creature of habit that I have frequently killed the finest and wildest gobblers merely by waiting for them on a certain old road at a certain time of day.

I remember once taking a friend to such a crossing. We got there about 2:30 in the afternoon. He asked if it was safe to smoke. I said: "Not if you want your bird. They will be along here about 2:45." At 2:50 they came, and he carried home what he came for. But he still thinks I made a lucky guess. Not so. The turkey goes through life on schedule, in much the same manner as the bobwhite does.

For two hours after leaving my car at daybreak I ranged the swamp, raising a few grouse, at which I did not shoot; still-hunting a good deal by just sitting on an old stump and listening. The day was warm; there was not a breath of air stirring. The woodlands were hung with the tattered gold banners of autumn. The world was fragrant with the hale aromas of wet mosses, dewy hickory leaves and damp laurel.

At such a time, amid such beauty, the hunter does not always feel that the primary business of life is killing something; indeed, if more sportsmen would take hunting as a game instead of a battle, their victories would be sweeter, and their defeats easy to bear. A man should not fight the birds and animals he is after; he merely uses his strategy in an attempt to outwit them at theirs. If they win, why, that's a break for them.

I get a good deal of enjoyment, after the season is over, in recalling the misses I have made, or the failures of other kinds that have been mine, for every one of these means the life of some wild thing. And it's good to think of some of them as still being in their native haunts after we have spent a whole season after them.

My still-hunting profited me nothing; hence I eased out of the swamp and up a little bench of the mountain. I like to get where I can look down a long stretch of woodland, especially when hunting turkeys. In the mountains, these great birds have an almost invariable habit of flying down-hill and then walking up; rarely do they fly up or walk down.

As I neared the top of the rise, slue-footing it through the damp leaves, I distinctly heard something on the farther side. Usually it is possible to identify footsteps in the forest, but a wild turkey and a man walk remarkably alike. I can always tell a squirrel by his little hops; a deer's approach can be distinguished, and that of a grouse. But repeatedly I have been puzzled to know if a man or a gobbler is coming. Nor did I know. I had to see with my eyes.

Trying to walk even more softly than I had been walking, just as I reached the crest of the rise I heard something run down the farther side. I knew then. And I knew likewise that I had probably lost my chance. A wild turkey may come to you; but it is almost a law of nature that you shall not go to him. If he ever runs away from you, he's likely gone for the day. I felt I had no more chance to get him than a homely girl has of making Hollywood.

Coming to the top of the hill, I looked downward on the other side; and there, 150 yards away, glistening regally in the morning sunshine, was the Rogue himself. He was standing in an old lumber road. With a rifle, I should have had a beautiful shot at him; but with a shotgun, it was hopeless. Well, "I'm 'way up hyar, and he's 'way down thar," as the song has it, and that was the situation.

There he stood in all his glory. I doubted his reputed weight and his prodigious wing-spread; yet, all in all, he was as fine a gobbler as I had ever seen. And he was no half-breed: long red legs, keen neck, and blue head; massive yet graceful body, and that indefinable air of the true aristocrat, an air that no bird of barnyard blood ever achieves. Well, there we stood. He saw me, and I saw him. You may hear of men who have stalked wild turkeys; and perhaps the thing can be done—if the turkey is blind. I remember one day walking up to an old gobbler standing beside a road. He did not fly until I was within thirty yards of him. When he was retrieved, he was found to have only one eye; and I had approached him on the blind side!

With the first step I took in the direction of the Rogue, he clamped in all his feathers, and, looking as tailor-made as if he had just stepped out of a Park Avenue shop, he raced down the old road and was lost in the glimmering distance. It was then ten o'clock in the morning. I took careful note of the time and place. On another morning he would likely be here—about at this same time. That day I saw him no more, and on my return home I kept discreetly silent about what I had seen.

Several days later I repaired to the haunts of the Rogue, but on arriving found that the swamp was full of rabbit hunters. As there is no affinity between beagle and wild turkeys, I went half-way up the mountain on the side toward the Game Refuge. I thought that if the dogs roused the old rascal in that dense jungle, he would most likely make for home and I would intercept him.

As I can't take the hills as I used to, and as turkey-hunting is a business in which the less a man moves about, the better, I sat in the kindly sun on an old chestnut stump and listened to the little hounds making merry with the bunnies. There was just a faint breeze blowing, causing the mountain pines to murmur and wave. Below me stretched the tawny woodland, through which I could see for two hundred yards.

Suddenly I heard a terrific commotion in the swamp; dogs and men joined in the clamor. But I heard more than their voices. I heard a turkey get up in thick brush, exploding the bushes like a covey of grouse. In a moment I saw a huge black shape rise over the tree-tops and head my way. It was the old Rogue, and the reception committee was waiting for him. There is no use to say I wasn't excited. My heart jumped like that of a debutante or a coffee toper. He looked too big to kill. I had a swift belief in that story of his six-foot wing-spread.

But instinct or his guardian angel made him turn away from me. Sailing down out of the sky, he swerved to the right, alighting on a big rock. There he stood grandly, stretched to his full height, sheeny and iridescent. He was just out of range. I don't know how it is with my brother sportsmen, but I have stopped shooting at game that is too far. I feel that is isn't exactly fair. It is all right to kill it; but when the chances are that it will merely be wounded and will escape, perhaps to die a lingering death or to fall victim to some predator, why, I just don't shoot.

A hunter knows, or should know, the range of his gun; and he ought to be able to estimate distances, both in the open and in the forest. I think that with any shotgun, in pursuit of any game, sixty yards is almost the limit of a certain kill. Some say forty. But I no longer shoot at anything over sixty yards away. A hunter ought to have a heart; and if the game gets that much distance between them, why, it's the game's break.

I lately hunted with a man who shot eighteen times at grouse, and he didn't bag a bird, though he feathered several. Investigating, I found that he had been carrying his gun over his shoulder, and had thus lost a few vital seconds when a bird rose. He was shooting at them just a little too far away. Every time he would miss or would draw feathers, he would make savage remarks about his gun and his shells. They were all right. He was just expecting too much of them.

My idea is that about half the ammunition burnt in hunting is spent on shots that are really hopeless. The Pennsylvania Germans have two expressions that I think well apply here. One is "horse," which means to strike, to wound; the other is "momick," which means to slay, and no mistake about it. Well, I think a man should not shoot at wild game unless he has an excellent chance to momick it.

That old Rogue stood on the rock in the broad sunshine. He was facing the refuge, and that, I knew, was where he intended to go. My only hope was to vanish backward and get in above him. I waited for him to make the first move before I made mine. With the superb grace of all true game of the wilds he stepped down and was hidden in the laurel. I stepped back, but even as I did so that tall neck and blue head reappeared and those beady black eyes nailed me. It was no use. I caught one more glimpse of him as he ducked up the hill, making himself very small. Then he was gone.

It must have been five days later that I found, unexpectedly, that I could get away from work late in the afternoon. I was in such a hurry to leave home that I took the wrong shells. I forgot my 2's, and arrived in the mountain, with but an hour of daylight to spare, to find that all the shells I had were 7's. It looked as if I had better hunt grouse. Rather unwillingly I started to do this in the Rogue's swamp. But he was in my mind all the while. I kept wondering whether he did not range far up on the mountain after feeding in the swamp and then return by almost the same route toward roosting time. The idea took hold of me like a premonition.

Though the sun was not quite down, the deep valley was all in shadow. Mists rising from the humid swamp made an early twilight there. I kept easing along as noiselessly as I could, feeling that something was near me. I stopped on the breast of an old beaver dam. Far up on the shaggy side of the big mountain a horned owl hooted. The stillness was almost dense, and was certainly eerie. Below me the crystal waters of the trout stream gurgled away from the dam.

Just as I was about to step forward into the brush, I heard something move in a wild tangle of grapevines and sumac. It might be a man or a deer, and the light was so dusky that I had to be very careful what I was about. But I knew from what I had heard of the habits of the Rogue, and from what I had seen of him, that I must be just about on his line of march back to his roosting place in the Refuge. Above the thicket where I had heard the step, great hemlocks loomed swarthily. It was not a nice place to shoot.

I heard the telltale crack of a dry twig. I saw a laurel bush sway slightly. This was neither man nor deer. It was the Rogue. I felt sure of it. If he ducked away, he would be gone. If I could startle him into rising, I might get a shot.

With my old fusee ready, I ran right into the thicket; and before I had gone ten yards, things happened. I heard a startled "put!" Then a great black form tore out of that tangle and hurtled upward. It was the old Rogue. Ponderous but powerful and agile, he gained the air and swerved into an opening between two hemlocks, heading up a faint alley of light. At thirty-five yards I gave him the choke barrel of 7's. It was as if lightning had struck him. Down he came in a cloud of feathers. If elephants could fly and we shot them on the wing, why, he fell as one of them would fall.

As I carried my great trophy out of the swamp in the fast-falling twilight, my feeling was not wholly of elation. I had outwitted the old boy at last, but what was left to give me sport? Any misgiving I may have had was forgotten when I reached home. If any of you boys are domestically out of standing, let me recommend bringing home a twenty-one-pound wild gobbler, slung nonchalantly over your shoulder. It will work wonders.

Magic Moments
~ Part V ~

Every hunter knows them—those days when fickle fate sees fit to shine, however briefly, on his efforts. Such fleeting moments we cherish for their magic, even as we stoically acknowledge that there will be other times which by comparison seem tragic. The resiliency and selectivity of the human mind is such that failures are forgotten as successes stand forth with startling clarity. Mental gymnastics are an integral part of the turkey-hunting experience, a fact that Rutledge recognized. He preferred to write of successes, when no excuses were needed, as opposed to the bleaker moments of sport. He was keenly cognizant that luck played its part in success, but that what was described as luck usually was a fringe benefit deriving from such qualities as superior woodsmanship, a sound understanding of the prey, fine calling skills and the virtues of patience. A proper blend of these skills, spiced by good fortune, could produce grand days of the kind found in the tales which follow.

Here we sample eight magic moments, all of them set in the environs of Hampton Plantation which Rutledge knew so well and hunted so wisely for close to eighty years. While he hunted turkeys elsewhere, including North Carolina, Virginia, West Virginia, and Pennsylvania, the sporting ways and outdoor days he loved best came in delta country along the lower Santee River.

In five of these stories individuals other than the narrator play key roles. There is Steve, a frequent sporting sidekick of Rutledge and a wizard when it came to understanding wild turkeys. We also meet Prince, the man whom Rutledge once described as "companion to my heart" and whose friendship he cherished above that of all other men. Both Steve and Prince were black men who lived on the grounds of Hampton Plantation (both are buried there, as is Rutledge). Joel, who figures as the protagonist of another tale, was an impoverished white woodsman. All of these men shared one important characteristic—they possessed exceptional turkey-hunting wisdom thanks to having lived for years in close communion with the wild haunts the birds prefer.

The role of these men in these stories is so prominent that one might be led, wrongly, to conclude that Rutledge was little more than a turkey-hunting "trigger man" for whom others did the calling and supplied the savvy. In reality, he was a superb hunter, and most of the reliance he placed on others had to do with their efforts as what might be called "scouts." Plying "Miss Seduction," his homemade call, he went on plenty of solitary hunts and "strutted his stuff." In these tales, whether Rutledge is hunting alone or with stalwart companions, he enchants his audience as the dulcet tones of Miss Seduction come to us across the years and we share the magic of turkey hunting in the world around Hampton.

WILD TURKEYS OF THE DELTA

In the mild dusk of the winter's evening I was sitting on the back steps of the plantation house, listening to the way the mallards were raising cain in the old rice fields across the river. Only 100 yards below me rolled the dark stream; and for some reason, at that moment it loomed darker. Was night coming on so fast? Oh, no. It was only Steve slouching up the dim pathway. . . .

Up to me he came, with that unmistakable air he shows when he has seen game.

I asked him how his still was running, but he had greater tidings.

"Cap'n," he said, "you done ought to been wid me just now."

"Who was after you?" I asked.

"I run into a flock of wild turkeys," he said soberly. " 'Bout sixty or a dozen," he added, "right on that ole causeway. They been gwine to roost."

"What time do we start?" I queried, getting his drift.

"Daylight," he answered, "or before dat."

"All right," I said, "I'm going to be drinking coffee at five o'clock. And if you aren't here, you'll have to eat crow for Christmas."

"My belly ain't got no suction for crow," Steve answered. "I will be here, Captain."

The Santee River, in Carolina, some fifteen miles above its mouth, divides; and the two branches, about a mile apart flow separately into the ocean. Between these broad streams is the mysterious and magic land of the delta, once cultivated from end to end for the growing of rice, but now for seventy years abandoned to nature and her children. Here are lazy, winding creeks, miles of weedy morasses, dense swamps where the footing is watery and muddy, canebrakes, old canals now bush-hung and choked with semi-tropical growths of wampee and duck oats. And here dwell deer, ducks, turkeys, wild hogs, black bear, bootleggers, snakes untold, snipe in myriads. It's a great place to hunt if you can take it. But

---

From *Outdoor Life*, January 1933. Later included in *An American Hunter* (1937).

don't hunt on the delta in your Sunday-go-to-meetings. However wisely you walk, you and your game are going to be covered with mud when you return home.

When hunting on the mainland gets too hot for the deer and turkeys, the deer swim and the turkeys fly across to the delta. It takes either a brave man or an idiot to hunt there. Steve and I belong in one of those classes.

The moon was still bright; the owls were still weirdly hooting; and the coffee was not hot when Steve shambled up to the back door and knocked softly. I admitted him, and together we had breakfast.

"Are you sure," I asked, "that they were not buzzards? You remember that time you took me to that wild field at sundown to shoot a big buck that you had seen, and I came near shooting a mule?"

"Great God, Cap'n, since when can a buzzard gobble? And a buzzard don't scratch in de leaves. If dem is buzzard, I is a preacher."

"Then they must be turkeys," I admitted.

Together in that mysterious twilight before the dawn we got in the canoe. Over the misty river we moved. Steve's a good paddler, steady and silent and skillful as an Indian. Up Push-and-Go Creek we went, heading toward the old causeway that used to span the delta. Washington crossed that causeway when he visited the South after the Revolution; Lafayette crossed it. Now a wildcat has a hard time fighting his way through those burly briars, with every now and then a break in the bank to negotiate, twenty feet wide and ten feet deep. But between breaks the dyke is fairly high. It was on this old bank that Steve had seen the turkeys; they must have been roosting ahead of us in the great cypresses and tupelos that tower out of the vast and melancholy swamp.

I know men who, the night before the season, roost a flock of wild turkeys, then sleep under the trees, and at the crack of day shoot the birds off the roost. I could never get any kick out of this sort of strategem; to shoot game while it is asleep is like shooting a tame pigeon padlocked in an iron cage.

As we were as yet at some distance from the birds, Steve was telling me about a bull alligator that got after his children the summer before.

"You know, Cap'n, I done got 'bout twenty or sixteen chillun. An' they will go down to the ribber. One day Mandy come runnin' to me, shoutin' and wavin' her apron. 'Whass matter wid you?' I done axe her. You know, Cap'n, how I kin talk to a 'oman. Well, sah, Mandy she come runnin' to me and she says, 'O Steve, a alligator done ketch one of de chillum!' And

I says, 'Mandy, ain't I done tole you las' month dat something wuz gettin' our chillun?' Yass, sah, so I done tole her."

We now came to a place on the causeway where we could land, and out we got, just as the Eastern sky grew pink, and just as the first mists of the morning began to rise eerily from the vast reedland. The weather was like early October in mid-latitudes. We never have any real winter on the plantation.

These delta turkeys, when they roost near the causeway, have a way of flying down to it from the roost, and roaming around on it for an hour or two to pick up the water-oak acorns. I asked Steve where he had run into them the night before. He indicated that we were within about 300 yards of them.

"There they are," I said, "and here we are. How are we going to get together?"

"I got a plan," Steve announced. "I gwine drive them to you."

Now you know that such a scheme doesn't sound very rosy; but it is a fact that wild game pays much less attention to a Negro than it does to a white man with a gun. I think deer and turkeys consider these plantation Negroes as natural objects of the landscape, like themselves, whereas a hunter is an alien and an intruder.

"But how will you get around them?" I asked.

"I gwine in de swamp," Steve answered undismayed. "I has done trabel dis swamp eber since hatchet was a hammer."

Into the wet bushes his dusky form insinuated itself and soon I heard him softly sloshing through the dim morass. He intended traveling on a wide arc, and would return to the causeway about a quarter of a mile from me, and then just loaf up toward me, driving the turkeys before him. In open woods such a plan might be just a lot of hooey; but you know how turkeys love to run a bank or an old road. The thing might work.

As I saw Steve disappear into the gloomy wetness of the swamp, I thought how humble and faithful a Negro can be, especially if he is close to nature and unspoiled. I knew what he would have to go through to make that circuit. I knew of the mud and the briars and the messy old ditches. But he just ambled right into it all. Good old Steve! He has his limitations, and he is not a domestic shining star, as his massive wife Mandy often testifies to me and the rest of the world. But I have had a lot of fun with Steve in the woods, and he understands game.

He had not left me three minutes before I heard the turkeys. Day was wanly dawning, and the swamp looked as if it were getting ready for eerie and witch-like performances, with that gray moss draping all the trees, those gray mists looming and vanishing, that heavy silence that was full of meaning. I heard a gobbler fly down from the roost; he always makes more noise when his wings are damp and the atmosphere heavy. As soon as he alighted on the causeway, he began to talk drowsily, asking the other members of the family why they didn't come down to breakfast. They came. Don't you always get a peculiar thrill out of hearing wild turkeys come off the roost? You hardly hear more than perhaps a creak of a limb, perhaps a wing striking the brush, and the soft "swish-swish-swish" of their wings.

By the time the whole flock was on the causeway, day broadened fast. The fantastic shapes of the mist took definite form as trees and bushes. I could easily see to shoot. There was a breast-high canebrake on the edge of the causeway, making a natural sort of blind. Into this I got, and was all set for the big parade. In my right-hand barrel I had 4's, and in the left, 2's. Some of my fellow sportsmen laugh at me for shooting these heavy loads, just as they sometimes spoof me about sticking to my old 12 gauge gun. But a wild turkey is a ponderous bird, and if you have to take him at any distance, you want to hit him hard; you want to break him down. I have seen many a heart-broken hunter vainly watch a fine bird flying on after being peppered at sixty yards with 5's and 6's.

Haven't you been on a stand when everything seemed in your favor? And then haven't you had something mess up the whole fair prospect? To me, standing there in the canes, serenely sure that I'd have wild turkey on the table for Christmas dinner, just such an experience came. At first the sleepy turkeys were the only sounds I had heard. But now, from behind me came grunts and little squeals and riotous sounds of ardent and promiscuous foraging. Up the edge of the bank came a whole herd of razorbacks, really wild hogs, ownerless, and as skittish as deer. They were going to traipse right down the bank and run my turkeys into the swamp. Turkeys are afraid of this brand of swine, for they will kill and eat anything they can get to, hide, fur, feathers, and all.

Just as I was in the act of stepping out from my hiding place to turn back the noisy intruders, far down the bank I saw the snake-like neck and head and the bulgy bronze back of the first of my intended prizes. If I showed myself, the game would be up. If I did not, the blamed hogs would play it their way. Something had to be done quickly.

The foremost hog in the drove was a handsome yearling, fat and sassy. With the 2's I laid him low in his tracks, whereat his fellows beat it violently down the bank for parts unknown.

The turkeys had been closer to me than I had thought. They often are like that. At my shot the whole flock rose in a ragged sort of tumult, flying in almost every direction. Most of them went right over Steve. Some I saw light on distant trees in the swamp. One stately bird headed for me. He was about fifty yards up, and had acquired his full momentum. I held for the very tip of his bill; and the 4's crumpled him. He fell high and dry on the bank, with hardly a feather ruffled. I had never seen more beautiful plumage—all soft brown, with jetty cross-markings, and a wonderful iridescence on his neck and shoulders. Later, when I weighed him, he sagged the scales to nineteen and a half pounds. I have seen them bigger, but not finer.

At my second shot, the rest of the flock quit the country. As an old hunter once said to me, "Mister, when a wild turkey says 'Put! Put!' he's going to leave them parts. He's going to quit that country. He's going to some other world."

These, of course, had only gone deep into the river swamp, which is, however, truly a kind of other world from the dry causeway. Being genuine wild turkeys, they would not call for a long time. I decided I had enough. Laying the gobbler beside the slain hog, I awaited the coming of Steve. I knew well enough that he had sensed that something had gone wrong.

Here he came shambling along like an old bear that has just taken a mud-bath. He was half-singing, half-muttering, "I done love a yaller gal, and dat yaller gal done love me." I suspect this sort of concert around home had gotten him in trouble with Mandy, who is as black as the inside of a tar barrel.

Disconsolately I walked up to meet him.

"No wonder Mandy is disgusted with you," I said, with the sternness of one who has just missed and is trying to put the blame on some one else. "Here you are yodling about a yaller gal when I thought we were hunting turkeys."

Steve stopped as if he saw a ghost.

"Ain't you done shoot, Cap'n?" he asked defensively. "I done say you got two."

"I shot the first time to make you quit singing, and the second time to let you know I was going home."

"Please God," muttered Steve, "ain't dat som'pin'!"

Just then he spied the porker, and what lay beside that brigand of the river swamps.

"Christmas bacon!" shouted Steve, doing a Brodie into the very bosom of the hog.

When he had the bacon shouldered, and I had the gobbler, we made our way back to the boat, each wonderfully light-hearted in his own way.

"It was a good hunt, Steve," I told him; "and calls for another soon. But you must cut down on the singing."

"All right, Cap'n. And please, sah, not to mention to Mandy 'bout dat yaller gal. She might not onnerstan'."

Women usually don't—about things like that.

STEVE KNOWS HOW

While I have often hunted alone, and have at times been successful as a solitary gunner, there have been other occasions on which I felt it necessary to call for some expert advice and assistance. For example, I well recall the time when I sent out an S. O. S. for black Steve. . . . If I am really baffled by some problem of hunting, I call him into consultation. Being one of them, he has the lowdown on wild things and their ways. He seems to ease in and out among them without their being alarmed. They don't mind him. He is as much a natural feature of the lonely pinelands and the deep river swamps as the cypresses and the old logs and the ancient mossy stumps. Being of them and belonging with them, he is a very valuable adviser. I need him and use him often.

Now, you all know how frequently it happens that game disappears from its accustomed haunts. It was here yesterday, but where is it today? This occurs in the case of deer, grouse, turkeys, and other things that do not ever go very far from the place where they were born. But they slip away, and we can't find them anywhere. This happened to me with my wild turkeys. I raised three fine flocks on the place. They were everywhere on the plantation throughout the summer and early autumn. Up to Thanksgiving, which is the opening day, they were in evidence. Sometimes I could see them from the house, crossing the peafields on the borders of the woods. But then they simply were not. They were not killed. I have no poaching. They could not have been disturbed, for they had not been hunted. But they vanished into the wilds. December passed, and January, and not a bird could I see. Nor were there any tracks or signs of scratching. It is far easier to tell if turkeys are about than it is to tell about some other kind of game: you see their tracks in this country in the damp sandy roads, the droppings under their roosts, their scratchings; and often you hear them. But I hadn't seen a sign. Therefore as the season was waning fast, although Steve had been avoiding me because certain of my hogs had assuredly disappeared into his cavernous belly, I

From *Hunter's Choice* (1946).

sent for him. If a white man sends for a Negro, unless he states his reason definitely, the chances are that the Negro will not come; for he always lives in mighty dread of the white man's mysterious laws. I dispatched a message to Steve to tell him that I had a quart of whiskey for him. I know what will bring him. It did.

Into the firelight of my dining room he shambled, cap in hand, mouth watering, profuse in apologies for not having been to see me in so long.

"After a man eats a lot of bacon," I told him sardonically, "he gets thirsty. I bought this bottle especially for you, Steve."

Steve understood my little joke; but he can think of but one thing at a time, and he was now absorbed in dreams of the bottle.

"Now, what I want to know is what has became of all the turkeys," I said to him.

"I dunno 'bout all," he said, "but I is know 'bout some."

I thought so.

"Well," I persisted, "where are they?"

"A big flock," he told me, "is usin' by Black Tom's Bay."

"I suppose they are feeding on the mash from the still that you fire there, Steve."

Steve grinned.

"I can take you to them," he said, overlooking my veiled accusation.

"When?"

"At dayclean tomorrow, sah."

"All right," I told him; "I'll meet you in the car at the crossroads before daylight."

And so it was. When I reached the dark crossroads, a darker figure than any night loomed there. Good old Steve! He doesn't need any alarm clock to get him up when we are starting early together.

For six miles we drove, turning in at last by Wildcat Branch, where we left the car. By now there were the first faint signs of day. The morning was mild and still and beautiful. I followed Steve toward the darksome edges of Black Tom's Bay, named two hundred years ago for a Negro slave. Steve walks like a panther; he just slews along noiselessly. We came to a place where a forest fire had swept the pinelands down to the edges of the wet branch. And, while I know that all ground-feeding birds like burnt lands, for the fire exposes the seeds that they love, I was not so sure that this was a good place to intercept turkeys. But I was in Steve's hands; and on such an occasion they are good ones.

Coming to where the dense myrtles and gallberries made out into the woods like a little peninsula, Steve halted and began to break some brush that he piled deftly in the shape of a horseshoe. So skillfully did he do this that a passerby would merely have thought that the bushes happened to be a little thicker there than elsewhere. Then we got around within the seclusion of the green semicircle. We sat down to wait. Daylight was broadening. I could not begin to fathom the thought of Steve, hulked there, but I was full of doubt.

While it was not yet fully light, I heard wood ducks fleeting overhead; a cardinal called; squirrels began to travel up and down the trees, gray nymphs of the morning's twilight. Owls gave their last demoniac hoots. I heard a great blue heron grunting raucously. But I was listening for other sounds.

We had been sitting there about a half-hour when I heard a very peculiar noise, one that I defy any human being to imitate. It sounded as if a frog with indigestion were giving utterance to his pain. "K-r-k-rak!"

I nudged Steve.

"Could that be a turkey?" I whispered.

"I ain't sho'," he answered. Then we both lapsed into tingling silence.

A full hour passed. The great forest was wide awake. Crows called, many birds caroled, two razorback hogs passed me. Steve's mouth watered, but I passed up his bacon. Then "Kouk!" Very subdued it was, and much nearer than the first suspicious sound we had heard.

Steve leaned over until his cavernous mouth was against my ear.

"Dat's dem!" he whispered.

For reasons that I need not try to explain, I got a bigger thrill out of those simple words than if Cleopatra or Helen of Troy had collapsed in my manly arms.

"Dat's dem!" I shall remember the sweet finality of these words as long as life lasts.

Without telling me why, but certain that I would understand, Steve laid his huge hand on my back and pushed me down lower behind the bushes. He did not have to explain to me that he would watch and then tell me when.

Twenty minutes more we waited, with my faith in Steve cooling a little. We have heard turkeys, I doubtfully agreed, but that was no reason why they should choose to walk right up on us. But now Steve eased down to me once more.

"Dey's comin'," he whispered.

I wanted to look, but his mighty hand held me down. But with infinite caution it began to relax. I knew that when the weight of it was wholly released, it would be time for me to perform.

From what Steve had told me of the regular route of this flock of turkeys, I judged that if they passed at all, they would come within thirty-five yards. With the right kind of shot, it is a perfect distance. I had 4's in each barrel.

Slowly Steve's hand relaxed its warning on my back. At last he removed it altogether. That was his signal that I might look. But, you know, a funny thing had happened to me. I had been sitting in the same position for nearly two hours. To see the great birds that Steve had silently told me were now near, I had to get to my knees. I lost precious seconds doing this, for my body was asleep from the waist down. When I finally managed to right myself, my knees cracked loud enough to scare every turkey. I eased up and peered through the thin fringe of greenery, expecting to see the flock not more than thirty-five yards away. But, old-timers, they were from forty-five to fifty. The moment I saw how far they were, and by the course they were taking I knew that they were not likely to come any nearer, I opened my gun, extracted the 4 from the choke barrel, and slipped in a 2. A gobbler is a big bird, and you have to break him down. If you merely wound a wild turkey, your chances of getting him are practically worthless.

The flock came wandering idly on, feeding sparingly on seeds exposed on the burnt ground. Few birds can look so utterly different in different positions. The wild gobbler, when he is on the alert, is the trimmest and most tailor-made aristocrat imaginable; but when he bends over to feed, his big shoulders make him look bulky and almost awkward. I saw three gobblers and eight hens. The latter, of course, were a whole shade lighter in color than the toms. It was up to me now to pick my bird. They were grouped so close that this was not an easy thing to do; and I knew that at their distance, my shot would scatter a good deal. I was after one big gobbler. I saw him. He completely satisfied my idea of what a wild turkey ought to be: a most beautiful and symmetrical body, suggesting massive grace; keen blue head; pink legs (most artists who have drawn or painted this bird have made his legs too short); rich bronzed plumage, full of iridescent lights. But as he is seen in the woods, and not examined in the hand, a wild gobbler looks black. He always looks very black coming to you. If he is going from you in the sunlight, he looks a silver-gray. In this manner you can tell a long way off whether turkeys are coming to you or leaving you.

My gobbler was attended by two hens that seemed to be trying to ingratiate themselves into his favor. A little behind was a second gobbler, almost the match of the first. A third was seventy yards away. I got my gun up; I covered my bird. But the hens were too much in line. I waited with my finger barely touching the trigger. The flock now moved a little past my front. Steve leaned over so quietly that I heard his breathing before I knew he had aught to say to me.

"Better shoot," he whispered. "Dey's gwine."

My problem was a hard one. I had to have the gobbler, but I didn't want to touch a hen. They were now nearly fifty yards from me; not alarmed, but just moving on.

My chance might come any second. It did. Coming to a big pine, the two hens passed on the farther side of it. As my big bird got directly between the pine and me, for some reason he threw up his head. And it was the last time he ever threw it up. The heavy 2's drove him. I heard a mighty commotion. Steve left me as if I ha'nt had him. As for the other turkeys, I never saw one again. All of them vanished running. As I came slowly out of the little blind Steve had made, still stiff from my long cramped wait, I saw Steve holding a mighty gobbler in either hand. I had killed two. Now, how did that ever happen?

"You see, Cap'n," Steve explained to me, "dat gobbler what was behind, he didn't like it for dem two hens to keep so close to de gobbler what been in front. And when they parted at the big pine tree, the one behind run up fast so as to get with dem two hens. So dat's how it happen you kill two. Dat's what he get," he ruminated darkly, "fo' foolin' wid 'oman."

"But it isn't the mating season, Steve," I said. "Gobblers don't fight now."

"Dey don't haul off and fight, but dey is jealous all de time; and dey fight some all de time. Dey is same like a man: dey can be sensible till a 'oman come around. Den dey do foolishness. Look at dis one: ain't he done run right into a load of shot?"

I asked Steve how he knew that those turkeys ranged along the lonely borders of Black Tom's Bay. But, while he will take me to game, he will rarely tell me anything. Indeed, as I have said before, after having associated with plantation Negroes for fifty years, I am convinced that they know everything about me, but I know nothing at all about them. Of one thing I am certain: they are far wiser than we imagine.

Joel's Christmas Turkey

Joel's place was the kind that one comes upon suddenly in the pineland wilderness of the Carolinas; the few meager fields and parched pastures leading up to it were unfenced, and appeared to be but an open stretch of the monotonous landscape. There were no groups of whitewashed buildings behind it, nor pleasant vistas of orchards and meadows; for Joel was a poor white woodsman and trapper, and his home was in the great pine barrens of the coast country of South Carolina. The nearest settlement was eight miles away, southward down the lonely, grass-grown road. His cabin, built of rough-hewn, sap-pine logs, already beginning to sag along their length and to be crushed where the weight of the structure caught them, squatted in a rude clearing not much larger than the building itself. Scrub pines and sparse patches of gallberry and low-bush huckleberry bushes grew almost to the door; a weedy path led from the road, along which few travelers ever passed, to the rotted doorstep-block. The reason why Joel's home was so unhomelike was simple: he had never married, and his real home was in the woods.

Joel was accounted the best woodsman in his county; and while he had many rivals, he had no peers. He killed on the average of twenty deer a season, and his record on wild turkeys was even more formidable. Joel always said that he had never been to school long enough to learn to count above the legal number of deer that the law allowed to be taken in a season; besides, his third cousin was game warden. But for all his craft, there was a wild turkey living in the tupelo swamp behind his cabin that had made Joel stretch himself, and, so far, stretch himself in vain. It seemed to the hunter that he had used every whit of his strength, woodcraft, patience, and tireless energy of pursuit in the attempt to win this royal prize; and doubtless the wild gobbler knew something of the relentlessness of Joel as a hunter, and just how wary he had to be to keep his distance from Joel's deadly musket. This turkey could not speak human speech as can some of the creatures about which our fanciful

From *Old Plantation Days* (1921).

naturalists write. He could not put his finger to his nose and scoff at Joel, saying, "O sad brother, I am the Wise One. Booloo is my friend. I shall meet him at the Council Tree at midnight, and you will never find us any more." He was just a plain turkey; but when that has been said all has been said that need be mentioned; for if a plain wild turkey is not the most intelligent bird afoot or awing, then the dodo isn't dead.

Joel had first seen him one sultry September day, when the pine-woods were fervidly hot, when the grass was as sear as tinder, and when the lush-grown swamps were sending up in steaming moisture the little water that the long drought had left in them. There was no wing stirring. The birds, hidden deep in the thickets, were still. Even the wood-cicadas had ceased their dry, insistent shrilling. Joel, coming down a sandy path through the scrub oak, not far from the west bank of the Santee River, heard a hen-turkey's sudden and startled "put! put!" Joel halted in his tracks, while his keen gray eyes swept the bushy savanna over to his left, whence the sound had come. He did not see the mother, but he saw the young one (there appeared to be but the one) as it came stepping from behind the shelter of a broomsedge tussock. A half-grown wild gobbler he was, remarkably large and well formed. He was so big as to be awkward; but, like all members of his hunted race, he was shy and swift and wonderfully gifted in the woodland art of silently and suddenly effacing himself. For a second he was in Joel's sight; then he vanished. When a wild turkey vanishes, after having seen a man, depend upon it, bank upon it, he's *gone*.

Joel came cautiously round the edge of the thicket, looking for others of the brood. But he saw none. Not far away was the sandy road, and toward this the trapper went; for if one cannot see the game itself one can at least have the dubious satisfaction of seeing its tracks. In the damp sand where a summer-dried stream had crossed the road, he found the turkey's tracks. There, lightly and springily set, were those of the hen; while beside them were great, sprawling tracks, with big, wide-spreading toes that mashed the sand.

"Well, now, jest look at that!" muttered Joel as he bent over them; "the young un's feet are bigger than his ma's!"

Then he stood up and looked toward the dark swamp into whose deep recesses the two turkeys had vanished. Knowing the pine-woods from the Santee to the Cooper, and from the railroad to the sea, the trapper knew where these turkeys would feed, range, roost. And he felt sure that by Christmas-time the hen and the fine young gobbler would bring him a big price from some epicurean clients of his living down in the village on the nearby coast.

The luxuriance of the summer passed into the mournful beauty of the autumn, and the autumn gave place to the winter; but still Joel had not fulfilled the plan he had made that September day when for the first time he had looked at the turkey-tracks in the road. A score of times he had seen the splendid wild bird; other turkeys fell before his gun; but the big bronzed racer of the pineland always escaped. The winter wore along to the early spring, but Joel was still unsuccessful. Late one March afternoon, on his return through a tupelo swamp after a trip for raccoon, Joel heard the gobbler down in a heavy clump of cypresses gobbling a provoked answer to a rookery of crows that were cawing away in their careless fashion. As soon as he got to his cabin the trapper took down from a smoke-blackened beam a small white bone, the radius of a turkey's wing. He washed it, blew through it, squinted down it; then, placing it to his mouth and hollowing his hand in front of it, he drew forth the soft and pleading notes of a hen turkey.

"That will fetch the old sport," he said to himself; "leastwise I never yet seen the gobbler that wouldn't jest streak it for me when I called."

It was still quite dark when Joel stepped out of his cabin next morning. The vast forest was sleeping under its mantle of mist. In the velvet-purple of the night sky the stars shone beautiful. High in the darkness the crests of the mighty pines murmured and waved. Fragrances of the wild and virgin woods moved subtly across the path down which Joel stepped, and met him also, more deep and rich, in the glimmering road. But the trapper, to whom such influences were too ordinary to be impressive, pushed on rapidly through the mist. Slung under his right arm, with its cap and priming kept dry by the flap of his old coat, was his musket; an ancient weapon, decidedly out of date as far as appearances were concerned, but one which had never yet failed Joel. On the few occasions when he had missed, he had never blamed his musket for it. No good hunter ever blames his gun, when once that gun has proved itself true.

A short walk down the road brought the turkey hunter to a blind sheep path, which an ordinary man would have passed without seeing; but, to him, the woods and their ways were as well known by night as by day. On he tramped through the bush-hung path. The gallberry bushes drenched him with their dew. The cool, misty tops of the bending broomsedge brushed him with a rainy fragrance. There were many odors of the coming spring wafted on the night air. Joel did not walk carelessly; he stepped with the easy stride of a woodsman, yet with caution and alertness. Only a woodsman knows how to be alert without being strained. Through these woods he was traversing there was danger; for on a certain day of that same week he had counted fourteen rattlesnakes, dragging themselves across his path, lying in loose coils between the tussocks of broomsedge, and sunning themselves beside fallen logs and sheltering stumps.

In half an hour Joel came to an airy ridge in the woods, and here he halted. Behind him lay the darksome forest, still dreaming in its mantling mists; but before him, like the effulgence from some distant fire, there was a living glow in the sky. Slowly the velvet-purple of the heavens changed to a velvet-violet, then to a velvet-blue. Beyond the vast tupelo swamp where he had roosted the gobbler, the red colors brightened and extended themselves along the horizon.

Joel sat down on a log, laid his musket carefully across his knees, took out his turkey call, and sounded tentatively a few trial notes. The sound was clear and sweet, and the atmosphere was just right for carrying it. He hollowed his big bronzed hands and drew luring music from the white bone; plaintive and pleading and feminine were the notes that came forth. In them were the tenderness and glamour of the voices of young love and the early springtime, voices of hope and of promise.

Far away, on his lonely roost in the huge old moss-draped cypress, the gobbler heard the sound. It pierced the solitude with a poignant sweetness that could not be resisted. Loudly and with masculine assurance he gobbled an answer to the yearning call. Then he launched himself out on his powerful wings, and sailed, straight as a quail flies for cover, toward the crouching hunter. The big turkey came to ground on the edge of the swamp; and there, being greeted by a further call, very soft this time, he put his head forward and down and raced for his alluring goal.

Joel had heard him gobble, but he did not see him coming. Had he known that his royal game was so near, he would have gone down on one knee in the grass. But instead of that he did something that was fatal to his success: he took the call from his mouth and shook the moisture out of it. The hunter had a flashing glimpse ahead of him of a broad bronzed back and a darting blue-black head. Before he could throw his musket up the vision was gone. Silently the great swamp, the sanctuary of the hunted, had taken back its own. Into its secure refuge the great wild bird had vanished.

"I knowed better'n that," said Joel disgustedly, still sitting on his log. "I might have knowed he would come a-pokin' up. But now he's gone; and by *gone* I mean he's *cleaned up*, quit the country, maybe quit the world. If a man doesn't shoot a turkey the minute the turkey sees him, it's good-by, Susie. And I could yelp here all day and he wouldn't even stop getting away from me. I reckon he thought I was shaking my finger at him. Gentlemen, he's a sundowner. But I don't deserve to have him."

The pineland hunter rose to his feet, knowing that his game had escaped him, knowing, too, that for a long time it would be practically impossible to get the wary old gobbler to come to his call. But there were other ways of getting this bronzed racer of the wilderness; and to a man like Joel the woods would not long deny another chance at the coveted prize.

But the spring and the summer passed, and he saw no more of his gobbler. But the autumn, with its bared forests and its fallen crop of acorns to attract turkeys to special places, brought Joel once more into distant acquaintanceship with the big bird. Once he had stalked him among sweet live-oak acorns under the giant oaks on a deserted plantation; but the wary monarch had been just a flash too quick for him. Again he thought he had cornered him in a big patch of high blackberry canes in the woods; and if Joel could have made him fly, the turkey would have been his. But the crafty bird refused to rise. After beating about the briars into which he had seen the gobbler skulk, Joel came out into the road, and there he saw the racer's huge tracks—the flying trail left by him in the sandy loam. Joel whistled incredulously as he stood up after measuring the tracks.

"Four inches from tip to tip," he said: "the biggest gobbler that ever ran these woods. And he'll be mine afore long, or my finger never touched trigger!"

But another whole year passed, and yet another, and Joel was still without his prize. His continual hunting of the big turkey had made that splendid creature abandon his old haunts. He no longer fed in the dense bays and gallberry patches of the Little Ocean; he no longer roosted in the tupelo swamp. Out of the pine-woods and towards the river swamps Joel had driven him. The hunter did not altogether approve of the turkey's new range, for well he knew that if once the gobbler took a notion to cross the river he would probably take up with other members of his own tribe in the swamps and pinelands on the North Santee side, never to return to his former home. This was especially likely, Joel knew, if he were not hunted beyond the river. During this last year he had been dividing his time among three or four old deserted plantations—Romney, Montgomery, Oldfield and Fairfield—that bordered on the Santee delta. It was on Romney, one November morning, that Joel had shot at the huge gobbler as he sailed off his roost in a giant short-leaf. But, as he said to himself with grim humor, "I kindled, but he did not curtsey." For a month thereafter he saw nothing of the object of his quest.

The twilight of Christmas Eve was falling as Joel, weary but hopeful, traversed the desolate, sandy field leading from the pine woods to the river bank on Romney Plantation. All day long he had followed the giant gobbler, and even the hardihood of Joel was sorely taxed. But before him in the sand he saw the fresh tracks which had been left by the wonderful bird he was pursuing. At length he came to a fringe of trees marking the bank of the river. Hardly had Joel paused to look and to listen when, from a thickety clump of elders, a hundred yards away, a great bulk rose heavily and beat its way over the marsh. Its flight took it upward, and bore it into a huge moss-shrouded cypress that stood on the very brink of the wide river. There it alighted heavily; clearly against the afterglow in the sky Joel could see its great bulk rock on the limb, lower its weight carefully, and at last settle on its perch. He had roosted the mighty bird! At last, after all those years, he was going to have a fair chance at the largest and craftiest wild gobbler that had ever ranged the Santee country.

For a half-hour, while the light died and the noises from field and fen wakened and were hushed again, Joel sat in the dry grass with his keen eyes riveted on the black mass that never stirred in the ancient gray cypress. At last the real darkness was at hand, and he must make his shot before it would be too late to see his game.

He could not cross the boggy marsh that lay between him and the big cypress. But a short detour, by way of an old check-bank, brought him almost under the vast bulk of the tree. Through the branches, draped with moss, he saw the Christmas stars; and motionless on a stout limb, to Joel's tingling satisfaction, sat the great wild turkey. All the hunter's stalking ended here.

Joel peered this way and that, trying to get his game clear of intervening limbs. It was tense work, as the light was almost gone. Finally, when he dared to step out on the edge of the marsh to get an unimpeded view, he was amazed and bewildered to see *two* black shapes in the cypress, where but one had been visible before. Moreover, they appeared to be of the same size, and they were undoubtedly of the same shape. Joel exclaimed under his breath. His first thought was there were two turkeys in the tree, but then he came to the conclusion that one was his gobbler and the other was a huge bunch of mistletoe.

But which was which? Joel peered and pondered. The light was going so fast that the great tree had taken on a more shadowy outline, and the two dark shapes were fast merging into the blackness of the cypress branches. Which object should he shoot? Which one was the royal bird, and which one was the bunch of Christmas greens? In vain did Joel crane his neck this way and that, straining his good eyes. Not even he could distinguish between the two dim objects so high up in the night.

As last he raised his musket, gripping it strongly with his bronzed hands. It roared out on the twilight. Its detonation rolled far up and down the misty reaches of the river. And Joel saw two things happen: first, a dark bulk launched itself out from the tree, directing its powerful flight above the river and toward what lay beyond; secondly, another dark shape swayed in the cypress, turned slowly, cracked, and came rushing to the ground. Joel had shot off the bunch of mistletoe. The king of the pineland wilderness had escaped across the river.

But Joel was a game sport. He picked up the bunch of mistletoe and slung it slowly over his shoulder.

"I'll take it home and hang it in the house," he said: "it will 'mind me of Christmas."

Magic on Mound Ridge

I have just described an adventure that befell me one winter twilight, but, much as I love the wilderness, as night comes, I like to be well within the reach of home. And if you were to ask me to name some of the places where I do not like to be caught after dark, Mound Ridge would take high rank in the list. Nor is it difficult to explain why this is so. All of us have heard of a "howling wilderness." This is the place . . . yet it doesn't howl. From time to time one hears noises of beast and bird, but it is the silence that gets the visitor, even the hardened hunter. And if a white man doesn't like to have the sun go down on him on Mound Ridge, what shall be said of a plantation Negro? It is in his nature to people the shadows with nameless terrors. I can get a reluctant consent from my good Negro, Prince, to go to the Ridge before daylight, for then the light is ahead of us. But when the sun touches the moss-draped funeral cypresses in the west, he is all for home, with bells on.

I want to tell you of a hunt that he and I had recently in this forbidding country. Honestly, if I were commissioned to find a dinosaur or some other prehistoric monster, I believe that my chances would be as good in this lonely swamp as in the wilds of the Amazon or in the papyrus jungles of Rhodesia. Yet, strange as it may seem, Mound Ridge used to be under a high state of cultivation. Before the Civil War, rice was grown there; many of the old banks and canals are still discernible, and, stranger still, though they have been standing in muddy water for nearly eighty years, and perhaps a hundred, some of the old cypress trunks (which controlled the flow of water into and out of the fields) are still in place. Somehow, a place is more lonesome if it displays some signs of former human habitation; it carries an air of having been forsaken.

Twilight had fallen over the plantation when I heard the heavy scuffing of bare feet coming up the back steps. These mighty feet, should they be shod, would call, I think, for about No. 19 shoes. Amiably, Prince shambled in. As I was drowsing by the fire, I told him to sit down and

---

From *Hunter's Choice* (1946).

unburden his soul. To afford his feelings full and genial flow, I gave him a full tumbler of muscadine wine.

"Well," I said, "You've something heavy on your mind."

The grapevine telegraph of a prison, the secret communications of the underworld . . . these are as nothing compared to the way in which Negroes get hold of news and circulate it among themselves. After living among them for more than fifty years, I am convinced that they know all about me, while I know nothing at all about them.

"Day befo' yesteddy," he drawled, "Mr. Raybun, he been huntin' hogs in de Ridge."

"Yes?" I queried. But I always have to let Prince take this time. He has only one thought in his system at a time.

"He didn' find no hogs," he reported.

"No?" I questioned patiently and solicitously.

"But dat fice dog he got—you know him, sah?"

"Yes, I know him."

"Well, Cap'n, dat dog done put twenty-seven turkey across Flag Creek."

He subsided, having told me all. A Negro will rarely make a suggestion to a white man. He will state a fact; then he will wait to see what the white man will do about it.

"You want to start before daylight?" I asked.

"Yass, sah. But don't les go too early."

I knew what he meant; he wanted some daylight to be showing before we landed on those haunted shores. There, on mild nights in the winter, a man might step on a cotton-mouth moccasin or a great diamondback rattler; there, as I myself had seen, roamed genuine wild boars, great hulking brutes, like no other creature of the swamp. Not that one of these will attack a man, but it is not pleasant to encounter one in the dark. There are bull-briars a half-inch in diameter, studded with wicked thorns. There are thousands of places where an unwary step may send a man crashing to earth, or may submerge him in mud of about the consistency of pea soup. These are some of the known reasons for bewaring of Mound Ridge in the dark. Prince had reasons far more fearful and occult. At any rate, next morning we drifted on the starlit waters of Flag Creek until faintly behind the dim shores the east blushed softly, and above us, the stars paled.

"Time," whispered Prince.

In a few moments we had landed, pushed our way through a 20-foot jungle of canes, and had come out on the high, dry, and open ridge. By then I could see about me a little; I heard wood ducks passing up the river. A cardinal called. Owls gave their last derisive whoops. Day was coming fast.

"Dis is de place," my Negro breathed to me, his voice making hardly any more sound than the ripple of the water over a bed of moss, a voice so attuned to the voices of nature that it never seems to startle a wild creature.

I asked him just what he thought we should do. This business of leaving one's bed at four o'clock, coming three miles up a great river in the dark, and then landing on Mound Ridge, a place too forbidding to most people, seemed to me to call for a rather definite course of action. To sit on a log, even a good log in good turkey country, and wait for an old swamp master to come to you, is almost as barren of hope as trusting that your mother-in-law will adore you. But long years of countless hunting experiences with this same dusky Negro had given me faith in him.

"Let's look and listen a while," he told me softly.

The first thing I heard was a slithering sound under my feet. Prince nonchalantly mashed a copperhead into the hard ground with the massive heel of his tramp-steamer foot.

"He done come right out dis log," he said (referring to the one we were sitting on). "Maybe there might be a fambly in it."

I heard the voices of scores of birds familiar to me, and the chattering of the gray squirrels was almost incessant. At one time there were eighteen within sight. Day broadened now, touching with a tender and dreamlike radiance the lonely reaches of white marsh, the somber cypresses, the giant water-oaks and sweet gums that towered nearly two hundred feet. Wild hogs we heard, and the strange scream of an eagle. I thought that, as far as turkeys were concerned, our effort was a bust. Prince evidently did not share my growing disappointment. He sat hulked like one of Rodin's statues.

"Shall I call?" I asked him.

"No sah. Wait till I hear one come down."

On a clear warm morning, wild turkeys usually come to ground about sunrise. On rainy cold mornings I have known them to stay on the roost until nine o'clock. It was now nearly half-past seven, and the sun was coming up. The day was slowly rising.

While I was listening to the weird sweet whistling of wood ducks in a pond near by, a hand like a haunch of venison but now as gentle in its touch as a spiderweb, was laid on my sleeve.

"I done see one," said Prince.

He said no more, but pointed to a spot some eighty feet up in a water-oak, and out of gunshot from me. In our Carolina coastal country the water-oak carries its foliage all winter, and this tree had not only a dense crown of leaves, but was veiled in heavy Spanish moss as well. I felt that Prince was pointing vainly. Of course, in looking for a wild turkey on a tree, a man should always look for what does not belong there. By observing this rule he will not be likely to shoot down mistletoe, or moss, or gnarled limbs instead of a great bird.

After spending several minutes in careful scrutiny of the swamp giant, I turned to Prince, confessing to him that his eyesight was better than mine.

"Look on number seven limb, right hand side, 'way up; then watch dat head turning against the light."

These were specific directions, and I followed them. When once I made out the gobbler, I could not understand why I had not seen him before. Huge and black, he bulked against the radiant sky. But it is one thing to see a wild turkey in a tree and quite another to get him. The hunter has about the same chance as an office boy, who meets his millionaire boss's daughter, has of eloping with her. There's some chance, but slender, old-timers, mighty slender, indeed.

Red over the whispering rim of the marsh came the sun, its long lances flaming into the mouldering heart of the mighty swamp. They lighted up the gobbler on the oak. He stood upright on the limb, craned his neck, then launched himself earthward. I knew that he had not seen me, and I had hoped when he came down for breakfast that he would come my way. But his flight took him toward the delta, and I heard him alight heavily in a desolate field of white marsh, three hundred yards away.

No sooner had his splendid form dipped downward than Prince was on his feet, straining his eyes. I believe he could have walked within ten feet of where the old bird came down.

"Now, Cap'n, now!" he said.

"Now what?" I asked, dumbly.

"Go to him as fast as you can without makin' no noise. When you gone halfway, sit down and call. But only call once. He's an old gobbler, and if you call any mo' dan once, he ain't comin'. Hurry, Cap'n. Don't call but once."

Well, boys, I'd like you sometime to try hurrying across Mound Ridge without making a noise. Centuries of dead leaves cover the ground. The heaped refuse left by great floods is everywhere. Also, there is the kind of mud that makes a racket like a wheezy suction pump every time you pull your feet out of it. But I obeyed my good Prince. I got perhaps a hundred yards, almost down to the edge of the vast field of marsh into which the gobbler had gone. Then I subsided on a mossy log, being careful to have in front of me a cluster of fan-palmettoes. They make perfect natural blinds.

Getting out my call, my Miss Seduction as I have named her, I touched it four times, rapidly and loudly, as if another gobbler had come to ground and was signaling number one. Of course, in the mating season, it is nothing to call a gobbler to you. Before it was against the law, nearly all the old birds were killed in this way. But in the winter it is difficult. Usually a gobbler pays no attention then to a call. Rarely will he answer. Occasionally he will bear your way without answering. But if he is just off the roost, and lonesome, he may call, and do so with a stridency that is startling. A few seconds after the notes from my willow box had sounded through the swamp, two hundred yards ahead of me, from the heart of the watery marsh, the old swamp king set up the noisiest gabble you ever heard. He called and called. Lazy sovereign, he wanted the other fellow to come to him. Sorely was I tempted to call again, but behind me, I knew, Prince would be listening to discover whether I had obeyed orders. The turkey's clamor kept up for three or four minutes. To make me more uneasy than I was, far up the bank of Flag Creek I heard another bird calling. But a wild turkey is full of curiosity, and, like that of a deer, it often betrays him.

The calling in front of me stopped. I had no way of knowing if the business was all over or whether some history was in the offing. Getting soggily down on one knee behind the palmettoes, with my cocked gun all ready, I waited. The birds sang. The squirrels chattered. Wild hogs grunted in the marsh. I began to feel about as full of hope as a suitor who has just been given the air. But a faint rustling of the marsh ahead of me caught my attention. I saw a shape that looked gray. Was it only a razorback? Then I heard steps in the watery morass. I was on the brink of the ridge, the marsh, thirty yards away.

If this was game coming, my time would be just as it cleared the marsh. Now I heard the comer, and now I didn't; now he vanished; then I caught an indistinct glimpse of him. Out of a little hedge of dwarf canes he stepped, a regal wild gobbler in all his glory. I sometimes think game has a sense that we do not understand. Often, when I knew that I was not seen, heard, or winded, game has suddenly become alert, even terrified, at my proximity. No sooner had the gobbler showed himself than he gave a hasty "put" of alarm, and, from the way he looked, I knew that he was either about to take wing or else to skulk back hot-footedly into the wild marsh.

I drove him where he stood. He never knew who heaved the brick. In a moment Prince was with me. He walked on mud as a ski-walker crosses snow. Slowly we retrieved the noble bird. Not a feather was ruffled. The

Mound Ridge turkeys are as pure a strain of the true wild bird as one will find anywhere. This one was all bronze and gleaming iridescence. Together in triumph we made our way back to the boat. Prince had told me that there were twenty-seven; we had killed only one, and that one fairly. Perhaps he did not belong in the flock, but was a lone old champion.

I have said that there is magic about Mound Ridge, that beautiful and desolate wilderness below the great Santee Swamp in South Carolina. Occasionally it is visited by black bears. At times, millions of mallards and black ducks, teal and widgeon resort to its lonely waters to feed on acorns. Wild boars are there also, and deadly serpents, minks and otters, woodcock and Wilson's snipe; and America's premier game bird, the wild turkey. I guess I almost forgot the deer; the Ridge is alive with them, and some of the bucks are burly old boys. Perhaps the magic of the place consists in the fact that the hunter there, so surrounded is he by the variety and the abundance of game, rarely knows for what kind to load his gun.

I claim that in these days any such hunting ground has magic in it. And it is likely to retain it for a long time, for, while accessible, it is hard to reach, and when you get there, you wonder where you are. As for getting caught there in the night,—well, I share Prince's feelings: he said that after dark Mound Ridge is a "man-stand-back place."

THE WRONG GOBBLER

You may remember that my good Negro Steve has a favorite prayer that I have fallen into the habit of using myself, and its beauty and all-inclusive nature are best understood if one will remember how Negro cabins have a habit of staggering when they attempt to stand. Says Steve feelingly, "O Lord, prop me up in all my leaning places!" I find myself repeating this prayer whenever I get in a tight spot, especially in the big woods, as I did on that memorable February morning when I found myself amid a disconcerting number of wild turkeys.

It's a man's job at any time to handle skilfully one wild turkey; but when they start simultaneously coming to you from every direction, calling at every step, as if you were some fatal siren and they were poor human beings, why, I say it's being in a jam for sure. It almost makes a hunter feel that, instead of being after them, they are after him.

The afternoon before, on the advice of Steve, I had gone with him to Hampton Island, a wild area of some six hundred acres that is a part of my plantation. As it is little more than waste rice-fields and overgrown banks, and little better than a watery wilderness, I rarely visit it. One reason why I am not keen about this hunting territory is because it is infested, at all seasons, with cotton-mouth moccasins, and these truculent devils take much of the sport out of hunting. But wild turkeys are on the island, and when food is plentiful they never leave it. So perfectly do they adapt themselves to that marshy and semi-submerged waste land that they may be said to have become semi-aquatic, for often they spend the entire day in the reedlands and tawny morasses, returning to the timbered ridges only to roost.

During the late hunting season, so uniformly unsuccessful had I been with wild turkeys that I had set my dusky woodsmen on their trail. If they are in the land of the living, Steve will find them; moreover, as they pay small attention to him, he never really scares them. It is a fact, at least in my country, that wild game is invariably less afraid of a Negro than it is of a white man.

From *Field & Stream*, November 1941. Later included in *Hunter's Choice* (1945).

Steve shambles amiably along, and deer and turkeys consider him harmless; he is, except that he relays news of their presence to me. It was so on this occasion. He said that he had been hunting hogs on the island (anybody's hogs) and had come across fresh turkey tracks in the old rice-field mud.

Here on the Carolina coast, along the great delta of the Santee, vast areas of former rice-lands are overgrown to white marsh, duck-oats, wampee, wild rice, smartweed, and other aquatic foods. In almost impenetrable cover like this most of our turkeys spend the day. In addition to the foods supplied by the natural growths, they get a lot that is drifted in by the tides. In the late winter, when most of the acorns and other seeds are gone, they feed much on the young green of springing plants. I have killed a gobbler of the marsh in late February that had in his crop nothing but young marsh blades and wampee leaves.

Hopefully Steve and I ranged the island that afternoon, and I did see all the turkey sign a man could wish for. There were tracks innumerable, droppings under the great cypresses and water-oaks, and on some of the ridges and banks whole acres of dead leaves were raked up in long windrows. For two hours we sat still, trying to roost a bird. But we neither saw nor heard a thing except countless gray squirrels and thousands of mallards coming in to the marsh to feed during the night.

At dim dusk we pushed our boat across the river and landed on the old Wambaw Bank, a huge earthen structure of pre-Revolutionary days, still strong and intact, and now grown to trees of immense size. We had hardly left the boat for our walk home when, right over my head, from out of a towering moss-shrouded cypress a gobbler pitched. He was closely followed by another. I did not see either one; but there was no mistaking what they were, and we could tell what direction they had taken.

I knew they would not fly far, and I knew they would alight in trees rather than on the ground, for when flushed from the roost at twilight a wild turkey usually makes an absurdly short fly and never alights on the ground. He may alight in a bare tree, presumably because he can see the branches. I have known a whole flock of sixteen, disturbed at dark, to fly not more than seventy-five yards. Taking Steve's arm, I whispered to him not to say a word, and we tiptoed away from the place. Under such circumstances, a hunt at daylight is the thing.

Let me add that, as far as my observation goes, of late years the turkeys are roosting more warily than they used to. Heretofore I often found them in comparatively bare trees, with perhaps a little mistletoe or moss in them; but now, for their abode for the night, they appear to choose the most densely shrouded cypresses and yellow pines, trees so heavily hung with moss that I have repeatedly stood under one of them, knowing a turkey to be above me, yet also being unable to make him out. I believe our turkeys travel considerable distances to discover trees suitable to their taste for roosting.

When we had gone far enough to make it safe to talk, I told Steve that by daybreak we should be back under the tree from which the two gobblers had been flushed. Thus it was that, while we got home with empty hands, we had a lot of hope in our hearts.

We left the house at 5:30 that mild February morning to walk the mile and a half to the magic spot we had in mind. There should be, I knew, more than those two turkeys that we had flushed. It was still, warm, and very beautiful in the woods, which were awakening to light and to life. I spend much of my time abroad in the wilderness at this hour and at twilight, for one can see and hear things then that he will never see or hear during the garish hours of sunlight.

In the dim swamp that sloped away from the old wooded bank toward the river I began to look for a suitable place for calling. Such a place is hard to find. I mean that the turkey caller should not be too much in the open (so much, for example, that even a slight movement on his part will be detected by an approaching turkey) yet not so hidden that he has a difficult time seeing what is coming. It is important which way he faces, for if one of these great birds is headed your way the slightest noise or movement will make him suddenly and radically change his mind.

At last I decided to sit at the base of a huge cypress, with my back to it, and about thirty yards from the tree on which the gobblers had gone to roost the night before. Steve, who had been shambling stealthily behind me, nodded approval of my selection of a stand, and eased off into the gross swamp. I had to smile when I saw him sit down against a black pine stump, a background that rendered him practically invisible.

Immediately before me was a thin screen of wild blackberry canes, with shielding moss draped over them. Just behind this screen was a small hardwood ridge. Behind me was a muddy swamp, densely grown to willows and alders. I know that it is sometimes bad policy to sit with one's back against a tree, but in this case I decided to face toward the place where the two gobblers had flown.

By the time I got settled, day began to dawn, all pearly and pink through the silent swamp, gradually tingeing everything with a roseate fairy light. Then, curiously, I heard a whippoorwill, for that bird is excessively rare here in the spring. Cardinals awoke, and Carolina wrens gave their rollicking calls; marsh-hens cackled raucously from across the river, and chickadees began to radio their companions. Light was coming fast.

Taking out my beloved call, Miss Seduction, I touched her gently.

Thinking at that time that I heard a slight noise behind me, I eased up cautiously to look. As I did so a masterly gobbler flew out of the cypress against which I had been leaning! He had been there all the time, camouflaged by the heavy moss, but I had not suspected his presence.

Especially in the dusk of the morning, a wild turkey will sometimes let you walk up under him; and this is commonly true if he thinks he is pretty well hidden. A wild thing enjoys as much as a human being a sense of security; give him this, and he will not rush away at your coming. I have walked within fifteen feet of an old buck curled up in dense brush.

Well, I thought, there are three big boys in this vicinity. I heard this latest gobbler come to ground far behind me; and, believe me, a big one can sometimes make a lot of racket doing that. I did not know whether I had disturbed him or whether he had come down of his own accord. As soon as he was on the ground I called again, at the same time looking at my watch. It was 6:40. I glanced off to my right and happened to see good old Steve, silent and inscrutable, trusting me. I must try not to disappoint him.

At that moment a thunderous sound came from the island—a long, low roar. The mallards and black ducks were leaving the marshes for a day in the salt creeks and bays down the river. For several minutes this little earthquake continued. Then all was still. Suddenly, behind me and a good way up the creek bank on my left, I heard a turkey. I answered softly, cajolingly. Oh, man! The whole country was full of turkeys! I heard them on every side of me. And they just happened to be in the right mood for calling.

I knew at once that this must be a good-sized flock, of which I had seen but three. The calm morning, the still wilderness, their own slight and unalarmed separation—all these conspired to make them loquacious. Suddenly, from across the river, a gobbler came straight for me. But he was flying well above the tall tree-tops, and I did not want to spoil everything by risking a most uncertain shot at him. But he was a grand sight, sailing high through the red dawn on those wide and splendid wings of his. He went over my head and alighted on the Wambaw Bank in a high water-oak, about two hundred yards behind me.

I heard four or five calling from the river bank on my left. Two were calling from the island immediately across from me. I heard one far behind me. Then one tuned up right in front of me. There were too darned many turkeys!

I glanced at Steve. The whites of his eyes were slowly rolling. Gently and coaxingly I touched Miss Seduction. I felt certain of an early chance to shoot. But in hunting this great bird almost everything is unpredictable. I have known a wild turkey to give a hunter a chance by making a stupid break; but he would be a foolish man who counted on his bronzed majesty's making a mistake. When it comes to blundering, a wild turkey isn't in a class with a man.

As soon as the gobbler in front of me began to call softly yet clearly, and I heard the turkey in the tree behind me calling him, I decided to quit my cajoling. I would concentrate on the one coming straight for me. It's all right to call a turkey; but if you really want one to come, let another of his kind call him for you. I knew that the turkey in front of me was coming right out to me, and might step from the shelter of the swamp at any minute.

I put up my gun. At such a time a man should have his gun at his shoulder; for if he waits to make that motion until the great bird is in sight, things may happen to make the hunter kick himself all the way home. For one thing, a wary gobbler is almost certain to vanish before the hopeful hunter can shoot—or at least before he can shoot with the accuracy essential in killing this finest of all game birds of the world.

So there was the layout: Old Steve rolling his eyes like a drunken gorilla; some six or seven birds now calling behind me—two across the river on my left; one straight in front of me—and all their yelps indicated that Miss Seduction had them in her power. They were closing in on me from every direction. And there was I, sitting flat, my call beside me, my gun up and ready for action.

I knew well enough that if I shot, the whole business of calling would be over for a long time. I only hoped that the rajah of the river bottoms was the bird coming straight for me. I had it all arranged very nicely. As soon as he showed himself I would collect him and go home in serene triumph. But weird things happen in the big woods, things which, years later, the hunter remembers with an "ouch."

While I was concentrating on the ridge before me, without a sound to warn me, a big gobbler walked up behind me, right up to my tree, and started to walk past me—not an inch farther than three feet from me, and on my right. He had come through the swamp on the soft mud, and he hadn't made a sound.

Turkeys make a lot of noise when they are in the water—almost as much as deer—but the approach of this bird had been noiseless. The first thing I knew of his presence was his great head stuck around the tree; then, "Kut! Kut!" in wild alarm. And just as I saw him out of the corner of my right eye I made out a black shape ahead of me, but dimly outlined in the fringes of marsh that lined the swamp edges. He was the gobbler on which I had designs, but this other old boy had broken into the picture. And I knew that one "Kut!" of his would change the whole aspect of things.

As soon as he saw me he jerked back and then made a prodigious leap that was half flying. He didn't run and didn't fly; but he made a marvelous slashing high jump that took him back and away to the left toward the creek bank. Meanwhile the gobbler ahead of me had vanished; and any man who knows turkeys knows that my chances of seeing that gentleman again were slight.

But the big bird that had, as you might say, been eating out of my right-hand pocket stopped within range, though partly shielded by stout alder stems. So silent and spectral he stood that if I had not seen him go there I would hardly have been able to make him out. Without lowering my gun, I swung it slowly around until I got the ivory bead on him. Since he had sounded the alarm, I was not counting on seeing any other turkeys. I touched the trigger, and one of the old monarchs of Wambaw was down to stay.

Of the ten or twelve other turkeys near me when I shot, I heard not a sound. After I had retrieved my grand bird, a 20-pound bird of the purest wild stock left in North America, Steve and I began our triumphant march homeward just as the rising sun was turning the broomsedge field of gold.

Said Steve, "Sometimes it is harder to kill a turkey when there is a plenty than when there is only one."

As I looked at the old strategist of the wilds slung over Steve's broad and patient shoulders I was satisfied, even though I had killed the wrong gobbler. The one that was coming straight for me will never know how close a call he had, nor how it happened that one of his own mates saved his life.

The Lady Was Kind

Some time ago I regaled the boys with a story entitled "Great Misses I Have Made," a piece in which I, with great candor, gave an account of some of my misadventures as a hunter. It might be as interesting to look at the reverse: to tell of certain of those times when Lady Luck was willing to be more than kind—when she acted like a girl who does the proposing.

Now, I do not want you to think that in these true tales I am setting myself up as a regular Deadeye Dick of a shot. You will soon discover for yourself that I personally had little to do with my extraordinary good fortune. And if you ask me how I happened to come home with far more than my share, my answer would be, "The Lady was kind."

While I was away from my plantation in South Carolina for most of the summer I kept getting frequent reports from Prince, my Negro foreman, of the game situation there. He had a lot to tell me about the deer; and as far as I could make out, I had apparently planted crops for them to harvest. He wrote me that whole herds would come into the peafield before dark. Deer have to be plentiful, tame and hungry not to remain nocturnal in their habits.

On the last day of October I arrived on the plantation to spend the winter, reaching there in the late afternoon. After I had unpacked the car, I loaded my gun and strolled down the avenue, a half-mile long, toward the woods. The avenue was flanked on either side by the big peafield in which the deer had been banqueting every night. In the sandy road I could see hundreds of tracks, most of them fresh. While most Negroes will lie just to please me, Prince had not lied. Big things had been going on here.

By the time I came within a hundred yards of the woods, the sun was down. But it had been a clear sunset, and a radiant afterglow suffused the whole world. Besides, at that time of year in the deep South, the foliage of the forest is at its height of color, and at sunrise and sunset the woods seem quietly ablaze. The leaves had not begun to fall.

From *Field & Stream*, June 1942. Later included in *Hunter's Choice* (1946).

To the left of the gate that is on a line with the edge of the woods, there is an especially dense thicket. Walking slowly, I was now within about sixty yards of it; that is, within gunshot. What was that yonder in the heavy patch of dogwoods and high-bush huckleberries? I couldn't really see body or legs. But I saw horns. Surely a buck, standing motionless there. He hadn't been hunted for ten months. For weeks he had fed in my field with impunity. Here I came down the sandy road, making no sound. Perhaps he did not even see me; certainly he never winded me.

Trying to walk up to an old buck is most uncertain business. Just as soon as I really made him out, I got my gun into position, at the same time edging a few feet forward. I probably was fifty yards from him when I shot. He acted as if lightning had struck him in the head. I saw him sink down, and I saw the glint of his horns as he lay dead on the ground. But I saw something else: a second buck, that before this I had not seen at all, jumped off as the first one fell. How close he had been standing to the first one, I do not know; but two old bucks that are consorting have a way of standing close together.

Slowly I walked over to the fallen stag. He was a fine one, and stone-dead. Somewhat idly I pushed my way through the fringe of the thicket, my gun ready. I was rather sure the second buck was gone; but sometimes when one falls, his comrade will stand around for some time. More than once I have seen two bucks running together; when one of them was killed, the other would stop.

A lot of wild creatures do not understand the meaning of the sound of a gun. In their natural haunts in the forest there are many familiar sounds loud enough to startle them, such as the fall of a tree. They don't like noises; they don't like a gun. But I often think they dislike it as a noise rather than as a gun.

In the twilight, on the open pond-edge beyond the thicket, I didn't see any wary buck waiting for his boy friend to join him. Of course, I was looking for a deer standing up, unharmed and ready to bound away into the dusky forest. I wasn't prepared to see what I saw: the second buck lying dead between two cypresses on the edge of the pond! He too was a fine animal, and had been killed by two buckshot that had struck him high up in the back.

It is fifty years since I began to hunt deer; but nothing like this had ever happened to me before, nor is it likely ever to happen again. A hole-in-one is the ambition of every golfer. Well, this sort of thing is like putting a golf ball into two holes at the same time.

In my country, along the great delta of the Santee, especially in the lower reaches adjacent to the ocean, there are a good many duck hawks in the winter. While I take a certain kind of delight in their power and grace of flight, their perfection of physical stamina, unabated through the long centuries, and even in the swift certainty with which they take their prey, I must admit that they are very destructive. They are one of the few species, even among the predators, that kill for the lust of blood; they kill more than they need for their own immediate use. There is a primal and savage splendor about a duck hawk, but he is a merciless killer.

At daylight one morning, some years ago, I was shooting ducks in that delta land, not far from the mouth of the river. A Negro was paddling me for jump-shooting through the mazy creeks and the old rice-field canals of the marshy wilderness. Every now and then my paddler, who knew about all that one ever learns about ducks, and who frequently advised me from the stern of the canoe, was given to muttering to himself, as if what he wished to express would be beyond my understanding. So when I heard him saying softly to himself, "Dat's too bad," I asked him what was too bad.

"I done see a duck hawk ahead of we; and where you see him, dat's bad. Look yonder now," he added as mallards and sprigs climbed the sky from the peaceful field. "He's coming dis way."

Up to that time I had not shot my gun, and it looked as if this marauder was going to ruin the morning's sport. If he came anywhere near, I would salute him. As the marsh was high on either side of the creek, and as the tide was rather low, I stood up in the canoe—a risky thing to attempt.

I was no sooner in that position than I saw a mallard drake flying straight for me, coming low and coming faster than I had ever seen a duck fly. He looked like a shell that had been shot out of a gun, and I was his target. I thought there was a second duck immediately behind him. I thought of the duck hawk, but there was not much time to think. Things were happening fast.

The drake could not have been more than twenty yards from me when I fired at him, head on, and his momentum was such that I had to dodge his hurtling body as it fell into the creek beside the canoe. Hardly had it struck the water when there was a second splash, and the duck hawk lay beside the drake he had been pursuing.

I claim no credit for anything. It just happened, and at that moment Lady Luck was very kind. I had one duck toward the day's bag, and I had the general disturber of the peace.

While I have never made any deliberate attempt to do so, I have more than once killed a good many flying quail at one shot. On the edge of a wheatfield in Pennsylvania, early in the season, a huge covey of quail got up on my right and circled around to my left to reach a patch of woods.

There were more than twenty birds, and they were not only flying bunched, but with curious deliberation. I felt certain of a double, and really didn't want to kill more than one barrel. But from that one shot I picked up eleven quail, and they were fine, full-grown birds. I did not honestly enjoy this experience; the Lady had gone too far in her generosity.

Another time, while coming down the mountain in the dusk, after a weary and fruitless grouse hunt, I heard a little scurry on the dead leaves. I was beside an old clearing near the foot of the mountain. Between me and the clearing there was a narrow but dense fringe of bushes and trees. The only real opening was a curious big hole through the heavy top of a red cedar, just such an opening as is made by the boys who string telephone wires. But there were no wires here. Although the light was low in the woods, I was facing the west, and the sunset sky was still bright behind the opening in the cedar boughs.

Almost as soon as I heard the noise in the leaves, a big covey of these mountain quail got up, and I thought at first that they were going clear over the fringe of trees. I really could not make them out in the shadows of the woods. By instinct I brought my gun up to the opening in the cedar, and the whole covey converged into it. In that perfect concert which is one of the wonders of the flight of birds, they closed ranks and tore together through that funnel.

I just shot at the sky through the opening; and in the edge of the old field beyond the cedar I picked up six of those husky birds. They were, of course, true bob-whites; but when they live in the mountains, they seem to get larger and heavier. This curious piece of luck not only made my feeble alibi unnecessary, but it supplied me with a good story to tell, all the better because it was true.

Next to giving a friend a shot at a fine buck, one of the hardest things for me to do in the woods has always been to get a wild turkey for some one on a given date. I think it is the poet Browning who laments that we never get "the time and the place and the loved one all together." He, of course, was writing about human lovers; but the same thing is true when the loved and coveted one happens to be a wild turkey.

I have an old friend in Charleston who used to be a great hunter, but for years now he has been an invalid. About a week before Christmas he wrote to ask me whether I could possibly get him a wild gobbler for Christmas dinner. Now, that's a real order in these days. This business of timing the killing of wild game in the howling wilderness is a master problem. To complicate it in this case, my wife had also ordered wild turkey for Christmas. I was pretty hopeful about getting one; but two wild gobblers at the same time are about twenty times as hard to get as one. Well, here's what happened, and I had really little to do with the way in which it turned out.

I knew where some turkeys were using, and it was within long walking distance of the plantation house. After dinner one day, at the critical period when I had to make good or go down in family history as an utter failure, I took my gun and slunk off into the woods. When it's turkeys you're after, you've got to slink. The woods into which I went are fairly open; there are plenty of oaks and pines, and here and there are big cypresses, growing on the borders of deep woodland ponds. Between the ponds are game trails.

It has been my experience that both deer and turkeys like to hang around water. Looking over the situation, I finally decided that I stood my best chance if I just picked a good spot, sat down, and kept perfectly quiet. This kind of hunting has the advantage of being both restful and strategic. A man may happen to walk up to a wild turkey (his chances are best if the turkey happens to be deaf!) but the real game is to let the old boy come to you.

I sat on a cypress log, partly screened by a growth of blackberry canes. All the leaves were now down; the woods looked bare; there was no wind. It was an ideal time for hearing footsteps in the forest. I had not been waiting long when I saw great blue herons, weird anhingas, a raccoon on the edge of one of the ponds; but so far there was no game. A covey of quail trooped by me, feeding and talking. But I was listening for the manlike walk of a wild gobbler. A deer, because of his four feet, makes a shuffling sound in the dead leaves when he walks; but you'd think a turkey was a wary hunter approaching.

At last I heard what I had come to hear. And only a minute after I heard the sound I saw the great bird himself, looking very black and ponderous. He was going to walk the ridge between two of the small ponds. Unfortunately I was on a farther ridge. He would pass me, but it would be too far—perhaps a hundred and twenty yards. For a rifle, the shot would have been a perfect one.

This old bird was walking slowly, keeping close to the ground, just like a grouse, but every now and then straightening up to his startling height. What a bosom he had! And what a beard! He was one of these old swamp prophets. If I had seen him sooner, I might have dropped back and gotten over in front of his approach; but it would now be folly to move. Practically all the wild turkeys that are killed are turkeys that never see the hunter. To show yourself is to lose your chance.

As I was getting a little negative satisfaction out of admiring the splendor of this old monarch of the wilds I heard another sound. Glancing warily to one side. I saw a second old gobbler coming. This one must have been hungrier than the first one, for he was investigating the possibilities of food along the edge of the pond. He looked as if he might come within range.

The first bird had now passed me, heading for the jungle-like thickets along the river. I forgot him to give all my attention to his burly partner. Once, when he was busily scratching in the wet leaves, I got my gun up. On he came, but most deliberately. I had 2's in the left. When he got broadside, at perhaps sixty-five yards, and was as close as he would come, I knocked him down. He began a great floundering on the ground, and for a moment I sat still, waiting to see if he were really dead or whether, badly wounded, he would try to hide under the nearest brush pile. I have known a good many wounded wild turkeys to escape because the hunter ran in too hastily after the shot.

Rather idly I had loaded my gun again. By now the gobbler was still flopping, but not so wildly. Suddenly, to my amazement, while I was feeling certain that I had a fine bird for my friend, but that we would have to eat sausage for Christmas, the first gobbler came running back at full speed, jumped on his fallen and flapping comrade, and began beating him! You know how chickens act when you kill one and throw it down among them. For a second time within five minutes I eased up my gun; and when it spoke, two families had wild turkey for Christmas.

As to why the first bird, the one that had walked past me, had not been scared off by my first barrel, I can only say that as I intimated earlier, wild game is by no means always scared into flight by a gun. It is usually startled, but it may not attribute the noise to the presence of man.

So while I have made some great misses during my days as a hunter—and it would be monotonous not to miss occasionally—I have had my share of good fortune. And now and then the lady has been very kind.

Miss Seduction Struts Her Stuff

For many years I have had a positive superstition about luck on the last day—sometimes during the very last hour. A thrilling and possibly dramatic experience that I had on January 2, 1933, has confirmed me in this way of thinking. True, the affair did not happen on the last day of the wild turkey season in South Carolina, for that is February 28; but it was the last day for me, as I was scheduled to leave for the North early on the morning of January 3.

That summer an old wild turkey hen raised a flock of sixteen birds on my plantation. I had had reports of them, and high hopes were mine that they would still be there on my Christmas visit. But certain turkey-minded friends and neighbors anticipated me; and while they killed only one or two of the birds, they succeeded in utterly scattering and demoralizing the flock. All through the holidays I hunted for them. Their tracks were found in the sandy roads. I once heard a hen drowsily calling at daylight; once I saw one about half a mile down an old woodland trail. But nary a shot was mine.

These birds were genuinely wild in every sense of the word: of the ancient pure wild strain, with no admixture of domestic blood—lovely bronze plumage, black heads, pink legs and a general aspect of being tailor-made. They were so keen of sight and hearing as to be able to detect a wink or a whisper at shotgun range; so silent and canny as to make an attempt at stalking a ludicrous thing. You know the feeling that I had as the precious days passed: that the game was unquestionably there, but that it was too smart to permit me to come up with it.

Finally my last day came. While I had had excellent sport with ducks and deer, it looked as if I were going to be a total washout on the turkeys. However, at about four o'clock that afternoon, with the kindly Southern sun shining genially and with no wind stirring, my three boys and I decided to try the last chance.

From *Field & Stream*, January 1934.

Scattered groups of the birds had several times been reported to me by Negroes as crossing an old abandoned road—usually at about five o'clock in the afternoon, evidently on their way to roost in the great river-swamp. I had not been able to discover their bedroom, yet had a fair notion of where it likely was. I posted my boys on the road and then walked a half mile down the river-bank. My idea was to call a little in order to lure any lonely birds toward the standers posted in front of me. It sometimes happens that for weeks at a time wild turkeys will follow the same range, day after day.

At the place where I stopped, two old rice-field banks converged and met the bank of the river. It seemed a strategic spot, though I had never tried it before. All about me were giant cypresses, softly alight in the rays of the setting sun; lonely abandoned rice-fields, grown head-high in marsh; solitary pines; thickets of cane and alder and birch. Except for the firm footing on the leaf-strewn banks, the country was very wet. As I sat down to call I heard a deer tramping round in the marsh across the river, gray squirrels barking and scuttling about on the leaves, wild ducks hurrying toward the delta, and the big owls beginning their weird hooting.

At a moment when some of these sounds abated, I touched my call.

This call is one of many I have made. Most of them have had faults of tone—either squeakiness, of a tone too high-pitched, or sounding more like something else than a turkey, or prone to emit a sudden false note that is always bad news for a turkey hunter. But on account of the depth, certainty and mellow tone of this particular box, I had christened her Miss Seduction. I have tested her many times, and I have found that she will do almost anything except actually kill my gobbler for me. On several occasions she has embarrassed me by calling up old turkey hunters to me. I like them, but there's a closed season on them.

For many years I have experimented with making box calls for turkeys from all kinds of woods. Red cedar I have rejected on account of the shallowness of its tone and its inclination to squeak; seasoned poplar is excellent, as is Western fir; dried maple and holly are good. I like willow best because of the quality of the wood, the smooth texture and high tension of the grain, and the mellow tone that can be drawn from such a box. Soft chalk is always applied to the calling-lip of the box and is used to cover the slate caller as well. I have made box calls with the shuffling tops, but the other type is handier and has been more effective for me. It seems a general principle that the best tone is to be had from a wood of medium hardness, such as chestnut or willow. If the wood is too hard, the qualities of depth and vibrancy will be absent.

To call a turkey one will perhaps do best if he will put himself in the place of the bird and will call in such a manner that, if he were the bird, he would come. A great many things are to be considered: the time of day (of course, they call best just after and just before roosting); the condition of the atmosphere (a windy day is bad, and a rainy day not so good); the place from which the calling is done, for it should be of such a character that the bird would naturally haunt it; and then the calling itself, which is a thing to be learned rather than told of.

I may say, however, that an amateur will call too often, too loudly and with too little variation in the tone. A wild turkey is a patrician, and he does not appreciate any member of his tribe's overflowing and drowning him with too much gushing. Of course, in the mating season few birds are more garrulous than wild gobblers. But in the hunting season they are almost as silent and non-committal as they are wary.

During the next twenty minutes I called about seven times. It pays not to be too urgent. Unless I am mistaken, it is the long, sweet pleading quality of the first note that usually does the work. I had had no answer; but, as every experienced hunter knows, a wild turkey will often come silently to a call. Some answer and come. Some answer and do not come. Some do not answer and come. Some never answer and never come. Some come running; some flying; some walking fast; some stealing along furtively. I have had an old gobbler come within thirty yards of me from behind before I detected his approach.

Down went the sun, suffusing the wild, sweet world with a golden afterglow. I had heard no gun from my standers. It looked about all over. But suddenly I heard a great commotion in the marsh across the river. At first I thought it must surely be a deer jumping in to swim across. Yet when I turned quickly to look, there came a splendid gobbler, flying almost straight for my call. I knew that I ought to get my gun up while he was flying; because if a wild turkey is on the ground near you, the matter of getting your gun on him is just one of those critical things that is awfully hard to maneuver. In the two seconds that it takes you to put it on him, he's going to be executing the greatest vanishing act you ever saw.

Fifty yards from the river-bank the glistening king of the swamplands set his wings and sailed, alighting high and dry about thirty-five yards from me. I made a clean kill with 4's. Miss Seduction had done her work. In forty years of hunting this was the first time I had ever called a wild turkey across a river. And any hunter can easily understand the thrill I got out of it—especially since it was sundown on my last day.

It is not usually worth while to call from the same place after a shot has been made there. But I love the river and the swamp in those mystic fading lights, and there might be a bare chance for more sport.

Sundown on a plantation has many compensations even if a hunter never shoots his gun. Winter there is kindly, and the coming of dusk does not mean a consequent fall in temperature. A man may sit it out without getting chilled. About me were primeval woods, beautiful with the full-foliaged water-oaks and the moss-bannered cypresses. I could see a little way up the river the immense and shaggy live-oaks, whose small sweet acorns wild turkeys prefer to all other winter food. Not until they have harvested this crop will they turn to the somewhat bitter acorns of the water-oaks. They also relish the hard black seeds of the American lotus, black-gum berries, gallberries and the fruits of the wild greenbriar.

In the old days of baiting turkeys, before beneficent laws were passed against this practice, the birds would come almost equally well to corn, peas and rice. I once examined the crop of a wild turkey that had in it a mixture of salted almonds and whole snails! The former he must have gleaned from the waste of some hunter's luncheon; the latter he probably ate, partly for the food value and partly for the grit in the shell.

It was now very dusky in the swamp. The river appeared wan and mysterious. Far up the stream I could see the lights of home shining in the twilight. Once more I touched Miss Seduction. It really seemed too late; yet while I have known some wild turkeys to take the roost long before sundown, I have known others to delay their retiring until it was almost too dark to see a limb on which to perch.

On the farther side of the old wooded bank coming down through the middle of the swamp, I had heard a brown thrasher scuffling in the leaves. This sound grew a little loud and unfamiliar. Save for his keen head, this turkey was completely hidden by the bank. But he was only thirty-five yards away, and coming closer. At the range which he had already reached, I would not have been afraid to try a chance at his head alone; but I had no shells save the two in my gun, and they were loaded with buckshot. All my turkey-shot, save the lone 4's I had already fired, I had given to my boys. Now, a man stands a beautiful chance of missing a wild turkey with buckshot, whatever the range; and to shoot at his head with buckshot is almost certainly to miss him.

The gobbler would pass me on my left. The old bank, behind the shelter of which he was walking, was perhaps of more advantage to me than to him, for I waited for him to get his head behind the bank and then got my gun up, leveling it through a small break in the dyke, across the aperture of which his majesty would pass.

The west was barely glimmering with the last streaks of day and the dusk in the swamplands was almost night when the great gobbler suddenly filled the opening in the bank. I could barely discern the white sight of my gun against his dark and splendid form. I touched the trigger, and immediately stood up.

What I saw was a big gobbler with a broken wing running for the tall marsh as if a dozen wildcats were after him on wings. I could not really lay the gun on him right, but I let drive with my last shell in his direction. Silence profound settled over the river and the swamp. It was my last shot of the hunting year.

A few minuts later I found my second gobbler, killed by a single buckshot in the neck. With my two wild turkeys over my shoulder, I was soon on the homeward road, along dim starlit paths, familiar to me since boyhood days, toward the old home that has always been to me a beloved sort of shrine for a thousand memories of the river, the pinelands, the broomgrass fields, the brooding solitary swamps and all their wonderful inhabitants.

BIBLIOGRAPHY

Although Rutledge dearly loved turkey hunting, virtually nothing has been written dealing with his involvement in the sport. To my knowledge there is only one published article bearing specifically on this aspect of his multifaceted career. This is my own "Fall Turkey Wisdom from the Old Masters" in *South Carolina Game & Fish* (November 1992, pp. 24–27, 52–53). This article looks at Rutledge's writings and turkey-hunting techniques along with those of another old master of the sport in the Palmetto State, Henry Edwards Davis of Florence.

Mention of Davis calls forth a tidbit of bibliographical information worth noting. As most students of the literature of wild-turkey hunting know, Davis was the author of what is arguably the single finest treatment of the sport ever written, *The American Wild Turkey* (Plantersville, SC: Small-Arms Technical Publishing Company, 1949). Details on Davis and his book can be found in my article "Henry E. Davis: A Turkey Hunter for All Seasons (*Turkey Call*, November/December, 1987, pp. 19–22) and in Brian R. Smith's *Samworth Books: A Descriptive Bibliography* (1990).

Interestingly, this was a book which Rutledge originally contracted to write. His agreement was with Thomas Samworth, the salty scion of the Small-Arms Technical Publishing Company and a man who carved for himself a secure niche in the annals of outdoor-book publishing. When Rutledge presented the completed manuscript of the book to Samworth, the latter found it unacceptable. Apparently Rutledge had compiled a collection of previously published turkey-hunting tales (quite similar to the present book) instead of writing an entirely original work. Samworth, of whom it could be charitably said that he was a stranger to diplomacy, let Rutledge know in no certain terms that he was unhappy with the collection.

Rutledge had already received an advance for the book, and he informed Samworth that the contractual agreement had never specified that he deliver an entirely original book. There matters stood, and the impasse was never resolved. In the end Samworth turned to Henry Edwards Davis, and Rutledge fans were denied a book which would have focused exclusively on one of Flintlock's favorite pursuits.

For those who are interested in more general information about Rutledge, pages 274–75 of the bibliography which concludes my *Tales of Whitetails: Archibald Rutledge's Great Deer-Hunting Stories* (1992) cover the relevant printed materials. The present bibliography is devoted exclusively to pieces by Rutledge that deal wholly or in large measure with wild turkeys. It has been compiled through consultation of all of his books, together with research in the major outdoor periodicals of the twentieth century. However, it should be noted that most of these periodicals are not indexed in standard reference sources such as *Reader's Guide*. Further complicating matters is the fact that complete runs of serials such as *Recreation* and *Outing* are rare, and this has meant that in many instances, even with help from some devoted collectors of sporting periodicals, my research has gaps. Then too, Rutledge wrote on turkeys (and dozens of other subjects) in such a wide range of magazines—publications for boys, scientific journals, those intended for general readers, and the like—that oversights are inevitable.

In spite of these considerations, the fact remains that the entries below offer a reasonably comprehensive listing of Rutledge's writings on wild turkeys. Certainly they suffice to give ample indication of Rutledge's abiding interest in the subject. The careful reader will note that there are more stories here that were never incorporated into books than was the case with Rutledge's writings on deer hunting, listed in the bibliography to *Tales of Whitetails*. The likely explanation of this is that interest in turkey hunting during Rutledge's most prolific years as a writer was not particularly widespread. He was at the height of his powers before one of this century's great wildlife management success stories—restoration of the wild turkey—became an accomplished fact, and publishers were less likely to accept stories on America's big game bird than those on other game animals.

In the list that follows where multiple publications are know, all are identified. Rutledge routinely made minor revisions in his stories when they made the transition from the pages of magazines to books.

The editor would appreciate additions to the bibliography.

"An Adventurous Day," *Hunter's Choice* (1946), pp. 200–205. Only the last portion of this piece, pp. 203–205, deals with turkey hunting.

"Ain't a God's Turkey," *American Rifleman*, August 1948, pp. 43–44. With minor revisions this piece appeared as "My Favorite Hunting Story," in *Those Were the Days* (1955), pp. 50–55, and was republished with this title in Jim Casada, ed., *Hunting & Home in the Southern Heartland: The Best of Archibald Rutledge* (1992), pp. 41–45.

"Any One's Turkey," *Old Plantation Days* (1921), pp. 75–83. Later published as "Wash Loses a Turkey."

"Baby Turkeys," *Wild Life of the South* (1935), pp. 109–11.
"Beautiful Wings," *Wild Life of the South* (1935), pp. 202–5.
"Big Tom," *Field & Stream*, November 1931, pp. 26–27, 64. Later published as "Bronzed Mountaineers," in *An American Hunter* (1937), pp. 335–43.
"Big Toms in Big Timber," *An American Hunter* (1937), pp. 79–89.
"The Bishop Earns a Gobbler," *The Woods and Wild Things I Remember* (1970), pp. 59–67. Also in *Fireworks in the Peafield Corner* (1986), pp. 81–88. First published in *Sports Afield*, February 1956, pp. 56–59, 127–28.
"But He Is a Turkey Hunter," *Those Were the Days* (1955), pp. 264–69.
"Calling a Wild Gobbler," *Wild Life of the South* (1935), pp. 209–13.
"Can the Wild Turkey Survive?," *Fauna*, 3 (1941), pp. 93–95.
"Catching a Wild Turkey," *Wild Life of the South* (1935), pp. 128–31.
"Daybreak in the Ocean," *An American Hunter* (1937), pp. 192–99. Also in Lamar Underwood, ed., *Hunting the Southlands* (1986), pp. 63–69.
"Fireworks in the Peafield Corner," *An American Hunter* (1937), pp. 192–99. Also in *Fireworks in the Peafield Corner* (1986), pp. 59–65. First published in *Field & Stream*, December 1932, pp. 24–25, 62–63.
"Four Bearded Men," *Those Were the Days* (1955), pp. 177–83. First published in *Sports Afield*, May 1946, pp. 46–47, 126–29.
"Gil-Obble-Obble-Obble," *Those Were the Days* (1955), pp. 436–43. First published in *Outdoor Life*, March 1942, pp. 16–17, 76.
"Give It to the Big Bird," *Field & Stream*, November, 1924.
"The Gobbler of Lone Pine Ridge," *Outdoor Life/Outdoor Recreation*, December 1930, pp. 14–15, 68–69.
"The Great Bird Comes Back," *An American Hunter* (1937), pp. 367–77. First published in *Field & Stream*, December 1926, pp. 32–33, 85–86.
"The Great Gobbler of Path Valley," in the Rutledge Collection (mainly tearsheets and typescripts), South Caroliniana Library, University of South Carolina, Columbia, S.C.
"The Great King," *Virginia Quarterly Review*, 11 (1935), pp. 518–28.
"How to Get Your Gobbler," Rutledge Collection, University of South Carolina.
"Joel's Christmas Turkey," *Old Plantation Days* (1921), pp. 198–212.
"The Lady Was Kind," *Hunter's Choice* (1946). First published in *Field & Stream*, June 1942, pp. 12–13, 58–59. Also in *Hunting and Home in the Southern Heartland*, pp. 91–97.
"Magic on Mound Ridge," *Hunter's Choice* (1946), pp. 46–53.
"Make Room for the Turkey," *Outlook*, 134 (1923), pp. 25–27.
"Miss Seduction Struts Her Stuff," *Fireworks in the Peafield Corner* (1986), pp. 91–96. Also in *Field & Stream Reader* (1946), pp. 76–81, and in Hugh Grey and Ross McCluskey, eds., *Field & Stream Treasury* (1955), pp. 165–68. First published in *Field & Stream*, January 1934, pp. 22–23, 53–54.
"Monarchs of the River Swamps," *Those Were the Days* (1955), pp. 279–86.
"My Craziest Turkey Hunt," Rutledge Collection, University of South Carolina.
"My Favorite Hunting Story," *Those Were the Days* (1955), pp. 50–55. Also in Jim Casada, ed., *Hunting & Home in the Southern Heartland: The Best of Archibald Rutledge* (1992), pp. 41–45.

My 339th Gobbler," *Outdoor Life*, January 1956, pp. 52–53, 70–72.
"Oh, These Hunters!," *Hunter's Choice* (1946), pp. 13–24.
"The Old Bronzed Men of the Hills," *Outdoor Life*, September 1934, pp. 20–21.
"Our Gobbler," *Plantation Game Trails* (1921), pp. 110–26.
"The Rajah of Bellefield," *Field & Stream*, January 1943, pp. 14–15, 53–54.
"Random Shots," *An American Hunter* (1937), pp. 229–50. Pages 236–38 and 240–41 deal with turkey hunting.
"Reconnoitring," *Children of Swamp and Wood* (1927), pp. 77–90. Pages 82–85 deal with turkeys.
"The Rogue of Orquic Valley," *Hunter's Choice* (1946), pp. 106–14. Also in *Fireworks in the Peafield Corner* (1986), pp. 67–74. First published in *Field & Stream*, July 1936, pp. 26–27, 66–67.
"Sometimes It Happens," *Those Were the Days* (1955), pp. 123–28.
"Stalking Wild Turkeys," *Plantation Game Trails* (1921), pp. 47–53.
"A Stalk on the Dunes," *An American Hunter* (1937), pp. 1–9. First published in *Field & Stream*, September 1934, pp. 28–29, 55.
"Steve Knows How," *Hunter's Choice* (1946), pp. 115–20.
"Talking Turkey," *An American Hunter* (1937), pp. 407–16.
"Tall Man of the Twilight," *Field & Stream*, March 1939, pp. 34–35, 65–66.
"That Twenty-five-Pound Gobbler," *Outing*, March 1919, pp. 305–7, 342.
"Their Baffling Maneuvers," *Florida Wildlife*, 13, No. 7 (1959), pp. 16ff.
"Those Bearded Men," Rutledge Collection, University of South Carolina.
"The Turkeys' Dance," *Wild Life of the South* (1935), pp. 30–31.
"Wash Loses a Turkey," *Outing*, March 1927, pp. 476–78. This is the same as the story published as "Any One's Turkey."
"Watchmen," *Children of Swamp and Wood* (1927), pp. 149–64. Pages 159–63 deal with turkeys.
"The Ways of the Wild Gobbler," *Field & Stream*, June 1970, pp. 85–86, 166–68.
"Ways of the Wild Turkey," *Days Off in Dixie* (1925), pp. 246–63.
"Wild Life in a Drought," *Outdoor Life*, November 1930, pp. 12–13, 82.
"Wild Strain in Turkeys," *Country Life*, June 1919, pp. 22ff.
"The Wild Turkey Stages a Comeback," *Independent*, 111 (1923), pp. 246–47.
"Wild Turkeys," *The Woods and Wild Things I Remember* (1970), pp. 239–54.
"Wild Turkeys in Pennsylvania Fifty Years Ago," Rutledge Collection, University of South Carolina.
"Wild Turkeys of the Delta," *An American Hunter* (1937), pp. 200–208. First published in *Outdoor Life*, January 1933, pp. 10–11, 55.
"Wild Turkey Stalking," Rutledge Collection, University of South Carolina.
"A Wild Warder," *Wild Life of the South* (1935), pp. 236–38.
"Wild Watchers," *Wild Life of the South* (1935), pp. 171–74.
"Wildwood Majesty," *American Forests*, 42 (1936), pp. 491–93, 532–33.
"Wildwood Majesty," *What's New*, December 1955, pp. 27–28, 41–42, 44, 47.
"Wingéd Mountaineers," *Children of Swamp and Wood* (1927), pp. 182–89.
"The Wrong Gobbler," *Hunter's Choice* (1945), pp. 143–49. First published in *Field & Stream*, November 1941, pp. 22–23, 73.